A Research Agenda for Corporations

Elgar Research Agendas outline the future of research in a given area. Leading scholars are given the space to explore their subject in provocative ways, and map out the potential directions of travel. They are relevant but also visionary.

Forward-looking and innovative, Elgar Research Agendas are an essential resource for PhD students, scholars and anybody who wants to be at the forefront of research.

Titles in the series include:

A Research Agenda for Media Economics
Edited by Alan B. Albarran

A Research Agenda for Environmental Geopolitics
Edited by Shannon O'Lear

A Research Agenda for Studies of Corruption
Edited by Alina Mungiu-Pippidi and Paul M. Heywood

A Research Agenda for Digital Politics
Edited by William H. Dutton

A Research Agenda for Environmental Economics
Edited by Matthias Ruth

A Research Agenda for Academic Integrity
Edited by Tracey Bretag

A Research Agenda for Entrepreneurship Policy
Edited by David Smallbone and Friederike Welter

A Research Agenda for Family Business
Edited by Andrea Calabrò

A Research Agenda for Critical Political Economy
Edited by Bill Dunn

A Research Agenda for Corporations
Christopher May

A Research Agenda for Corporations

CHRISTOPHER MAY

Professor of Political Economy, Department of Politics,
Philosophy and Religion, Lancaster University, UK

Elgar Research Agendas

Edward Elgar
PUBLISHING

Cheltenham, UK • Northampton, MA, USA

Published by
Edward Elgar Publishing Limited
The Lypiatts
15 Lansdown Road
Cheltenham
Glos GL50 2JA
UK

Edward Elgar Publishing, Inc.
William Pratt House
9 Dewey Court
Northampton
Massachusetts 01060
USA

A catalogue record for this book
is available from the British Library

Library of Congress Control Number: 2020944117

This book is available electronically in the **Elgar**online
Social and Political Science subject collection
http://dx.doi.org/10.4337/9781788977531

ISBN 978 1 78897 752 4 (cased)
ISBN 978 1 78897 753 1 (eBook)

Printed and bound by CPI Group (UK) Ltd, Croydon, CR0 4YY

For Hilary, as always

Contents

Acknowledgements   ix

1   Introduction to *A Research Agenda for Corporations*   1

2   The history of corporations and incorporation   19

3   Managing the corporation   39

4   Understanding the global corporate supply chain   67

5   The corporation's political agency   93

6   Can the corporation be reformed? Should it be?   125

References   155
Index   171

Acknowledgements

This book represents the culmination of perhaps two decades or more of pondering the corporation in political economy. As such I have been influenced in these reflections by more people than I can remember; so, if I have missed out people with whom I have discussed the sorts of issues raised in this book I apologise. Nevertheless, here is my attempt to recognise everyone whose ideas, views and suggestions have explicitly and implicitly found their way into this book; to you all I say thanks again. I have over the years had really fruitful conversations about corporations with: Louise Amoore, Isabella Bakker, Kurt Birch, Clare Cutler, Matt Davies, Randall Germain, Stephen Gill, Jeff Harrod, Virginia Haufler, Sam Knafo, Neil Manson, Johnna Montgomerie, Morten Ougaard, Ronen Palan, Nicola Phillips, Sol Picciotto, Susan Sell, Stuart Shields, Susanne Soederberg, Garrath Williams and many students who have studied political economy with me both at Lancaster University and before that at the University of the West of England.

While they had no input into this book, I would also like to acknowledge the good sense and support I have received in recent years from two of my colleagues at Lancaster: thank you Chris Macleod and Sarah Marsden for keeping me sane when sometimes it seemed like madness was/is all around us.

As always I also want to acknowledge the intellectual debt I owe to my late father, with whom I worked in our family business for nearly a decade prior to my academic career. Finally, but by no means least, once again I have dedicated my work to my wife of 35 years, Hilary Jagger, who remains an oasis of good sense, humour and love when it is most needed.

This book was finished during the (first?) period of coronavirus-related social lock-down in the UK. Already people are discussing whether this public health emergency may signal a rethinking of contemporary capitalism. If it does (perhaps sadly) the issues raised by the research agenda developed here are likely to be as apposite as ever.

Christopher May, 3 April 2020

1 Introduction to *A Research Agenda for Corporations*

This volume in the Research Agenda series explores a range of approaches to analysing the (global) corporation; the intent is to encourage researchers to adopt a more multi-disciplinary approach to studying and researching corporations. The research agenda proposed in this volume therefore has two distinct (although, of course, linked) elements: the first is a response to too much analysis of corporations being limited to (and by) its own academic or analytical silo. The approach adopted here is explicitly multi-dimensional and researchers are thereby encouraged to look beyond their own disciplines (or even closely allied disciplines) to seek out work on corporations that may further and differently illuminate puzzles and issues they are exploring. The second element is a call to establish a research agenda for corporations (and more widely business enterprises) in those disciplines that often merely assume or import uncritically an economistic account of business. This is not to argue that economics has necessarily got it wrong when it turns to the corporation or business enterprise, but rather to say that its analysis is only partial. Certainly, other disciplines and perspectives should not shun insights about corporations from economics, but rather should explore where they might add, modify and build in different analytical directions from economists' analyses. The discussion(s) in the following chapters will therefore suggest why an account of the corporation that engages with and combines a range of analytical approaches would likely lead to interesting avenues of analysis and research.

It is as well to be clear at the outset, however, that the intent of this book is to spur further research *into* corporations rather than necessarily offer a fully developed account of the political economy of the corporation itself or its future development, even if such an account might be inferred from what I have written. However, as will be clear from the final chapter, there is a clear strand of analysis that adopts a strong normative position, arguing that the contemporary corporation should be reformed. In this regard, a third element of the research agenda proposed herein is that research into the (global) corporation can (I would not be so presumptuous as to say 'should') be aimed at (re)thinking the political economy of the corporation itself. By doing so researchers could develop a political programme of reform that may gain some traction in the real world of economic relations of the business enterprise and specifically among those who seek to regulate and organise contemporary capitalism differently.

The need for the expansion of research into the corporation is further indicated by the exclusion of any extended discussion of the corporation as a subject of analytical interest in an otherwise relatively comprehensive recent guide to *rethinking economics*; firms and companies are mentioned in passing in a few chapters but nothing more (Rochon and Rossi 2017). As this suggests even though economic analyses of corporations may have some currency beyond the discipline, it remains an under-developed focus for those who wish to reform the discipline, reflecting a strange (albeit uneven) myopia in economics and political economy. Furthermore, it is nearly 30 years since Susan Strange argued that the study of international relations should (indeed *must*) include an account of the role of multinational corporations (Babic et al. 2017; Strange 1991), but there remains a noticeable lack of such attention. In both the study of (global) economics *and* politics, the corporation most often seems notable by its relative absence from the discussion. The following chapters will identify lots of interesting work, but often it seems to be at the margins rather than at the centre of focus of those (sub-) disciplines purporting to be concerned with the global system and its power relations.

It is important to stress that the discussions reviewed in the following chapters are not only relevant to those firms and enterprises formally constituted as corporations. Certainly some issues are legal questions that only directly concern corporations (firms that have been incorporated under various legislative arrangements in various jurisdictions), but others have much wider salience relating to issues that confront the analyses of non-corporate commercial/economic organisations. Indeed, it is not the case that across all economies the corporation is the dominant *domestic* form of economic enterprise (Whitley 2010), even if this is much more so in the global realm. I also accept Isabelle Ferreras' point that the 'idea of the corporation has managed to eclipse the idea of the firm . . . a *Reductio as Corporationem* [that] folds the firm into the corporation, despite the fact that the latter is merely the legal vehicle that structures capital investments' (Ferreras 2017: 5, 95). The corporate form (and a relatively exclusive discussion of it) obscures a range of other sorts of firms, an issue to which we return in the final chapter. That said, in this short book I often *do* conflate the firm and corporation, but nevertheless, I recognise that there is a need to balance the analysis of (globalised) corporate form(s) with the variable forms of collective economic organisation in national economies. Where an issue is of wider relevance, the questions raised will be relevant to partnerships, workers cooperatives and other ways in which collective economic activity can be organised. While this book is concerned with how we think about corporations' past and future, it seems to me that that in many areas the political economy of the corporation is not fundamentally different from that of other forms of business organisation.

Much of the available discussion of corporations has been undertaken in the various disciplines that find their home in management schools, but in critical social science(s) the corporation has been less readily *explicitly* included in analyses of the global system or of contemporary market society. Where non-management school social scientists have included corporations in their analysis this has largely (although not exclusively) been in the form of the recognition of (economic) power without responsibility, reflecting Ambrose Bierce's well-known definition from *The Devil's Dictionary* that a 'corporation' is an 'ingenious device for obtaining individual profit without individual responsibility' (Bierce 1911 [1958]: 25). Unfortunately, much of this critical analysis is relatively undifferentiated and therefore lacks a clear appreciation of the complexities of corporations' variable characters or practices. Indeed, as noted above, at times some critical social science seems to unreflexively import economic analyses of the corporation, which are then treated as viable depictions of a set of social relations such analysts wish to critique. This book is therefore intended to encourage the development of a more nuanced (or complex) understanding of corporations as political economic actors, building on existing research to suggest areas of potential further analytical development.

Establishing such a *research agenda* is necessary, as corporations have grown in importance in the (now) global political economy over the last one hundred years. At the beginning of the third decade of the new millennium, corporations with global reach control both digital platforms and informational resources that seem ever more central to everyday life and as such it should be no surprise that a new generation of students and activists is concerned about their power. However, the corporation (as an organised economic entity) has a long history encompassing international trading companies like the Dutch East India Company and multilateral clan- or family-based banking concerns such as those of the Rothschild family (and before them the Medici). That said, on the eve of the First World War, their economic activity remained *mostly* focused on domestic markets and economies. While there was international trading, this did not figure large in most enterprises' organisational considerations, but as the twentieth century progressed, so transport innovations, like cheap long-range communication technologies, and the standard-sized shipping container supported the growth of ever more complex and more widely geographically dispersed operations.

It is now a commonplace to say a third of all international trade involves multinational corporations at one side or other of a transaction, and a further third of international trade involves transactions *within* global corporate networks themselves. The character of the organisation of much of this trade into global supply chains, where intermediate goods circulate between countries in international production networks, can have significant effects on how we understand and measure the global economy. For instance, this intra-corporate trade can lead to (quite extensive) double counting of global gross domestic product, as value-added is often counted in more than one country's data. It can also distort the reported global economic shares of some industrial sectors, again through the double counting of value-added in intermediate goods traded *between* sectors (UNCTAD 2013: 123–32). Furthermore, shifts in the global economy (as measured by gross domestic product and trade statistics) suggest that while *economic activity* (and specifically manufacturing) is moving away from the core, the home of major corporations (as indicated by headquarters and place of incorporation) remains in the developed states and reflects their domination of the global economic system (Kellogg 2015: 284–9). Therefore, transfer pricing and profit shifting have an important impact on perceptions of productivity of various locations in the corporate production network (given that productivity is measured as a value-added in monetary terms) and may be having a subtle but nevertheless significant impact on development and anti-poverty policies. Governments' desire to enrol their economies in global supply chains can skew priorities towards the needs of non-national enterprises as opposed to the needs of the local community (Fischer 2018: 205–13). Unsurprisingly, as a result, the disconnection of activity and the location(s) of corporate power centres underlie much of the discussion of how we understand power and influence in the global corporate political economy.

As domestic economies have become more and more open to international trade, so the role of the globalised corporation has become clearer and ever more important to understand. How corporations operate, how they interact with (and structure) markets and the manner in which they thereby influence our political economy are issues of some importance. However, elite managers (and to an extent shareholders) want to present the working of business as opaque and the subject of specialised knowledge. Moreover, invoking commercial confidentiality or technical economic analysis, those who run corporations and other major commercial enterprises have often sought to place themselves in the role not of agents, but rather as non-judgemental communicators of some (neutralised) commercial logic of business (Davies 2017: 230). This move is intended to depoliticise the conduct and practice of business, and as such has led to a common lack of critical *political* analytical engagement with global corporate practice(s). It is this lack of a *political* element that most often renders economic analysis of the corporation (and by extension business enterprises more generally) partial and requiring further development.

The difficulty of this (attempted) depoliticisation of business is that (as will become apparent below) the corporation is dependent on the state for its very existence; it is not some neutral/natural facet of human organisation, rather it has been constructed by the (initially European and American) state. What is perhaps most striking about the new millennium is the manner in which states' governments have sought to 'outsource governance' to these very products of political origin. This outsourcing of governance can be identified across three dimensions: firstly, states have sought to facilitate a political economic environment in which global supply chains can thrive (see Chapter 4). Secondly, states have recognised and empowered private governance of the corporate sphere establishing it as a form of legitimate governance (see Chapter 5). Finally, states have embraced a market governance logic that individualises the causes of inequality and attempts to inoculate global corporations from responsibility for growing global and national inequalities (an issue that underlies the whole of this volume) (Mayer and Phillips 2017). The key point is that developed states (and their governments) are not helpless patsies in the face of corporate power, but rather have been instrumental and cooperative in its establishment, development and expansion. For developing states, the story is somewhat different with their semi-dependence on corporate-controlled technology and control of access to corporate production networks placing them in a much weaker position.

So, the core purpose of this book is to encourage (more) researchers, social scientists and analysts to look behind the 'corporate veil' to find out what is actually going on, and ask how that might differ from at least some of the stories that get told about the corporate sphere, by both its supporters *and* its critics. Another key message of this book is that those attempting to understand our contemporary political economy cannot really move forward with their analysis without a nuanced appreciation of the role of corporations collectively *and* individually. Reflecting my established pedagogic approach, however, there is a touch of 'do as I say not as I do' about this book, for which I apologise. Like my ongoing undergraduate course on *Economics for the Real World* and a past course on *corporations*, one of my central contentions is that we can only really understand global corporations by looking at *actual* corporate behaviour by *actual* corporations. I accept I do not do this enough in this small book, but would point to Intan Suwandi's *Value Chains: The New Economic Imperialism* (Suwandi 2019) as an excellent recent example of the combination of general analysis and focused attention on particular corporations' actions/practices that I regard as the most fruitful way forward. Nevertheless, this volume is an attempt to lay out a wide-ranging research agenda, with the hope that colleagues will use these themes, issues and prompts as ways to develop their own more detailed, more particular research into corporations.

The importance of corporate legal form(s)

Although this book is not primarily focused on the legally constituted form of the corporation, nevertheless throughout the question of legality and regulation will be key to understanding potential research developments. Indeed, John Ruggie has suggested that the 'disjuncture between [the corporation's] economic reality and legal convention is the single most important contextual factor shaping the global institutional status of multinationals' (Ruggie 2018: 329). I will return to the issue of the corporation's absence from international law below, but Ruggie's emphasis on the need to understand the legal aspects of global corporations' constitution and activities is well put; too often, the legal is treated as epiphenomenal rather than constitutive of corporations' political economy. As Joel Bakan forcefully puts it, corporations

> are legal constructs, created only through the operation of state law. They are rooted within and operate through domestic legal systems, tethered to and manifesting state sovereignty in every decision and action they take. There is no 'regulatory gap', no corporate space transcending state sovereignty, but only multiple corporate nationals operating in multiple nations – multinational corporations, but never truly transnational ones. (Bakan 2015: 298–9)

However, as we will see, considerable political capital is expended on both sides of the arguments about global corporate power to obscure this dependence.[1] Before moving on, therefore, I will offer an initial description of the legal form of the corporation, as this will be often relevant to the agenda for future research into the development of the corporation in subsequent chapters.

Even though corporations *as* enterprises are organisations made up of groups of people, various social and internal institutions and capital (and other) assets mobilised towards a set of economic (and sometime extra-economic) ends, once incorporated they are treated as having a single personality for legal purposes. This pays clear organisational dividends within contract law for instance: the corporation is an effective unitary signatory to agreements and undertakings (which will be of some importance when we look at supply chains in Chapter 4). Immediately, this should draw our attention to corporations' crucial dependence on the state; not just in their legal incorporation, but more generally in the dependence on states upholding and maintaining a fully functioning form of contract law (Pistor 2014: 234). While there is no single and universal legal form for global corporations, and there are many other modes of corporate organisation, the central aspects of Anglo-Saxon legal form have become increasingly influential and widespread in the new millennium, especially as regards this question of legal personality and the associated need for this to be exercised under contract law.

For many business enterprises the desire (or need) to compete to raise capital in London or New York, and thus seek stock market listings in the UK or USA, is a significant incentive to adopt the specific legal arrangements including incorporation that comply with these countries' accounting and financial reporting requirements (Hansmann and Kraakman 2000). Compliance with such regulations has effectively exported a particular legal form to countries with differing legal traditions and practices. This partial convergence of legal forms has not necessarily been beneficial for the accountability of business; the increasing adoption of Anglo-Saxon modes of limited liability within the governance of subsidiaries has shielded companies and their shareholders from accountability across their international networks (Sahni 2005). This rests on a key element of the contemporary corporate legal form: the ability to hold stock (or own) other companies (Muchlinkski 2007: 35). Like 'real' individuals, in most jurisdictions corporations are legally able to hold shares in other corporations (or their own 'subsidiaries') allowing the company itself to benefit from the protection of limited liability (originally formulated to protect individuals from excessive risk, not corporations themselves), in its role as a holding company.

The assumption of legal personality through incorporation was (and remains, formally) a grant of authority by the state to carry out certain purposes for the public good. In the seventeenth century, when this first became widely used, these public purposes were defined by the state with relatively little public participation or deliberation. Nevertheless, they were framed as public (or at least public-regarding) interests, and therefore counter-posed to any existing unencumbered rights to private enrichment. Importantly, it offered in return for serving the public good (however defined) protection from the state's regulation of monopolies. This emphasises that legal personality is not an issue of the corporation having some (natural) similarity to human persons, but rather was a legal mechanism to solve a logistical problem of how groups of people acting together could formally and easily interact with other such groups to serve purposes regarded as socially useful by the state. However, (as a legal concept) it has taken on a 'life of its own' (Hess 2013: 329). An important shift in the political shape of incorporation has been a move from being conceived as the state's delegation of certain powers, to seeing it as a mode of protection *from* the state (Picciotto 2011: 113). As a result, often we are now told that corporations' forms and practices are not political but merely technical, opening up an interesting question for activists regarding how far such corporations actually do fulfil their side of any (now forgotten) bargain regarding the provision of public purpose(s) in exchange for privatised enrichment (Bakan 2004). Underlying much of the discussion that follows is the argument that the treatment of the corporation as a legally constituted individual, and the assumption that it necessarily contributes to economic well-being, needs to be carefully scrutinised and subjected to democratic deliberation if business and democracy are to be reconciled within a nascent global society.

Most corporations do not have the institutional longevity of many established sovereign states, but their enjoyment of legal personality (and the attendant rights of that personality) allows them to deploy considerably greater social power than the natural persons on whose rights these corporate rights are often modelled. To be clear, three distinct legal personalities are generally recognised in law:

- naturally existing people (that is, individuals in a particular jurisdiction);
- the state (in its role as collective location of sovereign and legal authority);
- the legally constituted corporation, a collective organisation recognised for the purposes of state-derived regulation as having a single legal personality (most importantly an identity that is separate from its members at any specific time).

This division is hardly natural, and while the division between (sovereign) political authority and individual subject (or later citizen) might be said to have emerged almost organically from the historical and legal requirements of nation state politics, the assumption of legal personhood by the corporation was a politically engineered legal innovation, as will be discussed in the next chapter.

As Steve Russell and Michael Gilbert have pointed out, 'Corporations have many advantages over natural persons: effective immortality, superior resources, and with globalisation, mobility on a scale available to few human beings' (Russell and Gilbert 2002: 45). The divergence between the legal protection available to all (legally constituted) people, and the different effective position of the various types of individuals claiming the protection of the law has been central to much critical discussion of modern corporations. For instance, Steve Tombs and David Whyte conclude that it

> can act as a convenient shield for the key decision makers in the corporation. The corporation can effectively absorb the punishment, normally in the form of a fine,

while its directors and senior managers are relatively rarely exposed to sanction. (Tombs and Whyte 2015: 98)

The legal person of the corporation allows the natural persons who actually take the decisions to evade (legal) responsibility for these decisions. We have allowed the corporation to become inhumane by ceding judgements about its practices to markets and the impact on share price (or 'shareholder value') (Mayer 2016: 70). Again, this is not a necessary development but rather is a *political* choice about economic organisation and its legal constitution.

When discussing corporations' legal character, the focus by definition remains at the level of the national jurisdiction in which such incorporation is achieved. However, as I have already noted, this book is as much concerned with the *global* corporation, not merely the various national forms and the varieties of corporate practices one can detect around the world. So, while certainly corporations remain outside the scope of international law (like other persons they are subjects only of national law), it is crucial to recognise that corporations' recourse to legalised personality is a relatively internationalised legal norm even if it remains a national jurisdictional matter. Nevertheless, despite the general acceptance of this norm, the corporation remains without a *formal* personality as regards international law, which in one sense renders international law 'unrealistic' in its account of the political terrain over which it rules (Nowrot 2006: 572; Ruggie 2018: 329). Of course, for critics, this legal lacuna is not a historical accident waiting to be resolved, but rather is a specific outcome of the global political economy of corporate capitalism.

While corporations may be influenced by international 'soft law', little regulation at the international level has been solidified into (hard) positive law to hold them firmly to account outside national jurisdictions (Muchlinkski 2007: 111); rather a form of 'networked governance' has been developed with the aid of international commercial lawyers working with (global) corporations. Rendered as *depoliticised* technical arrangements, networked governance brings together interested actors and organisations in the 'gap' between formalised international law, and national commercial law to establish a range of guidelines, agreements and protocols that reflect 'functional fragmentation' and the decentralised political realm of the global corporate realm (Picciotto 2011: 17–24). This builds on previous forms of *lex mercatoria* (the law of merchants) to ensure that the global political economy has a regulatory structure that enables and facilitates corporations' preference for stability and predictability but allows its subjects extensive influence over its form(s) and practice(s) and denies states any power to sanction corporate behaviour in the international realm.

This has the advantage of offering corporations opportunities for organisational convergence with its posited associated efficiency benefits, but with few of the accountability costs of formal legislative development. This reflects the manner in which conservative and pro-business governments have reconfigured domestic laws to make them less constraining and more facilitative of corporate activity; moving away from protecting (however incompletely) public interests towards a focus more on enabling corporations and protecting *their* interests (Bakan 2015: 285). However, while the character of regulation has shifted and been refocused, this is not the same as any claimed *deregulation* of business. Rather, there has been a significant and ongoing process of *re-regulation*; this has not reduced regulatory instruments, as business interests often argue for, but has nevertheless reconfigured the proposed aims towards the interest(s) of corporate capital. In this, as Sol Picciotto puts it: 'regulation has become the tribute that corporate capitalism has been obliged to pay for continuing to maintain the private forms which allow its domination by a tiny elite, creaming off enormous wealth' (Picciotto 2017: 693). These moves, while advantageous to corporations, are also often an escape from effective and formal state regulation. As will be clear from subsequent chapters, much of the discussion of the political economy of the corporation revolves around how extensive this shift is in real terms and whether analysts see this as a problem or an opportunity for economic development.

Global legal variability *does* mean that multinational corporations are exposed to a significant legal tension however. They are constituted under the laws of their home country, and this will have some impact on their character and practices. At the same time, most countries require the local subsidiary operation of any corporation to be constituted under local (national) law, and as such frequently a global multinational corporation's legal form is highly diversified. This can lead to an attempt by governments of multinationals' home/headquarters states to seek to extend their legal reach (the extraterritoriality of their regulatory focus) through the demands that local subsidiaries should be governed by the regulations of the home country even if these conflict with those of the subsidiary's host jurisdiction (Kobrin 2009: 189–90). Conversely, host states may also seek to hold multinationals accountable through national legal mechanisms; these may be in tension with the manner in which the corporation expects to manage its affairs in its headquarters (home) country. Additionally, where bilateral investment treaties (BITs) are in force, the host state may have ended up constricting its own ability to regulate as a way of 'encouraging' inwards investment, an increasingly fraught issue to which we will return when we discuss treaty arrangements for investor–state dispute settlement.

While I would not necessarily self-identify as a proponent of legal institution-alism (see Deakin et al. 2017), my strong but not exclusive focus on the legal forms and structures that both support and constitute the (global) corporate sector means that there are distinct parallels with such an approach. The legal institutional approach emphasises that all firms (and thereby the corporations and business enterprises focused on herein) both are constituted in their specific form but require the law to operate – the law is unavoidable. The corporation is therefore a creature of the law, albeit with multiple (legal) parents; it is this question of how the corporation exists as a legal entity in the global political economy that in one sense lies at the heart of everything that follows. However, equally this does not mean that the law and legal analysis can tell us all we need to know about the global corporation.

The utility of a multi-disciplinary approach to the (global) corporation

One of the key reasons for adopting a multi-disciplinary approach to the analysis of (global) business enterprises is that as Julie Nelson has emphasised: 'business firms are not asocial machines operating in a vacuum, but are fully social entities with complex internal workings and which operate in deep interdependence with the ethical mores of the culture in which they partici-pate' (Nelson 2016: 188). While for Nelson this underpins a call for a feminist approach to economics that foregrounds 'provisioning' and human flourishing (Nelson 2016: 196), here it is a useful prompt to recognise that an exclusively economic perspective on corporate practices will miss significant and impor-tant social elements that contribute to the understanding and explanation of such practices. There are many ways that such a multi-disciplinary approach might be characterised, but here I will refer to this as 'political economy' partly reflecting my long-term practice of drawing from a range of analytical traditions or perspectives (see May 2014: 17–32). This also builds on Homa Katouzian's now four decades old definition of political economy which included as a key element the idea that political economists always 'recognise the importance of other "non-economic", social facts, categories and theories, in their analyses of specific economic problems' (Katouzian 1980: 182). This is to say, in seeking to establish a *research agenda* centred on political economy, I will reach out to a range of disciplines, and in this case perhaps most imme-diately to the legal study of the corporation.

As I have already argued, the key reason for this immediate interaction with legal studies is that the corporation is essentially a legal construct – it is what law (and lawyers) make of it. To ignore these legal aspects of analysis is to adopt an analysis that lacks key ontological elements as regards the subject of analysis. This leads Jeroen Veldman and Hugh Willmott to conclude that when we see the corporation as a 'separate legal entity' (SLE) we see

> a reified social construct formulated within a specific epistemological community whose concrete effects are mediated by processes of contestation over its status and significance ... Each historical stabilisation of the SLE has been conceived as a consequence of groups mobilising available resources that bestow and sustain material and symbolic advantage ... 'political contestation' and not 'community' is the key to the explication of the social ontology of the modern corporation. (Veldman and Willmott 2017: 1501)

The corporate form is maintained not by its social functionality ('community') as is often implied, but rather by the continued mobilisation of political interest. Moreover, thinking carefully about the social ontology of the corporation requires us to be alive to the contested place and character of the corporation as a distinct mode of social ordering; both reflecting sets of practices and organisational structures, as well as being something more than merely its material practices (Deakin 2017). Analysis of the corporation cannot be divorced from more ideational assumptions that are tied up with its legal form.

This volume reaches out across a range of disciplines and approaches to harvest insights and potential avenues for further research into the global corporate realm. This disciplinary inclusivity also reflects my long engagement with the work of Susan Strange, who even when not explicitly cited in subsequent chapters, remains perhaps the most influential background aspect to my political economy mind-set, albeit most recently in relation to work on the rule of law (May 2014: 17–32). Most famously, Strange was interested in the structures of power in which social relations took place; while immediate relational power issues were important, for Strange the context for such relations was the structure (or political economic context) in which these relations took place. For Strange, the political economy was patterned by four dimensions of structural power: security, production, finance and knowledge (Strange 1988). Strange saw no formal distinction between these structures; they are not ontologically separate spheres of activity. Indeed, her taxonomy of structures was not meant to identify hermetically sealed realms, quite the opposite: they are interpenetrated, and coexistent within a coterminous realm of political economy (Strange 1988: 24–8). They are an aid for identifying lacunae in political economic analyses rather than a closed account of the field itself, and are an invitation to a more permissive epistemology, one that does not necessarily promote one form of evidence, information or form of data above another.

It is within the interactions of all four structures that specific 'bargains' between authority and market as mechanisms of control will be struck. In any particular case there is an (albeit temporary) settlement, produced by the mobilisation of power, between the use of political authority to pattern the distribution of benefits and the use of market mechanisms. This settlement is never absolute; there is always an element of both politics and markets but the bargain made in a particular instance will allocate one or other as the lead distributional device. To have structural power over production, security, finance or knowledge is to have the ability to set the 'rules of the game', the agenda of possibility ruling some things as options and others as nonsensical or even impossible. In the production structure, the forms and focus of pro-ductive activity are shaped and shifted by agendas set by those with structural power over productive activity and present such an agenda as the common sense of contemporary economic development. In the security structure, the identification of the character and requirements of a secure society are shaped and particular conceptions of insecurity (and thereby policy responses) defined by structural power over politic-social agenda setting. In the financial structure, the normalisation of specific credit creating and financialisation processes is (again) normalised; while in the knowledge structure (in Strange's work this is less developed analytically), issues ranging from the manner in which knowledge is controlled and owned to questions of what is acceptable as 'evidence' for policy-making are subject to forms of structural power. This led to Strange's abiding interest in the practices of business and how corporations (and other enterprises) shaped the (global) political economy (Stopford and Strange 1991). Global corporations are able to influence all four dimensions of the context of structural power (albeit unevenly and inconsistently), and as such, for Strange, were a necessary element of any discussion of the contem-porary global system.

The intent of this approach is to avoid the silo thinking that has been identified as constricting analysis of corporations, and to establish a place for critical approaches (Baars and Spicer 2017: 4); this is clearly served by widening the remit of disciplines from which analytical substance is drawn. It is also a call to move beyond approaches that study corporations only to explain and/or understand their practices with a view to make them more effective, or only address the corporate form as a given social institution. As John Kay stridently argues:

> Firms are social entities and cannot be divorced from their social context . . . Reductionist accounts that see the firm as a nexus of contracts established in a com-petitive market, or as the expression of the will of the inspired leader, neglect the historically-determined pattern of relationships within any complex organisation

which explain why some firms succeed – for a time – and others, often the same firms, fail. (Kay 2019: 12)

Multi-disciplinarity not only allows for analyses of how corporations work and are governed, but also allows for an interrogation of why they exist in the form that they do. This can be both historically defined enquiry (see next chapter) or a more political approach seeking to explore the range of social forces that maintain our (global) corporate economy (as explored in the rest of this volume).

This is not a novel suggestion: the most plausible and convincing analyses of how businesses (and corporations) engage with society have always been multi-disciplinary, even when their main analytical intent has been comparative (see, for instance, Moran 2009) or focused on the internationalisation of production (see, for instance, Dunning 1988). Moreover, others have also called for an expansion of multi-disciplinarity in the study of international business, albeit from a different starting point (Geppert and Dörrenbächer 2011). Certainly, as Mats Forsgren argues, one can identify a range of contending approaches to studying (multinational) corporations – he lists six approaches to characterising multinational firms: dominating, coordinating, knowing, designing, networking, or politicising – but, as he implies, the most fruitful analysis comes from combining these approaches in specific instances to understand how corporations operate in the global political economy (Forsgren 2013). For any specific issue, pragmatically different combinations of analysis may prove best suited to delivering particular insights but the key thing is not to see a mono-analytical approach as preferable. The complexity of the global corporate realm/sector requires analysis to reflect the range and diversity of issues that contribute both to corporate practices and decisions as well as the variety of social, economic and political responses that these practices may engender.

In this volume this comes together perhaps most obviously in the chapter on the global corporate supply chain which is an ideal terrain for multi-disciplinary analysis of corporate practices (see also Haufler 2018). This also reflects Nicola Phillips' argument that global production networks (supply chains and value chains) are the key terrain over which global political economy power is articulated, but also are a major site for the production of global inequalities. Within these production networks, asymmetries of social power, market power and political power shape the potentialities for development, the distribution of benefits (monetary and other) and the control of key assets from technology to material resources (Phillips 2017). Much of this will be explored in the chapter on global supply chains, but it is worth stressing, as Phillips does, that to understand the global corporation's political economy, the characteristic patterns of a 'global value chain world' cannot be ignored or downplayed. The best way to develop a compelling analysis of this 'world' is to adopt a pragmatic range of method/analysis. Multi-disciplinarity therefore underpins the analysis and suggestions for future research set out across all of the following chapters.

To be clear, a multi-disciplinary approach is not a complete rejection of mainstream economics based accounts of the corporation, but rather a reflection of the partial (incomplete) character of such accounts. Certainly some critics have argued that the discipline of economics has produced a managerial class that *performs* their economic function based on the de-socialised (formally modelled) economics they once learnt and by doing so reproduces an anti-social form of capitalism. Rather, I follow David Spencer in seeing 'bad management' of corporations as reflecting particular responses to the structural and practical aspects of capitalism itself, not as the result of the (often rather basic) education of managers by economics departments, and what they remember of it (Spencer 2020). Therefore, by adopting a multi-disciplinary approach, including legal analysis, sociology, geography, philosophical and other approaches the aim is to illuminate more, understand more and explain more about the particularities of the corporate political economy. A fully developed defence of multi-disciplinary practices' ontological and epistemological grounds is beyond the scope of this volume other than by demonstrating through the following chapters the pragmatic utility of this approach.

What follows

This book both maps out the range of issues that make up a multi-disciplinary study of the corporation, from national contexts to its global political economy, and suggests future avenues of fruitful research. Each chapter explores a set of themes that it strikes me are crucial to a fully rounded account of the political economy of the multifaceted global environment in which corporations operate, as well as prompting analysis of particular corporations, and concludes with some questions that seem to require further exploration. Chapter 2 sets the global political economy of the corporation in an historical context. The chapter develops a brief history of the corporate form and specifically the legal innovations that led to the normalisation of the act of incorporation. This history is related to the analysis of varieties of capitalism and the development of the global supply chain or production network, and includes some discussion of the shifting relations (in a general sense) between managers and workers. The chapter concludes with a consideration of the history of the corporation as a reflection of organisational processes highlighted by transaction cost economics. The key argument of the chapter is that it is impossible to fully understand the contemporary political economy of the corporation without placing it in an historical context even if in everyday research this remains more implied than formally and fully developed.

Chapter 3 asks: what is entailed in managing the corporation? This chapter focuses on law and planning, but also develops at some length the need to have a *political* understanding of the internal organisational dynamics of the business enterprise. This leads to a discussion of the classes involved, and that are to some extent in conflict within the corporation; the discussion ranges from workplace democracy to how we might understand the conduct of corporate managers. Perhaps unsurprisingly, this then leads to the first of two discussions of issues around the idea of corporate social responsibility. The chapter concludes by setting out why a focus on the internal management of the corporation matters, and by extension why any critical account of the corporate sector, as well as being aware of the structural issues, should be informed as to the real-world conduct of actual corporations.

After exploring a range of issues related to the *internal* management of the corporation, Chapter 4 examines the key terrain of the corporation's external governance function. Here I seek to demonstrate the utility of regarding the contemporary global corporation as an agent of global governance itself. To this end, we examine the global supply chain or production network, and the character of the political economic relations between core corporations and the small and medium sized enterprises that make up most of the ecology of these networks. Focusing attention on the governance of these networks foregrounds issues, such as legitimacy and democracy, that are usually absent from supply chain analysis. The chapter then moves to discuss the role that 'enrolment' plays in the supply chain in developing states' economic upgrading strategies, before examining the relations between these states and corporations as a site of corporate political economic power.

Having broached the issue of power, Chapter 5 examines the corporation's political agency across a number of dimensions. Starting from the relaxed attitude of neoliberals to corporations' quasi monopolies, the chapter then looks at issues related to political influence, before focusing in on the contested politics of investor–state dispute settlement and associated arbitration practices. The discussion then moves to the wider context of global governance of the corporation, including the United Nations Global Compact and the OECD guidelines for corporate practice. The question of taxing corporations draws many of the chapter's themes together, and then finally, the chapter (building on aspects of the class analysis from Chapter 4) looks at the political economy of the transnational capitalist class.

Chapter 6 asks whether reform of the global corporate sector is possible, returning to legal issues originally discussed in this first chapter. The chapter also looks at what reform of the global governance of corporations might entail, as well as developing further the account of corporate social responsibility (here as a mechanism of reform) commenced in Chapter 3, before linking that to the possibilities of the private regulation of corporate activity. The chapter concludes by examining the reform of the internal organisational logic of the corporation through an expanded (democratic) role for the workforce, and then asks whether the gig economy or 'platform capitalism' is the sort of reform that corporate managers prefer if left to their own devices.

All of this is intended to suggest avenues of further research, interesting interactions between research foci too often kept apart by disciplinary boundaries, and to criticise the idea that corporate management is best treated as a rational response to cost control. I do not offer a well-rounded coherent account of the corporation; rather, I hope the reader, suitably intrigued by connections that emerge across the book, will find this a useful prompt for further developing their own research.

Note

1.   Here I should note that, like Bakan but unlike many books and articles on globally active corporations, I will not be using the term 'transnational corporation(s)'; like Bakan, to my mind this implies a level of disconnection from the world of *international* political economy that few if any corporations achieve. In this book I therefore use the term *global* corporations to capture the scope of their operations without seeking to claim they are disconnected from national jurisdictions, a claim which, as I hope this book will demonstrate, misses the corporations' continuing and crucial reliance on the intersection of national legal jurisdictions.

2 The history of corporations and incorporation

Although this book is about future research directions for the study of the (global) corporation, part of the multi-disciplinary approach I am advocating involves recognising that corporations (and by extension the global capitalist economy they have done so much to shape) do not exist outside history. Corporations are not merely a contemporary phenomenon which analysis should seek to understand on the basis only of their current character. Rather, we should start with some historical reflections to emphasise that many issues that are set out in the following chapters are both evident in the past (albeit sometimes in different forms) and owe their character, at least in part, to this varied and diverse history.

The origins of the corporate idea (that a group organised for a specific task or goal is for practical purposes the same as a single person) are far from clear. One account traces the origin of the *idea* of the corporate body back to 2000 BC and the Assyrian Empire (Moore and Lewis 1999). More commonly, the origins of the corporation are located in the merchant economy of the trade routes that expanded across the known world between AD 700 and 1600 (Gabel and Bruner 2003: 18–21). In both accounts, this relates to organisational issues rather than to any legal definition of the corporation, but nevertheless points to the perceived social requirement to treat economic (but also other) activity in certain social circumstances as the product of a collective rather than as the result of a group with individual (social or legal) identities. Certainly, even before the accelerated expansion of trade over distance(s), the Roman Empire developed a legalised recognition that not only settlements, towns and other colonies (as single entities), but also commercial or business associations of artisans organised by skill or trade, could formally adopt a legal personality (Williston 1909: 197). Indeed, this idea of associations adopting a singular legal identity, based on activity rather than on proximity or residence, was to have considerable influence in legal systems influenced by Roman law.

The rise of Benedictine monastic orders and the recognition of these organisations as collective/corporate individuals, and the rules under which they were organised, also play an important role in the development of the corporate form. The accumulation of wealth by Holy Orders was in many ways similar to contemporary corporate activities (Brown 2003). These religious orders were early examples of groups organised through rules and practices that transcended the individual's life and/or interests (here, of course, incorporating the will of God). Likewise groups of artisans organising themselves into what would become professional guilds also were moving towards a self-perception of belonging to a group that had some existence beyond the involvement of its individual members. In both cases, this involved the recognition of the legitimacy of the corporate body holding, controlling and, in the end, being able to divest itself of material resources.

Following the progressive establishment of a range of monastic orders enjoying a form of corporate individualism in the tenth to twelfth centuries, in Britain and on the European continent, this form of (proto-) incorporation mostly remained limited to organisations such as universities, ecclesiastical orders and boroughs. Artisan groups and guilds utilised some of these methods but often lacked the formal recognition accorded these large proto-corporations. However, all these organisations sought recognition as unitary agents beyond the lifespan of any specific set of members (Davis 1905: 35–88). As C. A. Cooke put it, the 'starting-point of the corporate administrative and commercial life of today was when the towns-folk broke the links with the old economy and jurisdiction, and became corporations of freemen, burghers or guilds' (Cooke 1950: 183). Therefore, incorporation established the separation of the organisation from its members, in a similar way to how the medieval state began to be distinguished from the personality of the sovereign and allowed an element of self-governance for the group concerned (Jussen 2009; Kantorowicz 1957 [2016]). Therefore, paralleling the development of the idea of the state as separate *politically* from the personal (divine?) authority of the monarch, early forms of (proto-) incorporation asserted an authority (and legitimate social existence) separate from any socio-political identity of those persons who were members of, worked for or benefitted from the operations of a collective endeavour.

This idea was highly influential, leading groups of merchants to further develop their trading relations (with the acquiescence and protection of monarchs) to include institutional elements that suggested some form of corporate existence. For instance, the Hanseatic League, later consolidated and formally established in Lübeck in 1358, was a group of merchants operating out of towns across Scandinavia, Northern Europe and England that sought to control and profit from the extensive trade between the various market towns of its network. The *Hansa* developed internal regulatory structures, include forms of *lex mercatoria* (the law of merchants) to govern the relations between the towns, and the merchants themselves (Gabel and Bruner 2003:

20; Husa 2018: 78). This model, in part adopted by the slightly later Merchant Adventurers, was corporate inasmuch as the needs of the network formed the logic of governance rather than the individual interests of the members. Likewise, and to some extent influenced by these merchant groups, early guilds were effectively corporate entities, seeking to establish rules and procedures relating to the control of specific trades, beyond the lifespan or involvement of any specific set or group of artisans. However, as new technologies and trades developed outside the traditional guild structures in the late sixteenth century, the common law assumption of a form of legal personality started to be extended more frequently to business enterprises that reached beyond the relatively local horizons of the guilds (Cooke 1950: 31, 39). To some extent then, the early development of incorporation responded to the needs to manage collective activity but also to issues of scale and reach of economic activity.

The Dutch East India Company and its British counterpart, the Royal African Company alongside the Hudson's Bay Company were among the first commercial (non-guild) organisations to incorporate by charter. These trading companies were also the first corporate entities to reach out beyond the borders of their home country strategically, rather than merely as an opportunistic response to particular trading circumstances (Gabel and Bruner 2003: 22–3; Jones 2000; Robins 2012). Previous commercial activities notwithstanding, these were the first international (or multinational) corporations, but because management and control practices were as yet under-developed, often these entities formalised family and kinship relations (McCarthy 1994) or were semi-detached extensions of state power (Robins 2012). Likewise, the Renaissance banking families, such as the Rothschilds or the Medici, also operated across Europe, but again were organised by kin, and as such remained essentially pre-modern. The modern corporation, while prefigured by these developments, still lacked its recognisable modern legal form, although by this time its outlines are clearly coming into focus.

In Britain, a specific law of corporations was only finally codified by William Blackstone in his *Commentaries on the Law of England* (published in the eighteenth century). However, as John P. Davis pointed out, he 'did little more than to bring together the principles scattered through [Sir Edward] Coke's Institutes and Reports, and to present them in a more compact and serviceable form' (Davis 1905, vol. II: 210). The previous developments (briefly detailed above) had led to custom and (legal) practice effectively recognising that collective endeavours had some existence beyond the personalities of those involved, and thereby was different to their associated politico-legal rights. Once Coke had formalised and reported on these practices, by the end of the seventeenth century the legal structures underpinning the singular identity of the corporate body had become standardised, encouraging incorporation to be utilised much more widely than the previous guild arrangements. Blackstone's formal consolidation of custom, practice and legality into a clearer guide to what was possible enabled a further expansion of the use of the corporate form.

The birth of the modern corporation

In 1702, the increasingly important role that corporations were playing in the British economy prompted the anonymous publication of the first book devoted to 'The Law of Corporations' (Williston 1909: 201). Both in this book and in the charters of the new corporations, one of the key corporate undertakings was the public goal of the better management and ordering of the trade in which the corporation was engaged, alongside any private goal of profit for its members. Hence, the legal personality of the early corporation was presented as conditional on a clear public-regarding role in promoting economic development (or some other public good); in return investors began effectively (if as yet not formally) to be able to limit their liability to immediate loss of their investments. Unlike today, however, where incorporation is seen as essentially a right unencumbered by any conditions, corporations like the East India Company had to regularly renew their charters, offering regulatory authorities (in this case Parliament) the opportunity to amend the structure(s) of incorporation (Robins 2012: 30–32, 190–93). The East India Company in many ways both pioneered the shareholder model of corporate ownership (discussed in the next chapter) and also prefigured many critics' concerns about the contemporary behaviour of (global) corporations through its ruthless pursuit of corporate gain (profits) and (political) power.[1]

The limitation of liability to the initial purchase of shares was a vital step in ensuring that joint-stock companies could obtain the widest possible market for their initial stock offerings. Initially established by custom and practice, in Britain liability was only formally limited by statute in the Limited Liability Act of 1855 and the Joint Stock Companies Act of 1856, followed by similar statutes in the various states of the USA over the next 40 years. The ability to shield wealth effectively from claims against corporate liability allowed investment in shares to continue to flourish, although not without early criticisms of the manner in which this also limited the moral responsibilities of owners. From the eighteenth century onwards the limitation of liability was a key mechanism underpinning the growth in size and resources of corporations, allowing them access to disparate and unconsolidated capital to a much greater extent than partnerships. Moreover, by ensuring that investors' risk was easily quantifiable and through their multiple shareholdings spread more widely than if they had only invested in a single enterprise, the growth of arms-length investment in business enterprise was encouraged and consolidated as a normal activity for the wealthy.

In addition to the imperial role of the East India Company (Robins 2012), during the second half of the eighteenth century, corporations were increasingly used by the British government to organise private finance for the construction of the national infrastructure that Britian's growing economy required. The development of the canal network and then the railways acted as a significant and further spur to the use of incorporation. The scope of operations and the magnitude of financial capital needed to conduct these extensive infrastructural projects were so great as to be beyond the resources of enterprises still organised as partnerships. As such, the need to raise large amounts of capital as part of the 'railway revolution' stimulated the further growth of corporations on both sides of the Atlantic. With the swift economic expansion of America in the nineteenth century, new corporations flourished (initially mainly in Massachusetts due to the particularities of its state legal system, but increasingly across all the states). Although the federal state was often willing to collude with companies in the maintenance of cartels, political opposition to such market rigging led finally in 1890 to the Sherman Anti-Trust Act (Kozul-Wright 1995: 104). However, paradoxically, this encouraged the development of ever-larger corporations through vertical integration (as single entities rather than trusts), able to reach across the continent to control economic activities. Relying increasingly on internally generated surpluses and the stock market, American corporations became larger and more powerful than any that had preceded them.

Freed from the traditional and historical economic limitations of Europe's relatively fragmented state system, the development of capitalist corporations in America proceeded unfettered. The expansion of the economics of scale (due in part to the expanding US domestic market) that were enjoyed by larger corporations also allowed significant gains to begin to be captured by workers and other non-capital-owning groups/classes during the late nineteenth century (Resnick and Wolff 2003). By expanding productivity through technology and organisation, but at the same time producing a significant rise in the standard of living of its workforce (however precarious such advances might be for individuals), American corporate capitalism laid the foundations for a new period of modern capitalism: now called *Fordism* in most accounts. Large corporations were able to dominate market sectors (nationally and increasingly globally) based on their technological and organisational advantage.

These organisational advances were enthusiastically taken up on the European continent in the first half of the twentieth century; the pressures of catching up in internationalised markets forced German entrepreneurs to adopt these innovations in corporate organisation, but in a different way. In both the countries that would become significant industrial competitors for Anglo-Saxon capitalism, Germany and Japan, the shift to banker-led corporate consolidation continued apace from the late nineteenth century, through two world wars and into the present (Micklethwait and Wooldridge 2003: 83–101). While in Germany, the numerous Mittelstand (medium sized industrial companies) balanced the power and influence of the larger corporations, in Japan the Zaibatsu created vast client networks based on cross-shareholding between corporate elements, smaller sub-contracting firms, and their banks. Although each developed their own particular national approaches, Japanese and German industrialists remained influenced by the basic organisational innovations of US corporate capitalism even if the financial structures that supported the major corporations were based within the banking sector rather than via independent (or sometimes collective) share-holding investors.

The significance of the US corporation is therefore most obvious in the manner in which production (or services) are organised, the application of 'scientific' management, but also how the entire corporation works, from accounting and personnel management to its interactions with partners and the global economy more generally (Noble 1977). Moreover, as John Kenneth Galbraith argued, the American corporation in the twentieth century often managed to position itself at the heart of the planning of society, as a crucial element in what he famously referred to as the 'technostructure' (Galbraith 1985). More recently (perhaps partly in jest) Leigh Phillips and Michal Rozworski compared Walmart to a socialist planned economy, citing its ability to manage an extensive range of non-market (and controlled market) interactions within its international network (Phillips and Rozworski 2019). We return to this issue of the ability of large corporations to manage, plan and (I will argue) *govern* global networks in the next chapter. The point to emphasise here is that recent history has not so much seen a decline in attempts to plan economic activity, but rather a series of shifts regarding where such planning might be attempted (from the private sector, to the public and back again).

This is not to say all corporations were/are the same, only that the largest had a clear potential to embed themselves within the governance mechanisms of modern society, but without any necessary linked political accountability. In the late twentieth and into the twenty-first centuries, this embedding developed a global dimension, leading some commentators to argue that the globalisation of the law underpinning the corporate legal form was first a major facilitator of imperialism and then, subsequently, a key aspect of the globalisation of capitalism (Baars 2015). Here, the development of international law reflects the requirements of the (globalising) corporation throughout the nineteenth and twentieth centuries. Indeed, the development of the international private law(s) of business, *lex mercatoria*, is a key element of the globalised legal system of the new millennium. It might even be seen as a set of non-national but broadly global laws that business has used to side-step the regulatory intent of states (Husa 2018: 84–5). We will return to this question of how corporations have shaped a global capitalism that suits their needs and interests when we discuss Stephen Gill's analysis of the new constitutionalism in Chapter 5.

The notion that business is shaping socio-economic and legal relations in its own interests is hardly novel. In the first decades of the twentieth century Thorstein Veblen set out a *Theory of Business Enterprise* (Veblen 1904 [2002]), which in the new millennium has become again an influential depiction of the strategic motivations of corporations (see, for instance, Nesvetailova and Palan 2020; Öncü 2009; Shaxson 2018). Veblen argues that underlying the history of corporate enterprise has not been the appetite for competition presented in many mainstream and orthodox accounts of how business people operate in markets. Rather, he argued (as do those influenced by his analysis) that corporations (and business more generally) may celebrate the value of competitive markets in public pronouncements, but in their actions do all that they can to sabotage such competition towards the establishment of sectoral monopolies (or at least oligopolies) (see also Harrod 2006). This sabotage can, of course, be regulated through various forms of anti-trust/anti-monopoly legislative actions, but the demands for light regulation from collective business representatives need to be seen in the light of a history of corporate sabotage of 'free' markets. This sabotage also extends to the limitation or constraint on certain forms of technical advance that while welfare-enhancing may be detrimental to profitability. The balance between Veblen's 'sabotage' and the regulatory state's interest in competition itself has a long and varied history, which also helps to reveal different 'varieties of capitalism' and their regulatory settlements.

Varieties of corporate capitalism and the post-colonial corporation

For many commentators the history of the last one hundred years of global capitalism has been the consolidation of an increasingly monolithic (now often termed 'neoliberal') capitalism. Conversely, a well-developed line of critical analysis disputes the identification of a single form of modern capitalism. Starting with the consolidation of a range of research by Peter Hall and David Soskice into the framing of the institutional varieties of capitalism (Hall and Soskice 2001; Hanké 2009), it has become a relative commonplace in political economy analyses that capitalism is not monolithic across space any more than it is across history. While not wishing to embark on an extended account of this specific institutionalised political economic approach it is worth noting that different varieties of capitalism are to a significant extent differentiated by how the state and the corporation (or business sector more widely) interact, and how this interaction is regulated. As this suggests, a key institutional element in the comparison of varieties of capitalism is the legal system through which contemporary capitalism(s) are grounded and facilitated. Thus, as this volume emphasises, any political economy of the variable geometry of the (global) corporate sector will need to accord a sufficient weight to issues of law and legal systems that underpin global corporate networks.

Richard Whitley has suggested, from the perspective of the enterprise or corporation itself and aside from the issue of relative internationalisation, that there are three interlinked dimensions to understanding both the variance and commonalities between specific capitalist organisational forms that pattern the global political economy (Whitley 2000). The first dimension is the institution-alisation of what he refers to as *business systems*: this focuses on the manner in which ownership is coordinated; how other (non-owning) coordination takes place (which we will return to in detail in the chapter on supply chains) and how work and employment relations are managed (which will be discussed in the next chapter). This first dimension is linked to four forms of institutional actors, external to business: the state, the financial system, the skill develop-ment and control system, and the (perhaps more nebulous) social institutions of trust and authority relations (Whitley 2000: ch. 2). If this is the external environment in which business operates, Whitley is also keenly aware that there are important additional internal dimensions that also pattern different forms of capitalist economic organisation.

Therefore, the second element of his analysis focuses on the form of enterprise governance and its capabilities and strategies. This leads Whitley to identify five types of firm – the opportunistic and the artisanal, which are essentially owner-manager small firms; and three larger forms: isolated, cooperative or allied hierarchically organised enterprises (Whitley 2000: ch. 3). Whitley links these forms of enterprise characteristics with the external environment before relating that to how they structure their work systems. His third dimension then encompasses a broad tripartite typology of working systems: the Taylorist (scientific management) form of organisation, systems of delegated responsibility, and systems that focus on flexible specialisation (Whitley 2000: ch. 4). There is significant analytical complexity here to suggest that the idea of one global capitalism in which corporations operate is too generalised and is largely unhelpful.

As Whitley's analysis implies, while the expansion of US corporations overseas certainly spurred the development of the modern global corporation, this has not been the only organisational model followed; other political economic histories have prompted other hybridised settlements around the *politico-legal* place of the corporation or business enterprise. For instance, British and other European firms have utilised 'free-standing' companies as a way to invest and develop business in foreign territories (Wilkins and Schröter 1998) and this alternative (less-integrated) mode of cross-border organisation has remained a significant element even for relatively integrated global corporations. 'Free-standing' companies often have been able to combine the advantages of corporate organisation, alongside the particularities of their home economy, with the network advantages of a globalised organisational structure, not least as regarding (so-called) 'tax efficiency' (of which more later).

These forms of internationalised production to some extent find their origins in the colonial control of under-developed states and economies, where these sites of domination were utilised to underpin profitability and the expropriation of surpluses from these territories in Africa and beyond (Bairoch 1993: 88–98; Rodney 1972 [2018]: ch. 5, *passim*). Certainly, any discussion of the early economic relations between European states and those areas that they brought under their imperial rule would be incomplete without some discussion of the commercial enterprises that were involved and indeed often dominated the process of domination. Both the Dutch and then later the British East India Companies were de facto political powers in the regions they worked in, far from the metropole (Robins 2012: 203, *passim*). They moved from a purely commercial standing in such territories to effective colonial administrating organisations of their home states (especially in the case of the British company). Across what we would now refer to as the developing world, corporations worked to manage local economic organisation and development, and even after the de-colonialisation of the 1950s, 1960s and 1970s, maintained significant local economic control in the face of well-developed efforts by newly independent states to wrest the control of important aspects of their economies from them (Udofia 1984). There remains much to be explored around the corporate role in imperialism, colonialism and their attendant forms of domination and exploitation, but most importantly it would be mistaken to see the post-colonial, globalised economy as having abruptly disrupted or destroyed such relations of corporate domination and influence. Moreover, the nationality of imperial powers remains significant and influential for the variety of capitalism that has developed in these previously vassal states.

This is to say, the international reach of national corporations was enhanced through the utilisation of Export Processing Zones (EPZs), once the newly independent states began adopting such EPZs as part of their focus on economic development. As Patrick Neveling has pointed out, in the decades immediately after the Second World War, developing countries were 'hotspots for experiments and innovation in labour relations, the organisation of production processes, and regional and national economic policies' (Neveling 2017: 27). These were the places where the organisation of the new corporate multi-site, networked production system, building on interactive pathways already established over many years of more imperialistic relations was developed to become what we now call the globalised supply chain. Although we will examine the supply chain in some detail in Chapter 4, here it is worth briefly noting the origins of these supply chains in developments in communication and transportation.

The transformation of the global shipping sector by the development and then mass deployment of standardised containers in the 1970s can hardly be overstated. The move from loose and insecure freight to the secure and standardised *twenty-foot equivalent unit* (TEU) shipping container allowed the development and expansion of secure and scalable shipping around the world (Levinson 2008). Standardised and secure shipping facilitated the extension of supply chains in both scale and scope, and made the shipment of intermediate goods and components more efficient and less exposed to degradation (from shipping conditions and theft). Likewise, continuing post-telegraphic transformations in communication technologies throughout the twentieth century allowed the development of real-time coordination of economic activity. These developments (in retrospect) were necessary for the development of global supply chains, but it is important to stress that they were not sufficient; rather, corporations took advantage of these developments to respond to cost and regulatory pressures that emanated from politico-economic developments, and these networks were built on existing patterns of international operation(s).

The development of global supply chains, leading to what might be referred to as 'concentration without centralisation' (Arrighi et al. 1999: 149), is perhaps the defining characteristic of the contemporary large (global) corporation. In its most general sense the modern corporation (whatever its nationality) owes much to the development of the American corporation and its production networks, but with separation of ownership and management the most significant element. However, for Mark Casson, this overstates the internal drivers to the development of global production networks: his *internalisation* approach explains the development as a normal, cost-based response to the changing economic environment where technology developments change the calculations of profitability from any specific production location (Casson 2018). Here, the supply chain develops as corporations seek to internalise (into their network) those aspects of their production that are more costly if subject to market supply.

There is a clear parallel here with the transaction cost analysis developed by Oliver Williamson, to which we will return below. Certainly, the history of the specific organisational form of any corporation can be presented as a response to the issues raised by transaction cost economics. Corporations are constantly making choices between making or buying in: what is best carried on inside the firm (and thus outside the market), and what can be more effectively or efficiently supplied by contracting in a market for provision of materials or services? However, these decisions are, of course, made by managers, whose decision-making may well include a range of non-cost issues, responding to the particularities of the regulatory environment provided by the state. So before looking at transaction costs as a historical explanation of corporate form(s), we now turn to the actual people making corporate decisions.

The rise of the manager and the decline of the worker

Whatever the form of these calculations, corporation managers need to make informed decisions if their corporations are to remain in business; in the last one hundred years this has led to the professional manager becoming the key corporate player exercising the rights of the corporate personality on behalf of its owners. Thorstein Veblen referred to this development as the rise of 'Absentee Ownership' where those who interacted with the corporation had no chance of meeting an 'owner' (and final beneficiary of corporate profits) and thus were distanced from the effective power of such owners. Drawing a direct parallel with absentee landlords, Veblen wanted to stress the corporation's carelessness of the interests of the small-holder, supplier or customer. He concluded that in effect the corporation is 'a method of collusion and concerted action for the joint conduct of transactions designed to benefit the allied and associated owners at the cost of any whom [its actions] may concern ….… the joint-stock corporation is a conspiracy of owners' (Veblen 1923 [1997]: 409). So for Veblen, the shareholders seldom have any direct interest in the affairs and practices of the corporation beyond its ability to offer a return on investment.

Once again, it is worth stressing that that this was not a natural development. Rather, the development of a secondary market for shares (where shares are bought by those who have made no initial investment in the enterprise) was a direct result of political lobbying of the Dutch East India Company. When it became likely that it would not be able to fully honour the commitments for repayment to the original shareholders, a means by which the original investors could transfer this risk to others was required, which would allow them to recover at least part of their investment (Macaulay 2015: 10–12). Once this seventeenth-century innovation had been established it became embedded in the burgeoning European (and then global) model of stock-market and shareholding management. Thus, while 'shareholder value' (a proxy for the variable interests of actual shareholders) has increasingly become the key justification for corporate actions and strategic decisions in some major varieties of capitalism, its link to the *original* investors' decisions and interests was severed almost from the start (despite proclamations to the contrary).

The maintenance of the idea of shareholder value has been the result of the (hard) work of the financial services sector and their emphasis on a specific 'efficiency'-focused form of ownership and by extension management; what Alexander Styhre has called 'the single most successful managerial innovation over the last four decades' (Styhre 2018: 146). As will be explored later, while certainly formally accountable to the board of directors and through them to the shareholders, a new highly rewarded professional global business class has grown that, while not necessarily completely separate from owners, nevertheless has great latitude for independent management of the (global) corporation. Non-specialist investment bankers and fund managers have often (utilising market mechanisms) forgone the direct involvement in businesses that one might expect and only responded to the most immediate quarter-year's financial reporting. This can be typified as a move from 'retain and reinvest' where management focuses on the long-term growth of the corporation to a management focus on the extraction of value (money) for shareholders, sometimes termed 'downsize and distribute' (Lazonick and O'Sullivan 2000). This has led both to a focus on those aspects of the business that impact directly on market sentiment, while also allowing considerable independence to managers who, provided they stoke the share price, are rewarded whatever their other impact on the *actual* business of the corporation may be. It is this independence that has sometimes bred corruption, scandal and illegal activities and with it, a growing interest in the activities of this cadre of (international) managers; this will figure in the following chapters in a number of different guises.

Of course, corporations also are major employers and at the same time managers (and executives) have managed to gain increasing levels of control and discretion over their managerial aims and practice, while the power of labour (workers) has been, broadly speaking, moving in the opposite direction. In Europe, the plight of the corporate workforce, whether this is in pay and conditions or security of employment has generally worsened in the new millennium. Workers' share of the surplus generated by capitalist enterprises has declined, unionisation (by which workers' collective interests could be mobilised) has declined, and the discretion available to managers to shape and govern the everyday industrial relations of the corporate sector has increased (Baccaro and Howell 2017). Of course, this is not so much a new development as the end of a period in which labour was able to enhance its interests in the corporation by various means and a return to something that looks more like the capitalist model of the late nineteenth century. It has become clear that unions were more reliant on legislative and institutional support than their leaders may have realised; as labour law has been 'liberalised' so unions have lost power and influence. In many jurisdictions (in the developed states, at least) workers have considerably more developed employment rights than in the nineteenth century, for which they must thank previous generations of union organisers. Nevertheless, it is also clear that the political direction of travel has been away from the maintenance of a collective worker interest in society and the (re)development of a more atomised labour market.

Across the global political economy, corporate labour confronts the same issues; workers find themselves under-represented in corporate decision-making, through either a lack of unions, or only weak 'company unions' being recognised. Therefore, frequently across the global supply chain, workers find that full-time jobs need to be supplemented by casual extra work due to wages failing to provide enough to live on (even as supporters claim multinational corporations raise wage levels in countries in which they operate) (Råthzel et al. 2014). The liberalised, deregulated and (often) insecure conditions and practices of employment that have (re-)emerged in Europe and North America in the new millennium are not merely converging among these states but are also converging on the forms and practices of employment that multinational corporations have maintained in developing countries for decades.

On one level, as Nora Råthzel and her co-authors suggest at the end of their survey of labour relations in three major multinational corporations' sites in the Global South:

> Should workers realise and act on their own power, should they see that corporations need them more than they need corporations, then they and their communities might be able to gain control not only over those corporations but over their own lives. (Råthzel et al. 2014: 278)

Undermining the appeal of such a call for worker empowerment, corporations and their supporters have worked hard to ensure the legal environment makes the recognition and enacting of such potential power very difficult, while also utilising their discursive power to delegitimise the concerns of labour (and the legitimacy of unions). The rise of the 'gig economy', the decline of unionisation and the ability to shift workforce demands away from the developed countries (through the development of globalised production and supply networks) have shifted the balance of power in global capitalism significantly towards the corporation in the new millennium.

As this suggests there is the possibility of writing an alternate history of the corporation that presents it not merely as a response to the organisation of economic activity at an ever larger scale, but also as a response to the 'danger' of an autonomous workforce. In this framing, each development discussed above might also be seen as the manner in which the owners of capital have sought to exploit the work of labourers and workers, but also sought to control and minimise the ability of workers to act independently of capital. Perhaps the most influential proponents of this analysis are Harry Braverman and Michael Burawoy: indeed Braverman explicitly links the development of the strategy of 'de-skilling' which encompasses an increased technical (enterprise-level) division of labour to the organisation of capital investment through incorporated enterprises (Braverman 1974: 257–69). The key aspect of de-skilling is the fragmentation of work processes to enhance the technical division of labour within any enterprise with the express intention of improving the substitutability of labour; any worker can, in theory, be replaced by any other. While these methods of managerial control to some extent preceded the widespread utilisation of incorporation, nevertheless the development of the division between ownership and management (typical of the modern corporation) underpinned the intensification of the division of labour inside the corporation.

While, subsequently, this form of *Fordist* mass-production has been at least partly displaced by 'flexible specialisation', this remains limited to enterprises at the high-skill, high-technology end of manufacture. In the realm of global supply chains, the de-skilled highly controlled workforce remains much more evident. Already in 1979, Burawoy saw the management structures that maintained and expanded managerial control over fragmenting industrial practice as being an 'internal state' that needed to establish at least a minimal level of workforce consent to be managed in this way (not least through financial incentives) (Burawoy 1979: 109–20). This analysis will be picked up when we discuss legitimacy and the democratic deficit in the global supply chain. Even if the contours of corporate practice(s) have become more complex and differentiated both within and between enterprises, the de-skilling analysis identifies a key aspect of the history of the corporation: the integration and control of knowledge about process with the express purpose of managing for profitability. However, it is not always the case, as we will now explore, that enterprises (including corporations) have sought to directly control all aspects of the economic activity that contributes to profitability.

The history of the corporation through the lens of transaction cost economics

Having suggested there is a labour-focused history of the development of corporate capitalism, in this last section I want to look at the development of individual corporations to suggest *transaction cost economics* offers a useful set of analytical tools for considering *particular* corporate histories. For the transaction costs approach to the economics of the business enterprise (corporation), the key organisational driver is the desire to reduce costs associated with the activity undertaken (or planned). The focus on reducing costs is because (all other things remaining equal) this will raise profits for the enterprise and therefore its owners. Transaction cost economics is an approach that seeks to understand the shape and character of the enterprise (firm or corporation) as a quest for efficiency defined as cost-effectiveness. Indeed, Oliver Williamson has asserted that the 'progressive evolution of the modern corporation records the imprint of transaction cost economizing at every stage' (Williamson 1985: 295). Transaction cost analyses put the organisational aspects of the business enterprise at the centre of analysis and while not displacing technology-led accounts, do much to modify any singular focus on the control and deployment of specific technological advantage.

As Ronald Coase pointed out in his founding analysis, the 'main reason why it is profitable to establish a firm would seem to be that there is a cost to using the price mechanism' (Coase 1937 [1993]: 21). These market-related costs include those incurred in 'discovery'; how to calculate and assess the 'correct' price for any given input. Other costs involved in contracted market relations include dealing with uncertainty in demand and/or supply conditions. However, transaction cost economics argues that we can observe that these costs are reduced (although not necessarily eliminated) by bringing activities within the 'border' of the enterprise and removing them from the external market. However, as Coase also emphasised the cost advantage gained from internalising functions and activities may not last, and the gain through the exercise of direct authority may recede, encouraging the return of the function or activity to the market (Coase 1937 [1993]: 22). As this implies, even as this analysis of why firms or business enterprises exist and develop was in its early stages, the idea of 'outsourcing' (if as yet not so termed), when external expertise or specialism makes contracting more effective, was a central part of the account. As this also makes clear, and as Tony Lawson has recently pointed out (Lawson 2019: 110), actually Coase and those who have followed his lead are less interested in the *nature* of the firm (for instance, its legal/institutional character) than why it has developed to have the shape or boundaries that it has.

Moreover, while Coase does not offer a historical account of these developments (he largely deals with them in schematic and abstract terms), in a short final reflection he asks 'whether the concept of the firm which has been developed fits in with that existing in the real world' (Coase 1937 [1993]: 29). This question is answered positively through the suggestion that the firm/enterprise finds its origins in the expansion of the legally constituted inter-personal relationship between employer and employee, where the key issue is not so much the right to payment as the authority of actions ceded by the latter to the former as part of the employment relation. For Coase, the legal constitution of the firm (corporation) is merely this relationship writ larger, but as Scott Masten has demonstrated (in relation to employment contracts) actually the cost advantage identified by Coase is dependent on the *difference* between inter-personal contract relations and those mandated by employment law alongside the characteristic employee behaviours these incentivise (Masten 1993). In other words, the particular legal constitution of the firm (corporation), here as regards employment but also more widely, is what enables transaction costs to be reduced; the existence of the firm, enterprise or corporation and its specific organisational character is dependent on the relations between various regulatory measures in the particular market realm in which it operates.

More recently, the resurgence of transaction cost economics is a response to the work of Oliver Williamson, whose motivation in part was to explain the vertical integration of enterprises, not least of all in light of the US Supreme Court's failure to understand any benign motivation in such integrative strategies (Ketokivi and Mahoney 2017: 5). Thus, contrasting vertical and horizontal integration, where the latter is seen as a move towards unwelcome market concentration (the consolidation of similar enterprises to reduce competition), vertical integration is presented in transaction cost economics as a reasoned response to the market environment's costings of various inputs or services. However, it is not necessarily clear how such boundary-changing choices are made; it may be they are calculated rationally or it may be by a more iterative process of organic discovery. Indeed, Peter Buckley and Malcolm Chapman have argued that it is managerial *perceptions* of cost that are actually the key element when considering transactions costs (Buckley and Chapman 1997).

There is considerable analytical advantage in including in the costs that transaction cost analysis should seek to capture as explanatory those 'costs' that are not financial. Transaction costs may take many different forms and any analysis of the current configuration of a corporation needs not only to assess what financial costs the current organisational settlement has avoided, but also other non-pecuniary costs that have influenced strategic organisational choices.

Williamson also stresses that transaction cost(s) focused strategy depends on a range of legal structures, of which the most important is contract law, to manage activities – whether these are contracts between enterprises or between agents within the corporation (Williamson 1985: 397–401, *passim*). The calculation of transaction costs (financial and non-financial) is dependent on and responds to the legal environment which the corporation or business enterprise is working within. To understand the history of a particular corporation, then, for Williamson and his followers there is a need to focus on the micro-analysis of corporate decisions and understand these as responses to transaction costs. Williamson stresses that this introduces the necessary analysis of 'friction', which has been more established in engineering than it has in economics. While both start from an assumption of an absence of friction (in pure theoretical terms), economics often retains this assumption in subsequent applied work (unlike engineering which has to work out how to deal with physical friction); transaction cost approaches, on the other hand, make economic 'friction' central to the account of corporate decision-making (Williamson 2013: ix–x). The history of the (specific) corporation then becomes in part (at least) how managers and others have dealt with the frictions that appear due to the complexity of dealing with real human beings, not merely rationally calculating cyphers.

This can become very clear when the transaction cost approach is used to explore the corporate utilisation of what is often now referred to as the 'gig economy'. As Mary Gray and Siddharth Suri (interestingly, Microsoft-employed social scientists) detail in their recent research, the costs of finding and managing large groups of freelancers working in an effective spot market for small-scale tasks has been transformed by platforms like Amazon's *Mechanical Turk* and Microsoft's own *Universal Human Relevance System*, alongside other sites with similar functionality (Gray and Suri 2019; 69–75, *passim*). This has enabled corporations to shift a range of tasks outside the legal boundary of the enterprise, as the costs of searching for and contracting with suitable workers is now low enough that there are insufficient cost or efficiency savings to warrant the expense of established employment. This could be seen as merely the outsourcing approach to business organisation moving into a more fine-grained aspect of business tasks; Gray and Suri detail a range of micro-tasks that can now be provided to a business via online work allocation and tendering systems. Conversely, as a number of the cases set out in their research attest, the focus on costs can result in new problems and renewed cost calculations can lead to a half-way house where corporations seek to maintain forms of managerial control they have developed *within* their established workforce for their 'preferred' contractors. This desire to both maintain corporate managerial controls while shedding responsibility for the ongoing employment (and its associated legal requirements) of the workforce is perhaps best exemplified by *platform capitalism* and its legal travails (to which we return in Chapter 6).

One thing is clear; the argument that *transaction cost economics* might develop for the origins of the corporation works well for the history of *specific* corporations, but for the transaction cost advantage to be realised the corporate form itself must already be constituted. Thus, while this approach can be a powerful lens for discussing particular corporations' history and organisational development, it only makes sense in the context of the existing pre-history of the corporate legal form. Again, as this demonstrates, we need this historical dimension to make sense of corporations' political economy, even if the wider history is not necessarily required for an analysis of a particular corporation. Certainly transaction cost economics might reveal the cost-related drivers that influenced early business operators to seek legal changes that would allow the effective conglomeration of activities that a transaction cost approach would suggest would be better achieved outside the market (within the enterprise). However, it cannot offer clear insight into specific corporations' development prior to the establishment of these legal structures themselves.

Why the history of the corporation matters

Having spent this chapter outlining a range of historical issues, it should now be clear that one of the reasons for any account of the (global) corporation to maintain some historical sensitivity is that not only does the corporation have a long and variegated history, but this history reveals the (politically) contingent character of the current corporate settlement(s). There is a significant element of path dependence in the history of the global corporate system. As Paddy Ireland concludes his recent history of incorporation (which parallels much of the above):

> The institutional arrangements that currently prevail – including the dominance of finance – are not the inevitable products of some all-powerful, irresistible, universal, market-based, beneficent, purely economic logic . . . . [H]istorically the tensions

between the socializing and financializing tendencies inherent in the corporation, with its detached hybrid owner-creditor shareholders, have been resolved in different ways at different times. *These different outcomes have been determined as much by political decisions and their impact on prevailing institutional arrangements as they have by the economic logic of either capitalism or the market.* (Ireland 2016: 97; emphasis added)

Therefore, while approaches like transaction cost economics offer a powerful and useful analytical tool for understanding the shape and development of corporations, they do not adequately (and in fairness do not often pretend to) represent the legal-historical route by which the response to market cost issues would come to inform strategic decision-making. To a large extent this is because too often the corporation is tacitly understood as representing the 'end of history' of economic organisation (Baars 2016: 139); there is a teleological tendency to analysis that treats the current corporate form as the end point of a process of progressive (legal) improvement or refinement. Although business history as a discipline has focused on the practice of corporations, a more highly political (and politicised) history of the current legal settlement and the (albeit variegated) assumption of the normality of the contemporary legal form is required. This lack of historical reflection is a key aspect of what this volume is arguing: that analyses of the globalised political economy of corporations need to move beyond current limited practices.

Key questions for research(ers)

How does the history of the corporation continue to influence or even determine its contemporary political economy?

Are the 'problems' that critics identify with corporations historically 'baked in', therefore making calls for reform likely to be unsuccessful?

How do we understand the political motivations of the main actors and/ or groups that have shaped the legal, political economic history of the corporation?

How is our understanding of imperialism and colonialism modified by including corporations as active agents alongside states in its history?

Can a new history of (global) corporations be developed that focuses on the agency of labour, and balances management-centred or technology-centred account(s)?

Note

1. Space precludes an extensive treatment of the East India Company's over two centuries of activity, but Nick Robins' study not only offers a well-developed critical history of the enterprise but also is clear throughout regarding the company's place in the history of corporations' legal form and signature activities (see Robins 2012: *passim* but especially well summarised in ch. 10).

3   Managing the corporation

When we reflect on the management of corporations (both externally in the sense of regulation of activity, and internally as corporate governance), Teivo Teivainen warns that we should avoid *economism*, a 'strategy of defining certain institutions and issues as economic and using the doctrine of economic neutrality to produce a boundary between the economic and political spheres' (Teivainen 2002: 318). This leads him to suggest that we should judge the internal managerial structures of corporations by similar liberal standards that we deploy to adjudge more formally acknowledged democratic institutions. In other words, a 'more radical interpretation [of democracy] would extend democratic demands into formally private capitalist enterprises, especially those that because of their size or functions have significant effects on people's lives' (Teivainen 2002: 335–6). Therefore, he concludes:

> Once we start analysing transnational [*sic*] corporations and global economic organisations as inherently political animals, the extent to which there already exists a global political bureaucracy with intergovernmental bodies and 'private' departments of strategic planning becomes more obvious (Teivainen 2002: 338).

Certainly, one might suggest that corporations (and business enterprises more generally) are insufficiently like states to be remodelled along democratic lines, but this is not necessarily as clear cut as critics of workplace and corporate democratisation argue.

Indeed, Hélène Landermore and Isabelle Ferreras (2016) have countered the incommensurability position (that corporations cannot be held to democratic norms) across five of its key elements. They argue that, firstly, despite the superficial difference between 'profit' and 'welfare', actually if one sees both as the way that firms and states (respectively) gauge their sustainability then they are working to comparable ends. Secondly, arguments that utilise property in shares to suggest corporations and states have different mechanisms of control misunderstand the division between ownership and control in the modern corporation. In both cases a quasi-'independent' executive actually controls the organisation (albeit with differing forms of political oversight), making a clear managerial distinction difficult.

Next, Landermore and Ferreras focus on workers: it may be true that unlike states' citizens workers are *voluntary* members of the organisation, and are 'free' to leave at any time. However, due to the social structures of capitalism (the need to work, the state of the labour market, the difficulty of finding replacement employment promptly) in effect workers are *practically* in a relatively similar situation to citizens, who of course can also migrate and/or reject their citizenship. Likewise, they reject the limitation of the extension of workplace democracy on the basis of cost and conflict of interest, citing the success of other forms of organisation (which we will return to below). Lastly, while accepting that in abstract terms corporations are more fragile (more likely to disappear) than states, they also note that there are significant numbers of global (and national) corporations that are older, and more stable than many now stabilised European and post-colonial states. This all suggests that objections to the analogy between states and corporations as regards political organisation are less than self-evident. Therefore, this chapter focuses on how we might best understand the political dimensions of the management of the corporation. This is to pose the question: *how might we fruitfully understand corporations as institutions of (political) governance and by doing so expand the analytical tools available to address their (political) powers?* As such, this chapter focuses largely on the politics *within* the corporation, leaving the *external* facing aspect of corporate political power to Chapter 5.

In thinking about the governance (and management) of the corporation, much analytical work in the twentieth century, especially that which adopted a law and economics perspective, assumed that the key questions concerned the dispersal of ownership through shareholding, resulting in among other things, the development of a market *for* ownership. Here, research and analysis often focused on the relations between principal and agents, the fulfilment of fiduciary duties and the question of managerial incentives. There is a large technical and legal literature that explores and analyses forms and practices of corporate governance; I do not intend to rehearse these discussions at length here, rather I will concentrate on issues that allow us to widen the focus of attention away from approaches that would seem likely to attract Teivainen's accusation of 'economism'. Indeed, while such a governance model, responding to a market for ownership (shares) is widespread in Anglo-Saxon economies, it is much less dominant elsewhere in the global economy, even when forms of incorporation are being utilised (Goyer 2010: 426). Nevertheless, as the contemporary law and economics approach focuses largely on a universalised set of governance contexts, it remains a reasonable place from which to start.

Inside and outside the corporation

Perhaps most importantly, while in the first half of the twentieth century the law and economics approach (centred on Chicago University) was at least partly concerned with the problem of monopoly and the issues of corporate domination of sectoral markets, in the ten years after 1946 this concern was largely displaced (Styhre 2018: 28–30). Thus, as Rob van Horn concludes, by the mid-1950s,

> advocates and converts no longer regarded monopoly as the great enemy of democracy, much less a force to be broken up . . . Rather they argued that not only was monopoly not deleterious to the operation of the market, but also that it was a negligible symptom attributable to ill-functioning ham-fisted activities of government. (Van Horn 2015: 229)

Large and dominant corporations began to be seen as largely benign actors whose market domination would only survive as they continued to serve their customers. Law and economics as an approach therefore became more interested in the regulation of the internal governance of corporations to ensure they continued to respond to market incentives, and considerably less interested in the manner in which corporations might shape, and (re)form, the markets in which they operated.

As such, contemporary law and economics work has sought to develop analyses of the role(s) of agents within corporate structures – the motivations of, and incentives for, directors for instance – while remaining relatively under-contextualised either historically or socially (Goyer 2010: 429–30). To some extent this reflects the general criticism being developed throughout this book; that research into corporations needs to be historicised (and open to a range of analytical perspectives) to deliver real insight. Nevertheless, approaches rooted in law and economics analysis have suggested a key (if partial) aspect of corporate governance that requires exploration: the relations between the owners as principals and the managers of corporations as their agents. The management of the relations between shareholders and executives, sometimes widened to include more general issues of corporate governance has been a focus for work that explores how firms (and specifically corporations) are managed aside from their externally facing market relations (Stout 2017). There are a number of ways that law and economics approaches have sought to develop this analysis, but here I will mention just two: the firm as a nexus of contracts, and the centrality of the 'problem' of principal–agent relations.

In the nexus of contracts approach, the corporation is the sum of all contractual relations between its component actors/agents (Jensen and Meckling 1976). This analysis looks like an increasingly attractive proposition as global supply chains and (international) outsourcing have become more widespread and developed, as we will examine in the next chapter. These arrangements, it is often also noted, are also affected by the incomplete character of contracts themselves. Contracts can never completely predict and specify future events/developments between the contracting parties that might need to be managed (Zingales 2002). This approach, then, explores how these contracts both incentivise and obstruct beneficial practices between the parties and the impact this has on the success or otherwise of the corporation, where problems may be resolved through improved forms of contracting. This has prompted a linked interest in how principals (here, shareholders) might constrain or control the self-regarding, self-interested actions of their agents (in this case, corporate executives and managers). Indeed, much of the critical discussion of corporate governance now focuses on the potentially perverse incentives that 'solutions' to principal–agent issues have introduced to the corporate sector. The most obvious has been the attempt to align managerial interests and practice with shareholder interests through the utilisation of rewards systems that include elements of share-transfer to executives and other high-level corporate employees. Bringing these approaches together, law and economics has seen the corporation as a legally constituted entity, governed by explicit legal/formal agreement(s) between contracting parties (Cohen 2017). However, while certainly a plausible analysis of certain elements of corporate practice, it remains a partial analysis that seeks to exclude normative concerns as non-actionable (Langlois 2016). Such approaches can only be useful, inasmuch as they relate to other perspectives and to the actual management of business enterprise(s).

This, then, brings us back to how we might understand the variations within the general global corporate sector. Leaving aside small (owner-operated/managed) enterprises, as noted in the previous chapter, Richard Whitley suggests there are three broad types of large(r) firms: ones with an isolated hierarchy, those with a cooperative hierarchy, and those with an allied hierarchy. In the first type, enterprises are best understood as effectively controlled by absentee owners (subject to the market from ownership and control through stock exchanges) who function as isolated economic actors. In the cooperative and allied hierarchical categories corporations have links of various types with other economic actors, be they similar or differing in their own capabilities and strategies (Whitley 2000: 67–72). Therefore, one key differentiation between corporations is to account for the level/extent of the interpenetration of governance functions across their business practices.

Broadly speaking, we can see three dimensions where governance effects and functions can be identified. In this chapter I will be mainly focusing on those within the corporation itself, usually discussed under the term 'corporate governance'. In Chapter 4, I will explore the other dimension, the externalised governance function that can be identified across corporations' global supply chains. My analysis of supply chains in that chapter will suggest that corporations exercise a significant governance function across their networks and perhaps as importantly, despite the claims that modern capitalism is patterned by (and indeed depends upon) competition, what is most often evident *inside* the corporation and its production network is a significant amount of economic *planning*. Given that (whatever your preferred form of comparison) many corporations approach (or even exceed) the size of state bureaucracies and economies, it should be no surprise that the actual use of economic planning is widespread. However, as so often for many analysts, there is a distinction to be drawn between planning by states' governments, and planning by capitalist organisations, with the former often seen as market interference while the latter is seen as prudent management.

Large corporations (as transaction cost economics would suggest) remove interactions from the market where the associated transaction costs are too high, and bring them within the corporation's own organisational domain. Once the market, as an organisational and allocation mechanism has been removed, all that is left is one or other form of planning, even if the rhetoric continues to refer to the 'internal market'. Thus, as William Dugger argued in the 1980s (when the growth of corporations' role in society was already becoming clear), when we think about the power of the corporation, we should not miss that its internal capital and labour 'markets' are significant bases for power to be both developed and mobilised. The ability to move capital around the enterprise (perhaps most significantly the ability to cross subsidise activities between divisions or units), as well as the ability to frame and control the lives of workers through corporate choices about opportunities made available to the various (stratified) elements of the workforce and their conditions of employment, all underpin the political economic power of the corporation and its senior managers over the realm in which it operates (Dugger 1985). As this suggests, the key 'technology' deployed by corporations to enhance their power is *organisation* (Dugger 1988: 85) or, as I am discussing it here, *governance*.

This reflects the realisation among managers that what is required for them to control corporate activity and strategies is not the brutal exercise of power (which can be both inefficient and ineffective) but rather the inculcation of corporate insiders (from workers to managers) into the governing values and norms of the corporation. However, there must also be some acceptance of the legitimacy of such authority to govern, both within and outside the corporation. This requires analysts to see the corporation as an organisation conducting political governance as well as managing technical economic relations (May 2015). Thus, the general concerns about management *as* governance developed below will then inform the more focused discussion of the corporate supply chain or production network in the next chapter.

It is also worth stressing that the ability and power to *internally* organise the global corporate network allows managers to not only cross-subsidise units for strategic purposes, but also to move (via accounting protocols) profit to where it will attract the lowest tax rates (Ylönen and Teivainen 2018). The question of taxation and its reform is one of the key issues for many commentators on global corporate affairs, but here it also signifies the financial/economic organisational element of global corporate power. Indeed, as we will see, when we discuss the global supply chain, power based in organisational functionality is key to understanding global corporate power. The history of the global tax regime for business has always focused on the avoidance of unfair double taxation, with considerable effort by states' governments over the years put into establishing a regime that guards against such 'danger' (Avi-Yonah 2019: 3–6). However, the complexities of the system have allowed many corporations to actively manage their tax affairs, and by doing so to radically reduce their level of global exposure to tax on their profits.

As this suggests, and as Katharina Pistor has argued at some length, multinational corporations are essentially 'central planners':

> While we like to think of global markets as an open space in which economic actors freely compete based on the price mechanism, in reality we find that a substantial part of all transnational commerce takes place within transnational [*sic*] firms. Inside firms' resources are allocated by means that only remotely resemble open markets, notwithstanding the widely used language of 'internal markets' – a contradiction in terms. (Pistor 2014: 247)

The governance functionality which is central to understating corporate organisation is utilised, when possible, to transfer risk, costs and adjustment to external parties, while capturing the benefits (financial and organisational) for the corporation. An approach rooted in law and economics approaches sees this as a result of the legal systems mandated by the forms of corporate governance established in a specific jurisdiction.

Additionally, a third dimension of governance (which I will also discuss in Chapter 5 on corporate politics) is now clear: corporations are also instrumental in governing the external economic environment in which they operate, by managing the balance of activity they control or govern *between* the internal and the external (by managing the transaction cost-related boundary of the enterprise). To give one contemporary example of such balancing, for instance, especially among the various social media and platform capitalist corporations that work across the Internet, we might identify an active governance function where consumers use social media services. Ori Schwarz has used the example of Facebook to argue that it has developed a set of rules and practices that effectively govern an external space of what might now be referred to as 'generalised social capital' (Schwarz 2019). On one level, one might see such rules as part of a high-tech barter economy by which in return for free social media services and benefits we agree not only to provide our data for re-use, but also to follow the 'club rules'. However, it may be much more political than that and so I will return to this issue in Chapter 5. More immediately, this concern to recognise the *political* in corporate practices can also be directed towards the other two dimensions, and so it is the corporation's internal forms of governance that I will focus on below.

Inside the corporation

Space precludes a full review of the wide range of attempts to make sense of the internal organisation of the corporation. However, to demonstrate that discussing the internal *politics* of the corporation is hardly novel, I will start with Earl Latham's depiction of its body politic from the late 1950s and James March's argument that the firm is actually a political coalition, from the early 1960s. Drawing on political science more generally, and arguing that economists have mistakenly ignored its *political* aspects, Latham argued that the corporation has five essential *political* functions as regards its own organisational realm. Firstly, it has a management that can authoritatively allocate its principal functions around the organisation. Secondly, there is some form of system for the ratification of these decisions, most obviously the board of directors, although as will become clear, issues of legitimacy of decision-making around the various 'communities' or 'publics' of the corporation may require negotiation not merely imposition. Thirdly, there is a system of command that communicates decisions and fourthly some form of reward or punishment (which we might now more readily discuss under the term incentives or performance management). Lastly, Latham also rightly notes that there must be some capacity for the enforcement of the decisions and ongoing operational norms (Latham 1959). As Latham's second point makes clear there are always going to be forms of negotiation *within* the corporation.

Here, James March's suggestion that it is best to see the business enterprise and/or corporation as a political coalition that only moves forward through negotiation and conflict resolution, provides the context in which Latham's political processes take place. As March points out, this shifts analytical focus from the relations between owners and the entity (i.e. issues of shareholder control) to a consideration of the manner in which the enterprise's internal organisational practice is managed when there are groups within it that have differing interests, aspirations and priorities (March 1962: 674). This also points to the context-dependence of much corporate and enterprise decision-making as well as the contingency of solutions that are developed. By seeing the corporation as a political coalition constantly subject to negotiation and conflict resolution, differences between corporations and inconsistencies within them no longer seem anomalous or surprising. Again, this suggests that the focus for the study of the corporation should be more on forms and practices of *governance* than *management*.

Likewise, and more recently, Elizabeth Anderson has focused on the internal governance of the enterprise to argue that a political analysis reveals much hitherto under-appreciated by a focus only on *management*. Discussing the situation in America, but identifying aspects of the control of the workforce that would be much more widely recognised, Anderson suggests that the best analogue for a corporation's governance structure is a *communist dictatorship* (Anderson 2017: ch. 2). She argues that while there are final sanctions that back up the orders received by workers, nevertheless there is significant political power in the organisation (partly based on performance management of various forms) to ensure high levels of compliance, and indeed workers are socialised into an acceptance of the legitimacy of the power managers have over the workers' working day. Certainly in many ways the private governance of the firm or corporation does not approach the power of the state, however private governments 'impose a far more minute, exacting and sweeping regulation of employees than democratic states in any domain outside of prisons and the military' (Anderson 2017: 63). The extent of the deployment of this private governmental power may vary between enterprises (and societies), but the basic political point for Anderson is that for workers this is a more onerous form of government than they would be prepared to accept beyond the employment relation.

This leads Anderson to conclude that private government in the workplace

> embeds inequalities in authority, standing, and esteem in the organisations upon which people depend for their livelihood. Those consigned to the status of wage worker for life have no real way out: while they can quit any given employer, often at great cost and risk, they cannot opt out of the wage labour system that structurally degrades and demeans them. (Anderson 2017: 130)

Certainly, there may be legal limits put upon the exercise of such government (governance) by the state, but for Anderson this does not diminish the limitations on political autonomy that would be regarded as both legitimate and mandatory in other spheres of a market democracy. This leads her to argue that what is required in the corporate workplace is a more extensive form of democratic accountability, an enhancement of workers' ability to voice their interests and concerns, and for these concerns to be accorded real political weight in any governance structure. This is why I have identified a 'democratic deficit' as a key political problem for corporate managers and, given the possible counter-intuitive direction of this analytical approach, have developed such an analysis below and in the following chapter's account of the terrain of the global corporate supply chain.

More generally, as Isabelle Ferreras puts it: 'All contemporary capitalist firms are governed nondemocratically [fn. del]. Their government might be described as "capitalo-cratic" in that capital investors hold power over the firm via the corporation' (Ferreras 2017: 114). When power within corporations is discussed, there is no real dispute that investors have legitimate power (albeit delegated to senior managers) over the enterprise (although, as noted in the introduction to this volume, Ferreras disputes the elision of the firm and the corporation).

Developing workplace democracy?

The above discussion *could* be re-framed as a response to Friedrich Hayek's well-known criticism of attempts to plan in a world of complex and variable information and knowledge. For Hayek, the impossibility of knowing everything that would be required for successful socialist planning, suggested that unfettered markets (subject only to facilitating regulation) offered the best hope for efficient and effective social coordination. However, given the removal of enterprises' internal relations from the market the problem Hayek identifies remains active within the large corporation. This leads Theodore Burczak to argue that actually Hayek's question about the accessibility of tacit knowledge might be best solved *inside* the firm or corporation, by forms of worker representation and involvement in planning, as even internal quasi-markets do not function in the 'free' manner that Hayek's analysis would require (Burczak 2006). While this might slowly lead to an expansion of worker cooperatives best able to mobilise such knowledge, equally it is an interesting defence of workplace empowerment as an efficiency enhancing measure, rather than only a political issue of workplace justice.

This can be seen both in a technical sense of the place of the worker's voice in the governance of corporations but also in the consideration of what benefits forms of enhanced representation might bring. In other words, shifting to more democratic forms of internal workforce governance might have effects both on the corporation *and* on the workforce. The organisation of the workplace is not only an economic issue but has clear political dimensions as well and given the strength of the norm of democracy, adopting this perspective would imply that workplace democracy needs to be more widely institutionalised (although of course in some jurisdictions it is, however incompletely this is subsequently achieved) (Dejours et al. 2018). This requires a move beyond the standard economic notion that work is merely instrumental and thereby is the cost of obtaining leisure; work needs to be seen as having intrinsic value, which has been widely recognised beyond mainstream economics and suggests that different forms of management might be more effective than a focus on labour price/cost.

There are many current and past models/forms of democratic management of the workplace, from the experiments with self-management in Yugoslavia in the 1960s/1970s, to continuing forms of cooperative management, with perhaps the most high-profile examples being Mondragon in Spain and the John Lewis Partnership in the UK. In his often cited comparative analysis of forms of ownership of enterprises, Henry Hansmann suggested that the choice of ownership structure between investor-controlled firms and those owned by other groups associated with the enterprise (from professions' partnerships to cooperative/worker-owned enterprises) was, and is, related to cost. The costs of contracting for financial capital relative to the costs of contracting for other required/necessary inputs (including labour) inform organisational settlements. Where the contracting costs for finance outweigh other costs, then investors will organise an ownership structure (shareholding) that mitigates those costs. Equally, investors are often the key corporate owners because their social practices allow the development of a collective *political* interest that is more easily exercised than other groups that are in one way or another engaged with the enterprise's operations (Hansmann 1996). Of course the second aspect, especially, is directly related to the political context (and its associated regulation) in which an enterprise sits. Thus, if we briefly examine the case of self-management in the 1960s and 1970s in (then) Yugoslavia, a different set of possibilities is evident, not least as the state developed alternative approaches to the financing of corporate enterprises.

Nowadays, this relatively short-lived system of workers' self-management in Yugoslavia has been largely forgotten by economists, or political economists for that matter. At the time, in the 1960s and 1970s, this 'experiment' with self-management was seen as an interesting organisational alternative, with even the World Bank publishing broadly supportive analyses. At the end of the 1970s a team of World Bank researchers concluded that aspects of the planning at plant/organisational level were 'rational' and had clear benefits. However, the ability to manage the wider development of an economy dominated by self-managed enterprises would, they expected, produce a number of problems around coordination, especially if the economy maintained an openness to world markets (Schrenk et al. 1979: 77–81; see also Dubey 1975). Likewise, writing a little after the high point of self-management, Stephen Sacks argued that the system worked well as there was effective transfer price negotiation between enterprises and this provided a mechanism to ensure opportunism did not replace the social solidarity (in respect of the enterprises' collective aims) fostered by the socialist government. Indeed, for Sacks (deploying a transaction costs-related analysis, not dissimilar to Hansmann) the self-management system worked well when workers were able to manage their enterprises in ways that to a large extent paralleled the judgements that would be made by non-worker management (Sacks 1983). Here the allocation of capital for investment became the key issue: how individual enterprises managed (re)investment against the conservation of capital reserves was a set of decisions that was subject to negotiation between the enterprise and the state, which could lead to decisions at enterprise level being frustrated by national 'priorities' or capital rationing.

At the heart of self-management of such decisions was the workers' council. Despite legal restraints on the autonomy of managers and the constitutional establishment of workers' consultation, in reality the ability of the councils to effect enterprise's policy was uneven at best, and at times honoured in the breach. Nevertheless, the context enabled workers who were so interested to develop collective responses to managers and to ensure there was a political space where such engagements were regarded as legitimate (Ramović 2018: 178–80). However, even at its height, the system of self-management maintained significant differences even within any particular enterprise, with gender and age divisions among the workforce affecting how workers interacted with the systems of self-management; dominant, elder (often more skilled), male workers largely controlled the councils and to some extent captured the rewards of self-management (Archer and Musić 2017: 47–51). Self-management did not automatically remove divisive issues (and prejudices) within the workforce, even if the opportunities for resolving such tensions seemed more open. Moreover, as self-managed enterprises competed and entered international market relations, so the Yugoslav model looked ever more like forms of worker involvement being experimented with in sectors of the Western capitalist countries.

It is this convergence that both underpins the World Bank's relatively support-ive reports in the 1970s and Darko Suvin's negative assessment in his recent *X-Ray of Socialist Yugoslavia*. In the latter Suvin regards self-management as a top-down imposition on the working class of Yugoslavia, that empowered a particular element to join the managerial (middle) class, omitted many workers from actual self-management and by the 1970s had lost any of its rev-olutionary potential (Suvin 2017: 259–63, *passim*). Indeed, it seems clear that whatever the assessment of the self-management of enterprises in Yugoslavia, a key abiding element was the difficulty of removing the managerial function from the enterprise, inasmuch as such managerial needs always required some form of hierarchy within the decision-making process, whatever the legal constitution and expected practice of the workers' councils. Many would argue that similar issues have always confronted worker-managed enterprises.

To some extent this has been resolved in the most successful worker-controlled enterprises by a focus on a set of shared values. In some interesting compara-tive work on eight such enterprises (including both the John Lewis Partnership in the UK and Mondragon in Spain) Richard Hoffman and Frank Shipper identify eight sets of values (across two levels) that contribute to the success of these worker-controlled enterprises. The first set of values is concerned with the establishment of modes of affiliation with the group, the encourage-ment of workers' sense of a collective mission or project. These are grouped under four headings: honesty/fairness, freedom/autonomy, empowerment and egalitarianism. Certainly, in their comparative study not all enterprises achieved similar levels of shared values in these four dimensions, but each managed to make them reasonably active for the enterprise. However, the key issue is that all enterprises had participatory mechanisms that ought to support these values. The second set of values shared across the comparator group is related more to operational issues and again are identified under four headings: accountability/merit, transparency, community and sustainability. It is here that hierarchies are justified by their ability to further the success of the business, while remaining within these value structures, and by valuing the members of the organisation, encouraging commitment to the enterprise's goals and by building trust in the organisation's practices and management (Hoffman and Shipper 2018). None of these values are necessarily exclusive to worker-controlled enterprises, but in corporations they have proved both hard to engender and often managers have shown little proclivity to be concerned about them at all. It is to the corporate managerial class that we must therefore now turn, to seek to understand why these values often seem foreign to them even when calls for corporate social responsibility would seem to be related to such values.

Managers: a class apart

Perhaps unsurprisingly, a focus on managers immediately leads us to a concern for *class* relations: Stephen Resnick and Richard Wolff offer an intriguing analysis of the internal class environment of the corporation suggesting class-based power relations are not only external to the enterprise. They focus on how specific groups within (and outside) the corporation/enterprise distribute the accumulated (and generated) surpluses; these groups distribute

> surplus value in the form of taxes to state officials, discounts to merchants, rents to landlords, and . . . are as important to the existence of the capitalist fundamental class process as are the distribution in the form of dividends to owners, interest to creditors and salaries to managers. (Resnick and Wolff 1989: 178)

Their argument is that the more formal Marxist analysis of the corporation, as *only* distributing surplus value (derived from its operations and specifically its labour force) via dividends, misses an important dimension of the corporate (enterprise) role in the reproduction of capitalist accumulation across the economy. One key aspect of this analysis is that competition *within* the enterprise to capture value from its operations is a normal (and expected) part of its political economy; each group seeks to distribute surpluses to its favoured recipients, be they landlords, merchants or creditors (Resnick and Wolff 1989: 192). However, not all of these groups are equally successful: certainly, in the USA and the UK, the focus on maximising shareholder value has enabled one key internal group not only to control the corporation, but to maximise the value that they (as a group) have been able to extract, at the cost of the other stakeholders.

In William Lazonick's analysis, the stock market might be regarded as serving a number of linked business-related functions, but actually ends up serving the interests of the corporation's management. Firstly, a stock market listing effectively separates control of the corporation from its putative owners. Secondly, at the moment of an initial public offering (IPO) of shares, or during subsequent corporate share 'offers' the stock market can be used to raise cash for investment or other activities. This links to the third aspect by which the stock market, through an IPO, is a mechanism for entrepreneurs to seek private equity funding for new ventures. The stock market also underpins the use of stocks/shares as a currency for the facilitation of mergers and acquisitions, enabling the combination of corporate enterprises for a variety of reasons. Lastly, the stock market's operations have increasingly been used as a part of the support for the compensation (payment) of senior managers (Lazonick 2018: 199–220, *passim*). Lazonick concludes that it is the combination of the first and last of these functions that actually is the key to understanding corporations' managers' activities and practices. While on one hand this analysis is most relevant to what might be termed *Anglo-Saxon corporate capitalism*, as noted in the introduction, the preference for listing shares on the New York and London stock exchanges has pushed many non-Anglo-Saxon enterprises towards this model even if it is partly or wholly alien to their national political economy.

So, while 'shareholder value' is, to a large extent, related to a specific and formalised legislative framing for business, this approach is increasingly widespread across the global corporate system. While not all jurisdictions require fiduciary duties to focus on the maintenance of shareholder value, nonetheless it is a common requirement. However, the potentially wider focus on the value tied up in the corporation has been reduced to the notion that stock markets 'price in' all value that the corporation might be said to encompass, and thus the share price has often become a direct, if simplified analogue for value. Therefore, managers, having largely freed themselves from the control of *external* shareholders, no longer respond to more abstract characterisations of the value of the corporation, and through their compensation packages being shareholders themselves, are often now focused on how to manipulate the activities of the corporation to enhance the share price, and thereby their own wealth. In theory this might lead them to direct their attention to ensuring the long-term success of the enterprise, perhaps seeking out new innovative technologies or working to expand the business' most effective operations. However, most stock market actors (usually institutional investors) focus on quarterly results, yearly returns and speculative trading (sometimes driven by portfolio management strategies). This prompts a number of practices such as stock buy-backs and cost reduction through 'downsize and distribute' strategies, that while flattering the immediate price of remaining shares do little for the overall economic health of the business (Lazonick 2018: 129–34). While other functions of the stock market continue to have impacts on the corporate sector's activities, it is this particular managerial response that Lazonick argues has increasingly (and adversely) shaped the conduct of many corporations.

Indeed, the logic of 'shareholder value' is that where managers are unable to find activities that generate returns that maintain the value of the shareholder's assets, here often indicated (perhaps erroneously) by the share price, then the resources freed by this lack of profitable options should be returned to shareholders so they can reallocate their assets/funds to corporations that *are* able to use these funds profitably (Lazonick and O'Sullivan 2000: 28). However, given that share prices are in part influenced by both dividends and (recently) programmes of corporate 'share buy-backs', this can have the clear (perverse) effect of draining the corporation of funds for future internal investment. Moreover, with senior executives increasingly being parties to performance management packages that are linked to share price performance or, more directly, are denominated in share transfers, maintaining share price increases at almost any cost has become a significant element of corporate managerial practice. This suggests that managerial value extraction has moved to the centre of corporate behaviour, at least among the largest enterprises, through the adoption of share-linked performance and compensation packages.

This analysis of managerial behaviour has been recently expanded into an analysis of the whole of society by Gérard Duménil and Dominique Lévy (2018). They argue that an elite group of corporate managers, working closely with financial capital, are the drivers of *financialisation* which Duménil and Lévy regard as one the key elements of neoliberalism. Here, they argue that while the managerial class aligned itself with the 'popular' classes after the mid-1930s and into the 1970s, during the last half-century managers have reoriented themselves to become allies of the capitalist class (specifically the owners of financial capital).

Moreover, managers under pressure from the financial sector's performance expectations seek assets and financial investment opportunities for the corporation; internal investments are squeezed out by better performing (by the metrics the financial services require) financial assets (Orhangazi 2015: 146–7). The interests of the financial sector (to which managers with significant shareholding might themselves be said to belong) are privileged over other stakeholders. Rather than being seen as merely an intervening group between the class interests of capital and labour, in this analysis the corporate managers have a specific class identity and specific class interests, in the Marxist sense (Duménil and Lévy 2018). To test and explore this position would require an analysis of the management of any (global) corporation (or large-scale enterprise) to assess the internal political economic dynamics of managerial practice, and also an examination of the externalised issue of whether these managers were a class for themselves (whether there is a clear self-identification of their existence as a class with its own interests).

Prompted by such analyses, much discussion of the *transnational capital class* examines this issue (of which more in Chapter 5), and is also now complemented by developing research into the personal (political) networks that are underpinned by interlocking corporate directorships (Sapinski and Carroll 2018). This perspective on the power of the global corporate class can be linked to the identification of *Davos Man* or the *Bilderberg Group* and has more recently been presented through a mapping of the links between corporate boards. Regular contacts between members of corporate boards are key routes through which convergence of political and economic agendas can occur in varying global policy areas, perhaps most obviously in trade relations and the regulation (protection) of international investment(s). Sharon Beder (2006) is far from the only analyst to date this shift from the period of the 1980s and the governments of Ronald Reagan and Margaret Thatcher; both governments are presented as shifting the focus of international negotiation and regulation towards the interests of multinational corporations.

While this is not to claim that this replaced a period of extensive global democratic regulatory politics, nonetheless there is a widespread perception of a shift towards a focus on a corporate-led political agenda (see, for instance, Barak 2017; Davies 2017; Gill 2003; Harrod 2006; May 2017). This agenda, it is often suggested by critics, stems from the development of a relatively coherent global corporate managerial elite who have not only managed to capture many of the rewards of successful enterprise(s) but have also built a significant and well-resourced politically influential community of likeminded 'business leaders'. This community is evident in global moments of collective deliberation, at Davos and elsewhere, but also through the cross-membership of global corporate boards. These contacts and communicative moments allow (perhaps informally) for the development of a political position – the business interest – and the construction of a powerful narrative of what is good for enterprise(s), which then informs lobbying and political influence of various sorts (both corporate and personal). Some see this as a *transnational business class* or global corporate elite who have been highly effective in furthering their own interest(s).

One of the key questions that might be focused on, as regards individuals within these networks, is what motivates managers towards particular ends/outcomes? We might argue, for instance, that managers seek security (in income and employment) through the growth of the firm/corporation. When growth continues, so do returns leading to a rising share price, making it less likely that the enterprise in question would be subject to a hostile takeover (Marris 1998). In some ways this dovetails with approaches to motivation that look (through the lens of principal–agent analysis) at how managerial incentives can be aligned with shareholders' interests in profitability and the maintenance of share price increases. However, it is far from clear, in a highly financialised corporate environment, whether shareholders can really be said to be actively pursuing their modelled interests. Certainly, the norm of shareholder value is clearly a dominant and a much deployed rhetoric, even if it is not universally applied across the corporate sector. However, institutional portfolio investors have diversified their investment risks being mostly only interested in aggregated performance data, and therefore the appeal to a largely hollowed out conception of shareholder value is focused almost entirely on quarterly, or more frequent, share price movements. This suggests it is unlikely that many investors have much interest in how the corporation is being run, other than that it turns a profit to underpin both dividend payment and share price rises. Even so there remains a considerable body of work that seeks to understand corporate governance as an issue of the relationship between principals and agents, as discussed earlier.

What about the workers? Non-managerial employees

Much of the analysis of the management and governance of corporations has concentrated on questions around the employment of senior managers and directors, with (it sometimes seems) much less interest in employment practices for the majority of staff. Discussions of employment and work are often conducted at the system level (society) rather than at the level of the enterprise. However, as Geoffrey Hodgson points out, this sort of economic analysis reduces the workforce to an undifferentiated factor of production, rather than a moral community *within* the corporation. Hodgson rejects the idea that the corporation is merely a 'nexus of contracts' held together by the transaction costs that make it most effective/efficient to internalise tasks rather than obtain them through open market exchange. There *are* legal aspects to continued employment (ranging from contract to employment law), but equally in contemporary corporations 'a moral culture of commitment is often crucial in retaining and integrating a workforce' (Hodgson 2013: 144). This includes appeals to moral duty, social involvement and trust between managers and workers.

While transaction cost economics focuses mainly on the financial and economic costs that inform the 'make or buy' decision, for Hodgson the value of enterprise-specific tacit knowledge and inculcated practices can be as important for understanding why the corporation has the workforce it does:

> Under appropriate conditions, particular moral values can be enhanced in enduring groups with high levels of ongoing interpersonal interaction. In turn, these values help to further promote cohesion and performance . . . Morality can act as a social glue, bringing groups together and focussing them on shared goals. Morality makes economic sense. (Hodgson 2013: 148)

This is not to say selfishness, opportunism or self-regarding utilitarian actions play no role, but Hodgson's point is that within enduring and successful corporations there is more than merely the actions of rational actors. As Hodgson himself teases out of this analysis, the focus on short-term financial drivers towards shareholder value undermines these aspects of real corporate practices and by doing so may (as is often observed) be detrimental to the very things that will in the long term enhance the success of the corporation.

To look in a little more detail at this moral community I utilise taxonomy issues developed by Jill Rubery to identify the four linked dimensions of the corporate employment relation that require attention: security of employment, (expected/contracted) working time, forms of organisation (unionisation; professionalisation) and reward systems (Rubery 2010). Each of these issues reveals important aspects of how corporations (and enterprises more generally) manage their central activities, and how they relate to their workers.

For much of the second half of the twentieth century large corporations either formally or tacitly balanced their need for a flexible workforce with the security of employment that workers (understandably) mostly prefer. Large corporations with large workforces managed changes of work patterns within the organisation and mostly offered the promise (if not always the actuality) of long-term employment: the *Fordist* employment settlement. This approach was based on the large-scale mass production of relatively standardised goods and was to a significant extent modelled on the organisation of the automotive sector (hence the name). However, after the 1970s, this industrial settlement began to falter (and of course had never been universal), with job security being sacrificed by managers seeking to reduce costs. As noted earlier this can be seen as a shift from 'retain and reinvest' where management focuses on long-term growth to a management focus on the extraction of value for shareholders which might be summarised as 'downsize and distribute' (Lazonick and O'Sullivan 2000). For many within and outside the academy this reflects the *neoliberalisation* or *financialisation* of the corporate sector where labour (workers) are no longer seen as a valuable asset worth investing in, but rather as a cost that needs to be reduced.

This has led to reduction of what is now often referred to as 'good work' and its replacement by more precarious (less secure) working conditions for corporate workforces (Blanchflower 2019; Taylor 2017). This decline in the quality of work can be seen *within* the corporation, with commentary building on the older labour process analysis that scientific management led to de-skilling and the alienation of the skilled operative from the product of their activity (see Braverman 1974). However, it is also seen as a labour market development in that a weakening of the political power of workers (through de-unionisation) alongside shifts (generally weakening) the legal protections around employment have led to the degradation of the character of unskilled and semi-skilled work. More recently, fears of automation and technological developments around artificial intelligence have led to widely voiced fears that such degradation will reach professional service and higher skilled sectors of the workforce before long; here I leave aside whether or not these fears are well-grounded and merely note they are frequently discussed in the media.

Much of the increasingly precarious working environment is a direct result of corporations seeking to ensure that their workforces are more flexible, to meet perceived increases in market volatility and competition. Here, the move to part-time working and the rise of the zero-hours contract are emblematic of the (largely successful) attempt by corporate employers to reduce their commitments (as regards stability of employment) to their employees. While in the immediate post-war period this might have been met by the mobilisation of workers' resistance, part of the context behind the changing priorities of managers has been a significant political and legal attack on unions. This has included both constraints on union activity, from limitations on the establishment of closed shops and stringent strike ballot requirements, to the weakening of protection from anti-union actions by employers. As such the reduction of tolerance for union activity in the private sector both reflects and has been reflected in a changing legal environment that has proved less conducive to successful union organising (Ahlquist 2017). This has led to a decline in union membership across the developed world and outside of Germany a marginalisation of the limited involvement that unions *had* managed to secure in influencing corporate activity and practices. Moreover, as unionisation and unions' political economic role has been diminished, so their moderating influence on inequality has been constrained.

This leads us to the fourth of Rubery's four dimensions of the corporate employment relation. In the last decades of the twentieth century and the first two decades of the twenty-first, levels of inequality as regards corporate rewards have become wider but also more commented on. To some extent this can be seen as resulting from the removal of pressure from unions, while (as noted above) approaches to corporate governance that have focused on principal–agent issues have transformed the incentive and reward practices of global corporations. Indeed, the character of the principals themselves has an impact on spiralling executive pay: short-term shareholders have little interest in controlling or capping executive pay, while longer term *institutionalised* investors pay much closer attention to any growing division between rates of reward for executives and the rest of the workforce (Connelly et al. 2016).

Here, the financialisation of the global political economy, the move to financial forms of corporate control, is often identified as encouraging short-termism and therefore less concern about the longer-term potential impact on corporate workforce morale and/or 'human capital' resources available to the business enterprise controlled by over-compensated executives. This returns us to the question of the ethical character of the corporate environment; should corporations' managers consider non-financial issues in decision-making? Should business enterprises act in a manner that is socially responsible, both as regards their own staff and towards their external stakeholders?

Corporate social responsibility

It often seems that the discussion of corporate social responsibility is a response (positive or negative) to Milton Friedman's famous declaration. In the *New York Times Magazine*, Friedman quoted the conclusion to his book *Capitalism and Freedom* to assert that,

> There is one and only one social responsibility of business – to use its resources and engage in activities designed to increase its profits so long as it stays within the rules of the game, which is to say, engages in open and free competition without deception or fraud. (Friedman 1970: 124)

Much has been made over the years of Friedman's suggestion that it is up to the state to set the 'rules of the game' such that corporations' managers are not required to choose between contending ethical systems but rather can rely on states' deliberative actions to set the limits of acceptable corporate practice. This statement's simplicity and recognition of states' legitimate regulatory role would be more satisfactory if the same people who quote Freidman then didn't also often argue that corporations should be minimally regulated as managers and owners are better able to judge feasible economic practices than states' legislators. Whether this was also Friedman's position is less clear, but in any case, few corporations have adopted a completely neutral stance on ethical issues, not least as for many it now represents a major route to establishing brand value(s) and thereby marketing advantage (even if managerial motivations can often be less instrumental than this implies).

While corporate social responsibility (CSR) will also figure in the chapter on reforming the corporation, and in the next chapter on global supply chains, it is worth noting here that much of the discussion above could be (re)framed as a discussion of CSR in its various forms. We should also avoid some of the more myopic accounts of CSR that see it as a relatively recent phenomenon. Rather, the history of CSR (and CSR-like activity, both organisational and regulatory) can be traced back at least 150 years and in many ways offers a counterpoint (but also an added dimension) to the history of the modern capitalist corporate form (Eichar 2017: 9). From Quaker businesses in the nineteenth century and the Owenite moves to develop better working practices and labour democracy (albeit top-down), to the Cooperative movement, some businesses have responded positively to ethical demands for much of the history of modern capitalism.

One might even see a dialectical relationship between corporate management's interests in unfettered activity towards maximising profit and the demand to embed such activity (and thereby moderate or modify it) by social actors responding to non-economic social mores. Conversely it is also possible to see the growth in the acceptance of the social responsibility of business and corporations specifically as the necessary underpinning to the argument that private regulation is a plausible and indeed preferable alternative to mandatory legal regulation of corporate activities (Bakan 2015: 291). As this suggests, even the demand to see an expansion of CSR can be presented in different ways, depending on how one reads the politics of such calls.

For instance, Colin Mayer has published two books in recent years (Mayer 2013; 2018) which argue for a re-focusing of corporate governance away from profitability and the service of shareholder needs/interests, and towards the notion of the corporate purpose (which while not necessarily excluding profit-ability *includes* a range of society-regarding objectives and effects). For Mayer, the disconnection between servicing shareholder value and the incidence of short-term share-holding (in the UK) has led to a

> futile attempt to rectify this by seeking ever more extensive contractual arrangements and imposing tougher regulatory requirements that constrain the commercial potential of the corporation. Rather, corporate governance laws should be creating a context within which [the corporation] can realize its full potential to perform communal and social as well as self-regarding purposes. (Mayer 2018: 166)

Here, the current framing of corporate governance undercuts any attempt to refocus corporate activity in those jurisdictions so closely wedded to share-holder value as the cornerstone of corporate governance through the requirement of executives fulfilling the fiduciary duties.

Indeed, for critics, such as Steve Tombs and David Whyte, in this legal environment, CSR represents a two-dimensional strategy of dissembling. They suggest this involves the exploitation of a *space* within the law that encompasses under-enforcement of corporate-facing regulation and the shifting of understanding of what compliance might entail. This might be best summed up as corporations seeking to adhere to the letter rather than the spirit of CSR-related laws. However, there is also considerable latitude for corporations to frame their practices in the spaces between laws, between the various regulations (differing by character, articulation and coverage) in different jurisdictions (Tombs and Whyte 2015: 122–7). Corporations *may* adopt CSR measures in good faith but experience suggests this is not always (or even often) the case. Moreover, it's plausible that an enhanced corporate accountability can be, for a corporation's management, a way of both quantifying the risk (in financial terms) of any action, while the maintenance of the corporate form (with the corporation as the agent of CSR) allows the beneficial owners (shareholders) to remain shielded from liability (Baars 2016). Here, CSR is a convenient way to manage *political* risk, not necessarily radically change practices.

As Douglas Eichar points out, this *political* use of CSR can also be seen as an attempt by corporations to improve their image to key consumers by 'diverting attention away from questionable practices in one area to more responsible activities in another' (Eichar 2017: 316). This is at least partly a recognition that the global economy and its forms of interest representation have begun to look more like previous relations between the state and the national demos (Backer 2017: 115). In the same way that politics has always involved the idea of 'bread and circuses', balancing off benefits with distractions, so the globalised corporate economy (floodlit by social media) now requires corporations, whose actions might attract adverse scrutiny, to identify forms of distraction. Of course, this diversionary activity is not always successful; recent difficulties encountered by BP in the realm of its arts sponsorship have emphasised that the separation between socially responsible philanthropy and climate impacting practices has not gone unnoticed by environmental activists who have sought allies in the art world to reconnect these issues.

Conversely, the utilisation of private standards, rather than formal regulations has opened up a space for social auditing of corporate activity by non-governmental organisations and other civil society groups. Although presented by business groups and corporations as an agile and flexible approach to assess levels of social responsibility in diversified and geographically dispersed operations, such audits hold significant risks of explicit corruption and less organised bad faith in their operation(s). Given the disparity of resources, such auditing allows corporations to frame standards and rules in their own interests, while influencing supposed independent assessment. Not least by deflecting political pressure for more formalised regulatory oversight, the auditing 'industry' might be said to be colluding with the promotion of a corporate profit-centred agenda (LeBaron and Lister 2016). The capture and influence over privately organised auditing allows corporations, in the colloquialism 'to mark their own homework'. This preference for private regulation is also clear in the observed tendency for corporations who proclaim their own social responsibility (and may accede to forms of CSR auditing) to also lobby directly and contribute to organisations that seek to restrain and argue against formal regulations around corporate activity (Vogel 2006: xvii, 164–73). Indeed, as will be developed in Chapter 5's discussion of the political role of corporations, frequently their impact (via various routes) on the political deliberation of policy approaches and associated national (and international) legal instruments has considerably greater social impact than the activities of any one corporation.

This leads Christopher Kutz to conclude that corporate (social) responsibility is caught up in a legal incoherence around the allocation of *collective* responsibility. He contrasts the law around conspiracy and the prosecution of accomplices with the manner in which shareholders, through limited liability, have often been shielded from any material responsibility for corporate activity that has attracted adverse legal and/or social attention. Given 'a general ethical framework of inclusive and exclusive accountability, it makes no sense to except shareholders from the reparative duties of corrective justice' (Kutz 2000: 237). This is to say that the extension of limited liability is a legal exception that needs to be justified on more solid ground than merely the investment–incentive-linked justifications most often deployed. Indeed, for Kutz this justification stems from a category error; while across the world the corporation is treated as completely separate from its shareholders, Kutz argues that it is actually a cooperative enterprise constituted by shareholders' willingness to choose to invest in specific corporations (and their managers) on the expectation of profit (Kutz 2000: 240–52). The 'corporate veil' can and should be pierced when it comes to the need to allocate responsibility for social harms.

This can be usefully presented as a distinction between 'blame responsibility' and 'task responsibility' (Goodin 1995: 100–113); the former is focused on allocating blame for outcomes from specific actions, while the latter is concerned with the manner in which the tasks which led to the (unwelcome) outcomes were framed and allocated to the agents involved. While Robert Goodin notes, but is less interested in, how tasks are actually allocated to agents with capacity/capability to act (Goodin 1995: 109–10), for the discussion here the issue of task allocation offers useful analytical purchase; it is this 'task responsibility' that limited liability seeks to separate out and neutralise. If we see the allocation of task responsibility as an important element of setting out where responsibility lies, then the allocation by shareholders of the task of making a profitable return to the management (and employees) of the corporation qua investment vehicle, would seem to suggest at the very least a *sharing* of responsibility for ensuring socially responsible corporate practice. This is the very connection that limited liability has sought to constrain and/or sever.

Obviously, considerable political effort has gone into maintaining this distinction between corporation and shareholder, and their responsibilities; however, Kutz argues,

> the corporation is the product of its shareholders. It is *they*, not a separate entity, who risk their money in order to pursue gain. For consequential accountability, there is no principled distinction between corporate assets and the private assets of shareholders [that can be called on to redress damage(s)]. (Kutz 2000: 253)

That said, even Kutz recognises that this (re)linking of corporate activity and shareholder responsibility may have a negative impact on investment, but equally, we might argue that it would require greater due diligence and attentiveness from investors. Might this be no bad thing?

Conversely one could look to forms of contemporary capitalism where the secondary markets for shares is not so dominant. This might lead you to conclude that the equalisation of influence between original investors and the short-term shareholders utilising the stock market to spread risk, and more problematically the speculation on share prices, may be at the root of the problem that Kutz identifies. Looking to countries such as Germany (for long-term family-related investment) or to Japan (with its networks of long-term cross-shareholding between enterprises) would suggest the model of extensive and volatile stock markets is not a *necessary* component of contemporary capitalism. Rather, it reflects a specific political history (Macaulay 2015) and as such may require further investigation as a *specific* cause of some of the governance issues raised in this chapter.

There is also considerable political pressure on corporations to further and support the recognition of human rights in countries in which they operate. In the end there are really only two issues here: (1) corporations and other business enterprises should refrain from violating human rights; (2) however, if rights violations happen then the victims must be provided with a remedy against such businesses that have acted to violate their human rights (Bernaz 2017: 296). Therefore, a key question becomes what responsibilities corporate managers have for the human rights of those that they interact with, directly and indirectly, as employees, suppliers or customers. While corporations certainly *do* have human rights-related responsibilities, these are not necessarily simple to frame or define. Arrayed over four dimensions – legalism, universalism, capacity and publicness – the extent of corporate responsibility reflects the particularities of the case, and where there is an absence of effective other actors, then corporations' responsibilities may be greater. In the legal dimension much depends on the manner in which the state (in which a corporation operates) is itself practicing the rule of law, while likewise the issue of universality suggest corporations should be (at least at times) reticent about the deployment of their home state's mores on other populations. However, it is also the case that sometimes corporations have significant capacities to effect positive change, and operate as quasi-public bodies that can garner significant public support for their actions (Karp 2014). It is best not to merely assume that all corporations should act in specific (supposedly) human rights-supporting ways in every state in which they operate. Rather, we should examine actual corporations' actions and relate these to the material conditions in which they are operating.

This is to say, we should be wary of assuming the worst from the corporate sector. John Ruggie (who was instrumental in developing the United Nations Global Compact as a way of helping corporations develop more socially responsible behaviour) has argued repeatedly that it is better to work with the corporate sector than against them. While assessments of the success of the Global Compact vary (see Chapter 5's discussion), it remains true that Ruggie has had some success in engineering a convergence between critics of global corporate practices and the corporate sector itself (a story told at length in Ruggie 2013). Likewise, Joel Bakan has been at pains to point out that one should recognise there is good corporate practice and enterprises that accord social responsibility significant strategic importance (Bakan 2004 and the film/ interviews that accompany that volume). As I stress again and again in this book, while it often makes sense to discuss the (global) corporate sector as a single terrain or field of interest, equally we (as analysts, as critics, as commentators) need to recognise that there is significant variation in corporate practice. While unacceptable behaviour garners widespread coverage, those firms quietly getting on with being (relatively) good corporate citizens can often be forgotten and their work down-played.

Why the management of the corporation matters

Having reviewed a range of approaches to what we might rather generally refer to as the 'problem' of corporate management, it is worth stressing that while corporate employees (from the lowest functionary to the highest paid executives) are all influenced by various forms of economic incentives and structural impediments, they remain human beings. Any analysis that treats them merely as economic cyphers misses many key aspects of their behaviour and priorities as regards the management of corporations and as such fails to appreciate both the real and potential differences between corporate practices. As Ciaran Driver and Grahame Thompson have put it: the governance of corporations 'affects the distribution of income, power and risk across affected parties, thus inviting a political discourse' (Driver and Thompson 2018: 4). The practices and behaviour(s) of corporations have considerable external consequences and as such cannot be reduced to issues of economic efficiency alone. From such a generalised understanding of the social impact of corporations comes an interest in defining and regulating corporate social responsibility.

As such, much analysis proceeds from the assumption that broadly speaking the management of a global corporation should (and can) have a reasonable idea about what is happening across its business. Unfortunately, this is actually seldom the case. Certainly across a global corporation's network there may be convergence of activity, but this is due not to shared norms but rather through the more pragmatic governance of operations. Therefore, while demands around the CSR agenda would require corporations' central management to have high-quality information about distant (and not so distant) subsidiaries and contractors, the frequent information lapses focused on by CSR-related critics are actually commonplace and to be expected. This is because even where there are clear business-related (and institutionalised) structures in place, the global corporation's operations are subject to extensive local negotiation related to the local economic environment (and which may not be seen or known) centrally (Forsgren et al. 2005). Here, management, or as I prefer, governance of the corporate network, is much more imprecise and less informed than might be presented in much of the analysis that focuses on the problems of corporate governance. Again, this suggests that to really understand what is happening in the corporate sector, analysts need at least partly to focus on what corporations are doing in their specific and particular networks. This means (as pointed out in this chapter) that a focus on corporate governance, which concentrates largely on the relations between shareholders and/or owners and their designated senior management team, misses much that is happening elsewhere in the corporation's network. These production networks are the focus of the next chapter's discussion of global corporate supply chains.

Key questions for research(ers)

Should corporate governance only be judged by the standards of economic efficiency or are there wider social values to which it should be held?

If governance and planning are central to corporate practice, what opportunities are there to introduce a more democratic element into corporations' organisational structures?

Does the distinction between primary investments (initial share-based investment) and secondary investments (the purchase of shares on the stock market) help our understanding of how corporations' managers make practical decisions?

How can we relate the specifics of the corporate business networks to the more aggregated information and data that is often available (relatively easily) on the global corporate sector?

What sorts of criteria help distinguish socially responsible corporations from those acting in bad faith?

Can we draw together analysis of the governance of the range of work strata across a global corporation's entire organisational network?

4 Understanding the global corporate supply chain

The terrain of the global corporate supply chain has already been evident across the range of issues discussed so far. In this chapter, I explicitly examine the supply chain through a variety of lenses to try to make better sense of this important realm of the global political economy. The supply chain is where the practices and policies of the global corporation are implemented and therefore most visible: the interaction of markets, governance and political power therefore make the supply chain a key site for research into how exactly the corporation shapes and impacts global capitalism (Haufler 2018: 117; Phillips 2017: 431). This is not to argue that the adoption of a multi-disciplinary approach to internationalised production is particularly new; John Dunning has always argued that global production networks *can only* be understood through the combination of a number of analytical lenses including (but not limited to) economics, politics, law, sociology and geography (Dunning 1988: 309–11). Likewise, the contemporary global supply chain is hardly novel, even if the scale and reach of production networks is more extensive than in the past. Nevertheless, this chapter draws a range of analyses together to re-emphasise the need to put global supply chains at the centre of our critical analysis of the global political economy of the corporation.

It is possible to present the shift to global-scale networks in broadly functional terms; relating it to moves in logistics (most specifically the development of the standardised shipping container) that enabled the cheap transfer of intermediate goods between distant locations.[1] Conversely, the expansion of supply chains can be understood as the result of global moves (resulting in, but by no means limited to, the establishment of the World Trade Organization (WTO)) to facilitate global free trade. This has been accomplished through both the reduction in tariffs and (perhaps more significantly) the removal or reduction of bureaucratic frictions at the border of states and elsewhere that impeded such intermediate moves (or made them too costly). The removal/reduction of *non-tariff barriers* is accorded too little importance in the analysis of the expansion of global production networks or supply chains.

For every corporation this presents a set of decisions about the benefits of continuing to embed its organisation in its home state versus the advantages of shifting activities abroad that then informs its particular global structure. The dynamic of expansion and increased complexity of global production networks might best be regarded therefore not so much as an issue of cost controls and drivers, but rather the organisation of corporate activity to maximise the ability to capture value from all stages of the productive process. Moreover, as Martin Heidenreich argues, global corporations have a significant level of agency regarding these choices:

> Faced with multiple institutional environments [they] are able to choose where, in what dimensions and to what extent they will be embedded in various institutional, political, cultural and inter-organisational contexts in which they operate. They can actively, strategically and selectively use different opportunities and constraints of their heterogeneous institutional environments. (Heidenreich 2012: 573)

Thus, while necessarily embedded within various regulatory regimes, the global corporation is always able to mediate between alternative contexts and materially shift the balance of its integration into various national economic systems. As developed below, this agency lies behind the development of complex and extensive global production networks of supply chains, but also behind the asymmetry of power over their impact on economic development strategies of a range of states.

Considerable analytical attention in previous decades has been paid to the discussion of ownership-specific (internal) versus location-specific (external) cost advantages (which of course stresses that labour costs are only one aspect of how corporations make their international investment decisions) (Barff 1995: 60). Here the disintegration of production finds its origins in the longer history of national economic organisation, but the link to globalisation is as much about a range of cost pressures and the access to new markets through (partially) localised production (Herrigel and Zeitlin 2010: 537). The shift to global supply chains (in some sectors) therefore can be related to the economic context in which the corporation finds itself; shifting cost structures (be they of transport or labour or resources) present enterprises with new opportunities to reduce costs. This is hardly a new phenomenon: corporations are driven by the same profit logic they always have been; what has changed is the character and location of costs and thus the opportunities to develop an internationalised division of labour (Casson 2018: 147). The global political economic context may be as important for understanding corporations' supply chain development as their internal strategic intent (its internal ownership-specific factors).

More strikingly, the supposition that the global division of labour, facilitated by global production networks, would retain spatial hierarchies, with high value-added work in the metropole(s) and low value (generic) work at the periphery has proved only partial at best. Increasingly complex production networks have seen the spatial (geographic) diversification of location for activities of all sorts (Herrigel and Zeitlin 2010: 542–3). However, equally, in the new millennium, various political and economic factors have led to some 'reshoring' – returning activities to the country from which previously they had been 'offshored' – further disrupting simple depictions of the spatial trajectory of global supply chains. What *is* clear is that there is an increasingly obvious vertical division of labour in production and supply networks (often delineated by value capture – hence the popularisation of the concept of the 'global value chain') which has largely supplanted any remaining horizontal forms of division across locations within which global corporations are active. For Intan Suwandi, at least, this reveals the continuation of global imperialist social relations. A focus on labour costs rather than the capture of value has in the past obscured the continuation of the metropole's domination of the client (imperially controlled) states through the depiction of neutral market structure and via the supply chain (Suwandi 2019). Here, the (re)focusing on value chains in the critical literature on global corporations' production and supply networks reveals the continuing disparities and operations of global political economic power wielded by globalised corporations themselves.

Global production networks and small and medium-sized enterprises

The global corporation governs the space of the supply chain to produce a politico-economic environment suited to its needs and priorities. Therefore, the small and medium-sized enterprises (SMEs) working in this environment may well find that the 'market' they are involved in is highly structured and regulated by the lead corporation, shifting and changing the opportunities and risks for contracting partners. These pressures range from simple cost-related demands to regulatory arbitrage, from requirements around technical up-grading to environmental regulatory needs (often reflecting concerns in the metropole, not localised priorities). Moreover, the everyday practices of large corporations (from late payments, to unpredictable but large purchase requests) can lead to considerable volatility for SMEs involved in supply chains. As a result, one key developmental policy intervention that is often identified is to make this environment less precarious for SMEs (FEC 2018: 140). In many supply chains large corporations are essentially monopsonic (single) purchasers/buyers, leading to considerable explicit opportunities to apply pressure on suppliers, but also a disregard for the impact of standard operating practices within the global production network on small firms working at its periphery as contract suppliers of intermediate goods and non-production services.

In most global supply chains SMEs are also the actual (if often ineffective) transmitters and enactors of global corporate policies and practices. Therefore, any study of global production (or service) networks needs to focus on the relations between large complex organisations (the lead corporation and its major/tier one contracting suppliers) and the further reaches of the supply chain largely (but not exclusively) populated by smaller and much more focused enterprises. As such, this will reveal that across the supply chain different enterprises may have very different priorities and motivations, driven not only by their location but also by their scale of activity and the manner in which their activity is managed within the network.

Summarising a range of research into SMEs in global supply chains, Eglé Stonkuté and Jolita Vveinhardt identified a number of frequently observed shortcomings. Perhaps understandably, given that these are smaller firms, they often lack a range of up-to-date technological resources, and often work to a short-term time horizon. Reflecting their frequent lack of bargaining power in the supply chain, SMEs have also often been found lacking in competent management and leadership leading to low levels of agility and responsiveness to change (Stonkuté and Vveinhardt 2016: 98, *passim*). This makes the management and governance of the supply chain more difficult for the core/lead corporation(s), but also reveals why it may sometimes be plausible that the lead corporation is unable to guarantee the effective fulfilment of its own policies within its network. For cynics, the fragmentation of the production network rather handily supplies lead enterprises with this perfectly plausible excuse for failing to fulfil their own commitments as regards corporate social responsibility (CSR).

Part of the problem for many SMEs working in global production networks is that the supply chain can be a precarious location for economic activity, undermining incentives to develop new approaches or follow specific network rules too closely (if they involve non-transferable investment). Often SMEs may find it difficult to access credit or other forms of financial support to rectify these shortcomings, in any case, and where credit is available, it may be costly (Wignaraja 2015). However, the problems that SMEs encounter (and suffer from) may not be visible far up the supply chain.

It is perhaps less obvious that in a complex, networked supply chain the contractual relations that contribute towards the governance function of the corporation across its supply chain are dependent on what Gillian Hadfield has referred to as the global 'legal infrastructure' (Hadfield 2017: 133–43; see also Baars and Bair et al. 2016). The supply chain depends on the stability and reliability of contracts, and as such the more developed the legal infrastructure is, the more likely (other things being equal) supply chains will reach into national economies (Dollar 2017). Conversely, unlike global trade outside supply chains and production networks, there is considerably less 'exposure' to multilateral governance; the WTO has little functional governance capacity for trade *within* corporate production networks (Stephenson and Pfister 2017: 66–7). Perhaps unsurprisingly therefore, global corporations have developed a wide range of supply chain management processes to both manage the contract relations with SMEs in their networks and, in recognising that contracts are necessarily incomplete, to build up further *governance* practices on the foundation of these contractual relations.

There is a clear appreciation that contracting, even with trusted ongoing supply chain participants may expose the lead corporation to extra risks, ranging from internal quality issues to brand damage from revelation of illegal or illicit practices in the far reaches of the contracted environment (Dekker et al. 2013). In response, corporations have built up a form of legal environment (infrastructure) to ensure that complex supply chains remain a realm governed by recognisable (and enforceable) legal instruments. Quite how extensive that dependence is remains a matter for debate. For instance, Larry Catá Backer sees the two realms as distinct with contracts 'existing side by side' with the regulatory systems of states and capable of being seen as a 'freestanding, autonomous, self-communicating system', which is 'binding on its constituency' (Backer 2008: 517). While the network's particular norms (an element of governance discussed below) are important, as Backer puts it, they 'have no legal effect, except, ironically as enacted into contractual relations' between the core corporation and its firms in its supply chain network (Backer 2008: 522).

While much of the discussion of global supply chains focuses on the production of physical goods, there are also extensive supply chains in services, and service elements to production networks. To some extent, enterprises have always utilised specialised contractors, now often referred to as business-to-business (B2B) services, such as accountants or lawyers. Much of the early shift to outsourcing took place through the identification of other non-core service activities which could be contracted to specialised service providers (ranging from advertising and marketing to cleaning and security). In the new millennium the move to new information technology-supported virtual markets has allowed a further fragmentation of service provision so that less complex tasks can be offered cost-effectively to contracting freelancers in a spot market facilitated by online service platforms like *Mechanical Turk* and others. In the past, service supply chains were often (but not always) made up of specialised corporations (themselves often larger than the enterprise contracting for services). The move to a more fragmented service supply chain, for some task clusters, has shifted the dynamic of organisation away from the dominant B2B model and towards, in some market segments and service areas, a model now often termed the 'gig economy'.

Behind many of the most contentious aspects of the gig economy's organisational structures is the tension between the need for supply chain governance and corporate managers' desire to externalise risks and responsibilities associated with an established workforce. Indeed, core enterprises have sought to shift the risk associated with (relatively fast) shifts in consumer service requirements to a disassociated/precarious workforce. Moreover, by framing shifts in requirements as driven by consumer demand, such corporations have sought to construct their commercial requirements as merely a reflection of external market conditions over which they have little control (rather than reflecting the working of their own chosen supply model). We will return to the gig economy (or 'platform capitalism') in Chapter 6 but here the focus will remain more generally on the manner in which global production and service networks are governed.

Governance and the supply chain

As discussed in Chapter 3 there is good reason to see the corporate supply chain as the site of governance activity. This goes beyond the specific management of contractual relations to include the governance of an environment of rules (within the supply chain) that is dependent not only on authority but also on the recognition of legitimacy across production (and service) networks. Without rehearsing the analysis of the previous chapter, here I *do* want to explore why it might be said that many global supply chains suffer from what can be termed a 'democratic deficit'; an idea that, of course, only makes sense if we accept the idea of governance being more than the *management* of the supply chain. If one accepts that corporations conduct *governance*, then the link between governance, legitimacy and democracy is worth exploring in the case of the supply chain even if normal economic analysis might regard this as a misplaced concern. This is to say, by making the case for governance, we can enlarge the space for political analytical approach to the conduct and practice(s) of corporations.

As production networks have fragmented, as markets have become globalised and technological developments have become less linear, hitherto hierarchical power relations between core/lead corporations and the companies in these networks have become less stable, less settled and perhaps less unbalanced (Herrigel and Zeitlin 2010: 553–4). As such, the governance of production networks is now looking a bit more like models of governance that have developed in other areas of the global system. Indeed, there is already a growing pragmatic recognition in policy circles that corporations are governing these networks, not merely managing them, and this is driving the sorts of ethical demands that governments and civil society actors are directing at lead corporations' partners' practices within global production networks.

Certainly, corporations have undertaken an explicit programme to assert expanded (political) control over the supply chain, and like other (global) governance institutions this represents a proactive institutionalisation of power over a specified realm (here the corporate network). Global governance has been characterised by a transformation in the manner in which states determine and follow particular political priorities (Hameiri and Jones 2016), seeking out multilateral and collective approaches to replace bi-lateral political practices (albeit currently being reversed in some areas). The shift to recognising that corporations also exercise a (significant) governance function within their own supply chains suggests that an analysis based merely on technical management misses an important dimension of political economy that has been foregrounded in discussions of global governance itself. Moreover, state legislators in corporations' home states are beginning to recognise (partly due to the expanded interest in CSR) that this governance function may be a useful conduit for international influence. For instance, despite considerable resistance, from 2018 large French domiciled corporations have been required to mitigate environmental impacts and address human rights abuses within their global supply chains (Evans 2019). While such extraterritorial requirements may be an imperfect and partial mechanism for social change(s), here its importance is that both civil society organisations and the French state recognise the possibilities of levering corporations' own governance practice for democratic and social ends. As this implies, understanding global corporations' control of supply chains as a form of (global) governance, opens up this realm of the global political economy to an interesting set of analytical tools already developed to examine more normally conceived forms of global governance. It may also offer a complementary analysis that indicates how global governance itself may be experienced across the global economic system.

By utilising insights from the study of global governance, we can develop a critical approach to assess how corporate rule over their supply networks is justified as well as the limits to legitimacy this governance function might confront. This perspective on the internal legitimacy of corporate network governance also feeds into debates about the corporation's social licence to operate (Morrison 2014), which we will return to in the final chapter. Here I note that while this perspective on the legitimacy of the corporation is focused on the external socio-economic environment, stakeholders and other social groups impacted by corporate practices, the social licence itself is often related to supply chain practices (specifically, but not exclusively around labour standards and environmental impact). The idea of the social licence therefore draws together internal and external aspects of legitimacy, trust and consent to underpin a political analysis of corporate global governance practices across production and service networks.

So, if we see the global corporation as a governance institution, then we need to not only take account of instrumental or compulsory power differentials in supply chain networks, but also to focus more fully on the manner in which corporations seek to constitute and produce a socio-economic and spatial terrain of agreed rule(s). Additionally, while incorporation and contract relations might often give credence to a reified view of the identity/personality of the corporation (that it is a singular entity), the corporation like many other institutions that practise governance is actually subject to 'bureaucratic politics', which is to say, internal bargaining, negotiation and the use of (internal) political resources to shape decision-making. This reveals the corporation to be the subject of similar issues that other governance institutions confront and as such underlines why a governance analysis may make sense.

If governance is to be seen as legitimate by those contracting enterprises that are within the network, as it needs to be if governance practices are to be effective, then they must be regarded as transparent and have modes of accountability to deliver the value that can be derived from these relations. This is in addition to any basic market-based form of contractual relations (that would be the subject of a more management-focused analysis). Certainly, the closer that the relations between network 'partners' approximate market relations (and are governed via market mechanisms), the less legitimacy will be required, as legitimacy of relations are then conveyed by the notion of the market itself. However, many relations in established global supply chains have moved significantly away from the spot market (where contracts are for a single transaction only) and rely on ongoing relations between contracting parties.

Once we adjudge corporations to be acting as (political) governance institutions, then a normative concern with their democratic legitimacy becomes appropriate (Ylönen and Teivainen 2018: 449–50). It might seem a little odd to refer to a democratic deficit in supply chain governance, but this *oddness* is likely the result of the discursive normalisation of market relations as being 'outside' democracy. The democratic community of the supply chain may not be its general population of individuals, but the corporate/enterprise members of the governed network (seen as political actors on their own account) certainly can be regarded as such. Thus, where governance is not limited to basic market mechanisms the reciprocity captured by the idea of legitimate governance is likely to be of some importance to these actors. We know that in global governance the response to perceived democratic deficits has often been to empower, or seek to empower, civil society; this directly parallels the moves in CSR monitoring and auditing (and is often used as an example in mainstream debates). However, here I want to extend this to the contracting network partners.

In general, we can evaluate the democratic aspects of (global) governance, and thus its level(s) of political legitimacy, across four general dimensions (drawing from prior political analysis):

1. How is participation mediated – how do groups (in our cases contracted partners and others suppliers) gain access to the network?
2. What forms of deliberative forum are available to network participants?
3. How accountable is decision-making in the network? In supply chain networks, rather than examining the wider context, it may be more appropriate to limit concerns here to the notion of stakeholder groups, but even so this would be wider than merely participating network members.
4. Is there a real potential for contesting governance decisions within the network and as such are sanctions applied where contests/conflicts arise or are they treated as legitimate concerns by the central (corporate) authority?[2]

While it is unlikely that any corporate network would expect to, or likely achieve a high rating across all four aspects, the relative legitimacy of governance across different corporate supply chain networks can and would be illuminated through a comparative assessment of their performance against these criteria.

As with other global governance institutions, if there is a fall-off of perceived legitimacy, suppliers (an analogue to members in other institutions) may seek exit options, moving to other more amenable supply chains if possible. Therefore, the issue of relative democratic legitimacy of governance functions may help analysts explore and explain aspects of volatility within some global production networks. Conversely, where lock-in issues are evident, other forms of resistance may be deployed and civil society organisations drawn in to engage with the legitimacy of specific elements of the governance function. As this suggests, a focus on democratic legitimacy in the governance of the supply chain would shift analysis away from considerations that are purely economic, and include a range of political-relational issues that may well further illuminate how and why particular production networks persist and their relative levels of effective enactment of various CSR-related policies.

This also implies that in supply chain networks the actors that might benefit from empowerment are not only civil society groups (labour, environmentalists, those seeking to promote human rights) but also the smaller contractors themselves, whose interests and requirements may be quite different to the usually identified civil society actors. This has led Kate Macdonald to conclude that future advances in establishing legitimate and effective governance in global supply chains must be multi-institutional and multifaceted. This is to say, recognising corporations' own governance functions in their supply chains offers areas of engagement for both private regulatory initiatives and (revived) state legislative involvement, which at times will need to be effectively extra-territorial. Here the politics of global supply chains (like other political realms) involves a negotiation between various political actors with differently legitimated interests seeking to reach a solution that best represents a trade-off between these different interests (Macdonald 2014). Crucially, this adds in the contracting supply-chain 'partners' as well as the more usual lead corporation and activist civil society organisation(s). This may happen on a sector-specific basis or be focused on particular issues, but at all times is likely to involve negotiation between differently empowered political actors (including the corporations themselves, of course) brought together in governing the supply chain or production network.

Interestingly, as Richard Locke points out in his discussion of how labour standards have been promoted in supply chain networks, whereas in early engagements auditing and inspecting was seen as a process for gauging the need (or otherwise) for sanctions for non-compliance, more recently auditors (internal and contracted-external) have regarded their work as developmental. It now often encompasses not merely judgement of the fulfilment of codes' requirements, but also, when failings are identified, prompts support to enhance existing and introduce new practices that are code-compliant (Locke 2013: 181, *passim*). Here, the acceptance of lead corporations' legitimate interest in local practices and local contractors' ability to explore how compliance can be achieved in local circumstances, are subject to negotiation and potentially compromise over the manner in which policy is implemented that includes the local contractors. While likely still the 'junior partners' in such negotiations, Locke's account alerts us to how governance requires the involvement of the governed not merely top-down supply chain command management.

That said, it may be that mostly labour in the network is caught between the plausible deniability for lead corporations and the inability/unwillingness of local (national) regulators in contractors' home states to raise labour standards to nationally or internationally mandated levels (Lane and Probert 2009: ch. 10). In these circumstances, the negotiation and socialisation of network participants and at least a partial recognition of their interests may be the most effective manner in which corporations can govern these networks when looking to further their avowed CSR commitments. However, there may be less need for time to be spent establishing governance norms if power imbalances between the lead corporation and contracting enterprise remain significant. Here corporations can benefit from often disengaged local 'competition states' that are only interested in maintaining production within their borders and unwilling to enter into more invasive forms of legal regulation locally; this leaves the lead corporation more able to impose practices rather than negotiate their uptake. Such competition states see the inclusion of local enterprises into global supply chains as a key element of their strategies of economic development, but may also see their only competitive advantage as costs-based. We will return to the link between global production networks and economic development after the next section, but first it is worth widening the focus explicitly to include services.

Services in the globalised supply chain

The use of a wider range of services as part of the organisation of global supply chains and production networks again emphasises that a focus on costs *management* is insufficient for understanding such networks. While it is also true for the flow of intermediate goods around the supply chain, contracting for services foregrounds the non-financial, non-cost concerns around quality of service supply in the network that respond to the manner in which corporations' governance function shapes the norms and understandings of acceptable (and legitimate) demands and activity within the network. For instance, Neil Coe and Henry Wai-Chung Yeung have developed a 'cost-capability ratio' approach that focuses on more than merely economic cost. It includes the manner in which costs are relative to the capabilities delivered in a specific network relation and how these capabilities feed into the optimisation of the network (Coe and Yeung 2015: 85–8). While this remains largely rooted in economic considerations of efficiency, optimal costing and financial management, it presents an opportunity to include non-economic aspects (managerial desire for an expansion of the scope of control, for instance) on which corporations' governance function in the supply chain networks is focused, as much as market price. Indeed, costs are seldom the most appropriate way of judging the efficacy and 'efficiency' of the services element of any production and/or supply network.

One aspect of the global environment that can drive the utilisation of service (or business process) outsourcing as part of a global supply chain can be constraints on the mobility of appropriate or available labour (for instance where skilled visa restrictions restrict the flow of migrant workers to the lead corporation's home state); here capability issues and cost issues interact. Such constraints may also underpin the price advantage of utilising networked delivery of various service requirements within the supply chain. However, the common proprietary element to such service networking means that only states that have robust intellectual property laws in place are likely to be seen as 'safe' locations for service-related supply chain development.

Here, adding to the other drivers and facilitating elements that have contributed to the development of global corporate supply chains, one would need to include the development (after 1995) of a more robust global system for the protection of intellectual property through the WTO's Trade Related aspects of Intellectual Property rights (TRIPs) agreement (May 2002). Developing countries have historically entered the services sector of supply chain(s) initially through the provision of 'transactional' services (low-level data processing, logging and storage roles). In some cases (of which India remains the most obvious example) this has been followed by a shift first into operational services (containing stronger managing and administrative elements) before aspiring to offer strategic services (ranging from consultancy to data-related research and development activity) (Mukherji and Rawat 2017). As one can easily infer, this requires considerable labour market policy intervention by countries' governments seeking to develop services and business process provision for global corporations, not least a major investment in the forms of (higher) education that will provide suitable semi-professionals for such work. This goes well beyond the skill-supporting policies that might be required to engage with many physical goods' supply chains. Here national policy differences between competition states become clear and have evident impact(s) on developmental trajectories and potential.

There are (broadly) two aspects of service supply chains: firstly, most if not all global production networks and supply chains have an element focused on the delivery of services rather than intermediate goods, mostly defined as various business processes. Secondly, there are those service corporations (such as the major global accountancy/audit firms or major advertising agencies) that have fragmented their organisation to allow offshore service provision as part of their core activities. However, whether fully service-oriented or feeding into material supply chains, the governance of service networks adds further complexity to globalised production networks, in at least seven different ways.

1. Intangibility: while some aspects of the service may be subject to intellectual property protection, it is also difficult to gauge quality and compatibility ahead of delivery, heightening the importance of effective governance against merely cost-based negotiation.
2. Perishability: as services cannot be stored, fluctuations in demand are much more difficult to manage than for material/intermediate goods – there is no buffer-stock option for services other than contracting to maintain reserve capacity which may be costly.
3. Simultaneity and coproduction: linked to the above point – services require the delivery to be coordinated with other aspects of the supply chains much more closely than material aspects of the process with implications for the closeness and attention of the corporation's governance function.
4. Heterogeneity: due to the specificity of most service provision there are few economies of scale available within the supply chain with each service interaction being relatively independent and requiring dedicated attention.
5. Labour intensive: while some functions are being automated, services, especially higher end provision remains dependent on flexible and agile human labour, with few opportunities for cost-reduction without impact on quality.
6. Non-transferability: services are seldom transferable between different functional or spatial areas of the production network and as such again offer few economies of scale.
7. Individual demand led: services tend to be produced/delivered in response to specific network demands and while to some extent they are predictable, they again offer little opportunity for the range of economies that may be engineered elsewhere in the network (adapted from Thakur and Anbanandam 2016: 334–6).

This is not to say that supply chain utilisation of service and business process outsourcing has no advantages, but rather that it makes very different demands on governance from the intermediate good(s) aspects of the production network.

It would seem clear that the aspects of supply chain governance that build legitimacy and trust into ongoing relations between network participants are vital for the effective introduction of services into global production networks and even more so in dedicated service supply chains. However, the character of services also makes governance a more plausible approach to understand this integration rather than regarding this as a cost–management function. The aspects of relationship development that governance may deliver to corporations is intensified in the services supply chains (full or partial) due to the final dependence within the service realm on interpersonal relations, both between contractor and supplier and also between actual provider and user/contractor for the service (Wang et al. 2018). So, as I suggested above, the idea that corporations practise governance, not merely management, of their supply chain is (re)emphasised by this brief consideration of the role of services within such global networks.

The globalised supply chain and economic development

One of the most significant ways in which global corporations contribute to states' economic development potential is through the opportunities for engaging with global production networks. However, for many commentators the benefits of this engagement are, at the very least, distributed unevenly between the major corporation(s) and the state(s) in whose territory subsidiary activity is undertaken. For instance, reviewing the role of corporations in sub-Saharan Africa, Rogers Tabe Egbe Orock identifies a wide range of corporate irresponsibility and profiteering, and little discernible benefits flowing to the host societies (Orock 2013). Offering a more balanced (read *positive*) assessment, a recent United Nations Conference on Trade and Development report on global supply/value chains reported both advantages to involvement in global production networks *and* a range of risks for host countries (UNCTAD 2013), paralleling the research explored below. Moreover, UNCTAD is not alone in discerning *some* advantages to developing countries from an engagement with global corporations.

A review of research on the economic and human rights impact of corporate inward investment by Elisa Giuliani and Chiara Macchi concluded that the last couple of decades have demonstrated there were few if any general effects of foreign direct investment by multinational corporations in developing countries. On the one hand, the strength and operation of host country institutions, from the state's capacity to regulate to social capabilities to negotiating civil society engagement with incoming corporations, can moderate and even ameliorate any negative effects. However, equally, many studies showed how the introduction of large, efficient and politically powerful corporations can have significant negative impacts on local markets and enterprises (Giuliani and Macchi 2014). In part this may be due to the impact supply chain involvement can have on local industrial sectors; as different firms compete to enter different global supply chains, so the collective interest of the sector may become fragmented and more difficult to discern by policy makers. This may lead to what has been termed 'interest shopping' where policy makers, shaping development policy, seek out enterprises whose interests align with prospective policy changes, thereby in one sense strengthening the ability of governments to enact their chosen policies for business even in the face of some sectoral resistance (Meckling and Hughes 2017). Of course, the global corporations involved in inwards supply chain-related investment are able to present a more unified lobbying position, offering the possibility of bypassing the local business/sectoral interest groups.

Nevertheless, these negative effects may only be short term. Although the evidence is somewhat thinner, the positive impact for developing countries of engagement with, and hosting of multinational corporations' investments may be evident in the longer term, provided the internal institutional element is supportive and is not merely captured by the incoming enterprise(s) (Giuliani and Macchi 2014: 500–501, *passim*). This is to say, where governments are able to both facilitate and manage supply chain involvement consistently over time, there is a clear potential for involvement of local enterprises in global production networks to deliver the more generally claimed developmental benefits (around technological up-grading and re-skilling of workforces). There are key distinctions between the ability of specific enterprises enrolled into production networks gaining some benefits, and the manner in which the claimed advantages of 'upgrading' are distributed more widely. While network participating enterprises may well find it difficult if not impossible to retain (or capture) value in global supply chains' operations, equally the pay-off may in the short to medium term be related to skills and (to some extent) technology transfer into the local economy (Coe and Yeung 2015: ch. 5). However, if as suggested above corporations have established a governance function across their supply chains there is clearly some potential for both norms and material arrangements preferred by the lead corporation to clash with those that the local state (or society) may wish to further. This may be resolved through negotiation, but would likely depend on the relative power and interest constellations between the corporation, the contracting enterprise(s) and the state.

States who see the route to economic development as including enhanced (and promoted) participation in global supply chains, have often sought to constrain uncontrolled impact on the host country's economy by establishing export processing zones or 'special economic zones' (SEZs).[3] Local companies conducting supply chain activity can be located within the SEZ and benefit from specific regulatory and fiscal negotiated settlements which differ from the rest of the country. This allows any negotiated advantages to be limited to a particular group of corporations and local enterprises that the state seeks to prefer or encourage (Moberg 2017). However, the key issue for economic development, conversely, is how porous the boundary separating the SEZ from the host country is. For full advantage to be gained from income generation to technological transfer and local labour market skills upgrading, the SEZ cannot be completely inoculated from the local economy (Narula and Zhan 2019). Thus, while policy advice to states' governments may focus on the spill-over effects of supply chain 'enrolment' it is also clear from the above discussion that many global corporations would (understandably) want to have some control or at least influence over the diffusion of experience from the supply chain. It is advantageous to have enhanced competition for (local) supply chain contracts and/or entry into longer-term relations, but equally with a focus on value-capture there are clear limits to the character and types of work that corporations might expect to cross the boundary of the SEZ into the local economy. Therefore, the forms of 'upgrading' discussed below are likely to be subject to negotiation between government and corporations, mediated through the ability of local enterprises to respond to the challenges of the production network. The facilitating environment in which this can happen may be initially limited to SEZs but with the expectation that the dynamic will carry upgrading into the rest of the economy in due course.

In some cases, SEZs may provide a location for non-national migrant labour to join the local workforce, but without the wider socio-economic effects that migrant labour might produce in the wider host economy. When such arrangements are put in place, global corporations have an opportunity to *combine* in one location cost (and other) advantages, in ways that may not currently exist outside the SEZ. Thus, for instance, this allows corporations (and/or their representatives) to negotiate favourable arrangements relating to infrastructure and service provision, as well as access to the labour market alongside the ability to bring in specialised labour available elsewhere to complement the (possibly) deficient skills environment of the host economy's labour market (Park 2016: 1402–29). Here, globally active corporations are not only able to play off different potential host countries against each other, for regulatory and financial advantage, but they can also shape their economic activity with less regard to the labour complement of the chosen location, again enhancing their bargaining position and ability to shape their production networks' spatial arrangements to their specific enterprise needs.

Corporations' supply networks have been built to enhance or extend a range of explicit economic and non-economic benefits, and given that the network itself is a significant (organisational) asset, as already noted corporations' governance of such networks is likely to be more sophisticated than merely an exclusive focus on market relations (Dunning and Narula 2004: ch. 9). As with any asset, the 'owner' seeks to both maintain its value and manage its deployment to gain further advantage; here the reasons for reticence about spill-over and skills/technology transfer out of SEZs become clearer. The ability to control access to the supply chain is a significant aspect of global corporations' political and economic power; this is not a directly coercive form of (political) power but rather the ability to block fruitful/profitable access to the network, and its associated resources (both material and ideational). Global corporations act as 'gatekeepers' to their supply networks, although the strength of this power may vary by circumstance: where there is competition to work with high-quality subcontractors and network partners (where the skill or technology base for this stage of networked production is scarce) then gatekeeping will be less obvious and/or effective. Conversely, where contracting firms are competing to join one or more networks best suited to their operational practices, then the lead corporation may well exercise considerable power as a gatekeeper (van der Ven 2018). Controlling access to, and the borders of, the corporate 'asset' of the supply chain is key to maintaining its overall value to the productive enterprise.

This is typified by the use of both product standards and standardised operational methods (Pistor 2014: 233), but also by a range of other intangible 'properties' (Durand and Milberg 2020). These intangibles include formal intellectual properties (patents on specific technologies, trademarks and copyright on aspects of the information and data flowing round the network); proprietary information and control technologies used to organise supply chain interactions/relations; and financialised products available to supply chain participants such as intra-network developmental loans. The use of intangibles to reinforce the network boundaries ensuring that there are clear costs to exclusion from the network and clear benefits from 'enrolment'. By maintaining a threshold for quality of output and a requirement for a commitment to operational practices, corporations can effectively ground their power over the supply chain in its regulatory (which is to say governance) practices.

This governing may be strengthened by 'channelling' of contracted intra-network trade. Rather than rely on local firms, global corporations encourage their existing network partners to invest in new supply chain locations (within newly constituted SEZs for instance) thereby taking advantage of the locational specific cost advantages but avoiding the need to find and negotiate new contract relations with hitherto unknown firms. As Mark Dallas concludes, 'domestic firms are rarely invited into relational-captive channels because they lack the capabilities and trust of foreign buyers, and they lack the capabilities and trust of buyers because they are never invited into relational-captive channels' (Dallas 2015: 903). Therefore, local firms are often unable to initiate the relations with global corporations that would allow them to progressively benefit from forms of upgrading, even as the local workforce is able (partially at least) to gain experience and enhancement of technical abilities. To be clear this can also reflect a lack of knowledge of, or ability to abide by, the norms which pattern and underpin the lead corporation's governance function, thereby potentially undermining local enterprises' aspirations to join a supply chain/network.

Upgrading and the supply chain

The standard (and positive) approach to the establishment of a corporate presence in a local economy in the Global South suggests that integration into these production networks offers potential for the 'social upgrading' of labour. As noted above, this happens both through the acquisition of new skills and techniques by the indigenous workforce, but also through the provision of (relatively) well-paid and (relatively) stable employment. This is complemented by a wider set of effects on domestic enterprises often referred to as 'economic upgrading'. For a range of international agencies/organisations from the World Bank to the International Labour Organization, the notion of 'upgrading' has often now replaced invocations of *Washington Consensus*-linked policies that emphasise an 'enabling environment' for economic development. This is to say, 'upgrading' has been utilised to encompass the legislative and policy changes that have been inherited from the *Washington Consensus* to build approaches that stress proactive value chain strategies as a key aspect of economic development (Werner et al. 2014; see also Coe and Yeung 2015). It is not merely involvement in the supply chain of global corporations that is claimed to deliver the economic development benefits, but a proactive strategy of seeking to capture stages in the process that allow more value to be added – a process of 'value capture'.

This is sometimes presented as a form of 'ratchet', where initial involvement in supply chains may reflect established national comparative advantage(s), but once engaged with the production network, both lead corporations and contracting local firms may have an interest in developing/widening the involvement rather than seeking new contractors. This partly reflects sunk costs in the relationship, and partly the inculcation of contractors into the particular corporate network's mores and practices; its culture of governance. Unfortunately this focus on the manner in which any 'social upgrading' is dependent on intra-supply chain relations has led to a down-playing of the role of states. Now, more often there is an increased focus on CSR (in supply chain or production network governance) as the key element in 'upgrading' (Fridell and Walker 2019). This shift to private sector provision of social benefits, for many critical commentators, would be linked to the manner in which contemporary *neoliberalism* privileges corporate interests over and above state interests (see the brief discussion of neoliberalism in Chapter 5).

It is also clear that local corporate engagement may (and indeed has) been more 'fleet of foot' than the 'ratcheting' effect of upgrading may allow. Corporations have seldom demonstrated unconditional (or even any) loyalty to a specific location for any production network node, with disinvestment a recognised moment in the overall character of supply chain trajectories, as corporations recognise (or negotiate) new comparative advantages for specific aspects of the network in new locations (Gereffi 2019: 244). Indeed, the transformation of communications (physical and informational) since the 1970s has led to a reduction in advantage from clustering separate elements of the production network in the same location, further reducing the longer-term commitment corporations might expect to make in particular SEZs now that co-locational advantage is lessened (Moberg 2017: 165). As this suggests, at best the upgrading ratchet is soft and conditional; at worst, it is not a ratchet at all.

Global corporations can also use various legal instruments, perhaps most obviously (but not exclusively) intellectual property law and contract law, to limit the ability of 'partner' SMEs in the supply chain to capture value (Baars and Bair et al. 2016). Business-enabling legal policies complement other national policy focused on upskilling of workforces and the enhancement of pre-employment education, but these legal measures are hardly likely to be neutral. Global corporations are adept (through experienced legal teams and political negotiations) at ensuring that the legal infrastructure provided by prospective supply chain host states serves their interests (even while facilitating the SMEs' involvement in the production network). Indeed, utilising various forms of intellectual property law to control intangible supply chain assets allows corporations to concentrate in their favoured network locations/ jurisdictions the intangible resources that would be central to any developmental pay-off for countries seeking to access these networks by facilitating local involvement (Baglioni et al. 2019). In one sense this may allow such supply chains to become analogous to natural monopolies where the lead enterprise (or enterprises) are able to capture the positive externalities of the network's activities (Durand and Milberg 2020). Global corporations' control of information, data and knowledge resources is multifaceted, underpinning their gatekeeping of global production networks and their governance of the contracted participants to their own ends and benefit.

The result of this legal and governance environment can, at its worst, produce a rather paternalistic approach to understanding economic development, and can render workers and enterprises as passive recipients of largesse from the corporation(s) in whose supply chains they are working. Looking back to the development of labour relations in the most developed countries, Ben Selwyn argues that we need a different conception of how the interactions between global corporations and local workforces can bring about the positive shift in the working environment envisaged in the positive narrative put forward, for instance in the International Labour Organization's *Decent Work Agenda*. What is required, he argues, is both the recognition that top-down approaches historically have seldom delivered major improvements in the plight of workers *and* that the key effective mechanism has been a focus by workers themselves on the labour process and associated collective action, most obviously through unionisation (Selwyn 2013). To deliver the forms of social upgrading that supporters of supply-chain integration in the Global South claim for the workforces, in Selwyn's view there needs to be both political and legal space for the formation of independent trade unions and a willingness (or a legal requirement) for corporations to recognise and negotiate with such unions. Or, in the terms I have been using here, there is a need to address the democratic deficit in global supply chains.

This combination of circumstances is not so common; more often states' governments have been uninterested in moving beyond rather basic levels of labour regulation and have not been willing to support the extensive expansion of unionisation to fill the gap, not least as corporations have utilised their ability to choose investment location to discourage such provision. To some extent, in response, forms of private governance (linked to issues of CSR, and external to the corporations' own governance function) have grown in importance, especially in commercial sectors where consumer sentiment (via brand values) has some salience. Where consumers have both discretion and choice, and can become informed around labour standards there are some opportunities for private governance to have an impact on the articulation, development and enforcement of labour standards, whatever the local legal situation. This can complement unions' work where labour organisation has been successful, and can to some extent substitute for unionisation, provided consumers are committed and there is a private governance actor/organisation in play regarded as legitimate by both consumers and corporate managers. However, the worst difficulties for labour lie in supply chains where there is both little opportunity for union organisation (or indeed it is constrained in one way or another) and the products of the production network are either unaffected by branding issues, or are for (or part of) intermediate component markets (Donaghey et al. 2014). Again, different corporations, and by extension different supply chains, have very different politico-economic characteristics. This is not to say a more general analysis is impossible, just that it needs to be tempered by an awareness and acknowledgment of the complexities and variances within the global corporate realm and between varying corporations' practices.

Power analysis for (and in) the global supply chain

This complexity has recently led Mark Dallas, Stefano Ponte and Timothy Sturgeon to assemble a very useful typology of the ways power works in global supply chains. This typology offers a helpful analytical tool for both understanding the general terrain over which power relations operate and allowing the location of specific power relations within such a terrain (Dallas et al. 2019). Utilising two pairs of concepts, direct and indirect (diffuse) transmission mechanisms of power, alongside dyadic and collective arenas of actors, they present a four-part typology. Each cell of the two-by-two matrix in Figure 4.1 represents a particular dimension of power in the global supply or value chain. Crucially, these cells are not mutually exclusive; rather, they are interpenetrated and any particular corporate network may exhibit different forms of power in different places across its production network.

Dyadic/Direct:	Dyadic/Indirect (diffuse power):
Bargaining power	*Demonstrative power*
Collective/Direct:	Collective/Indirect (diffuse power):
Institutional power	*Constitutive power*

Source: Adapted/simplified from Dallas et al. 2019: 673.

Figure 4.1   Interfirm power in the supply chain

Each of the cells represents forms of power relations that will already be familiar from the discussion above and I do not seek to develop each in any great detail here, but this framing allows a clearer understanding of how the opportunities to enact forms of power will shift as the character of particular elements of the production network develop. Most obviously, allowing that most (if not all) power relations exhibit both direct and indirect elements at any one time, the more important dimension may be the shape and complexity of the supply chain relations at any particular point in the production network.

As this analysis suggests, the direct power relations in dyadic (one-to-one) contracting in the supply chain will revolve around direct bargaining in the first instance; here standard negotiations to establish contracts are related to the needs and requirements of the lead corporation (including cost and quality issues) and the leverage (or lack thereof) enjoyed by contracting suppliers. Lead corporations utilise the opportunities on offer *within* the supply chain to both control competition to enter the network (gatekeeping), while also using competitive contracting as a pressure on existing network 'partners'. However, external to the supply chain a more diffuse *demonstrative* power can be identified when the entry conditions are known and understood even among putative contractors as yet not in the position to attempt to initiate contracts (Dallas et al. 2019: 678–9). Here demonstrative power may be enjoyed by a range of actors, including the lead corporation but also development agencies and state-based actors, who will shape, support, and frame enterprises' development and (re)organisation towards any attempt to bid for a contract to join (enrol into) the production network. Thus, business consultants, banks and others may also enjoy demonstrative power through their purported ability to aid any firm's supply chain readiness.

Once the supply and value chain relations become more collective, in the manner in which I have already argued that requires forms of *governance* to be developed, then as the lower cells of the matrix indicate, direct and indirect power relations take on different characteristics. Here, the direct form of power leads to the development of a range of institutions, from business associations and standard-setting groups through to the network effects of the deployment of particular technological platforms. This form of power also includes the institutions of the state, especially where regulatory form(s) have been subject to lobbying by corporations or their representatives (private and public) (Dallas et al. 2019: 679–80). Here, the power of particular corporations is less obvious as the institutions seem to express industry sector or national interests, but are nonetheless shaped by corporations' direct involvement, albeit collectively.

Finally, when power is both indirect and collective, Dallas and his co-authors suggest this represents a form of constitutive power; the power to constitute the economic environment in which the supply chain sits without explicit corporate involvement (Dallas et al. 2019: 680–81). I am going to discuss this final aspect of power in the next chapter in more detail as it represents the interaction between the particular political economy of any supply chain and the wider global corporate political economy. Here it needs, again, to be emphasised that these four forms of power in global supply (or value) chains are not mutually exclusive. Rather, this framing and typology allows us to see clearly that the power relations and power structures of production networks are complex, multifaceted and often specific to the shape and scale of *particular* globalised corporate production networks and their preferred forms of governance.

Why the global supply chain matters

As should now be clear, the global corporate sector touches or interacts with other elements of the global political economy frequently through the governance and management practices of global production networks. When we talk about the impact of global corporations beyond their home/headquarters state, then these impacts are often (although not exclusively) mediated and articulated through the variety and range of relations that make up each corporation's supply chain, value chain or production network. A failure to appreciate the political economy of these networks is a failure to understand how the global corporate sector actually operates.

Whatever the organisational advantages of a global supply chain, global production networks also allow a form of tax planning, tied up with what is referred to as 'transfer pricing'. Transfer pricing is the calculation of the price paid for by one stage of the supply chain for the intermediate goods (or business services) provided by the previous stage. When these supply chain stages are in different tax jurisdictions, shifts in price(s) charged will shift the tax exposure in each jurisdiction. Simply put, raising the purchase price of the sending stage increases the profit at the sending stage and therefore increases the tax exposure; conversely reducing the price at the sending stage allows a greater profit at the receiving stage, raising the profitability of the receiving stage and thus its exposure to tax. Pretty obviously, it is in the interest of the lead/controlling corporation to take the profit at the stage where taxation is lowest and thus prices are adjusted around the supply chain to effect that outcome.

Tax authorities are not blind to such attempts to minimise exposure to local/national taxes and therefore usually require transfer prices to be calculated on the basis of an analogue to an 'arms-length' commercial relation; as if the corporation was party to only one side of the transaction and not (effectively) both buyer and seller. There are three methods by which this calculation is made: the comparable uncontrolled price, which is the price that might be identified in an open market where the corporation was buying the good or service; a cost plus calculation (where the issue becomes what an acceptable rate of return/ profit is); or a resale price. The latter two formulations calculate the transfer price on the basis of 'normal' profitability for the sector (Avi-Yonah 2019: 32). Of course, this leaves considerable room to 'game' the system as many aspects of the information needed to calculate stand-alone profitability of a production/service stage are complex and often commercially confidential, if not wilfully obscured or distorted by corporations. Thus, even with these mechanisms in play, the general presumption is that transfer pricing allows extensive 'tax planning' and significant under-taxation of global corporate activity and profits. We shall return to the politics of global corporate taxation in the next chapter, but it should be stressed this is not an accidental outcome but is often planned into corporate network development.

One further key area of politics needs to be mentioned before we move on, not least as it has a direct and recent impact on the organisation of supply chains; and that is the revival of protectionism as mainstream economic policy (not that it ever really went away). If you are resident in the UK, during the discussion of the potential (or otherwise) disruption of leaving the European Union, you will have seen the discussion of various automotive supply chains and the criss-crossing of the English Channel by various intermediate products. Most famously, this focused on a BMW/Mini automotive drive train that crossed the channel three times before becoming part of a finished car. Much supply chain analysis is premised on continuity of relatively free trade; however, the raising of effective tariffs (for instance as the UK leaves the EU or as the current trade war between the USA and China deepens with discussions of an associated global economic 'decoupling') will disrupt and change the organisation of global production networks. Unsurprisingly, this relatively recent political development is often absent from the existing literature on supply chains (Dong and Kouvelis 2019: 9–10), but will have a range of impacts.

Protectionism may reverse the fragmentation of networks and make the clustering of a number of sequential stages in one location of SEZ (again) more cost effective. Additionally, as policymakers clearly intend it may result in the 'reshoring' of production and activity back into developed country homes of global corporations. Finally, following on from these two potential shifts, the developmental policy of economic upgrading through supply chain enrolment and involvement may be dealt a significant blow. Therefore, as we enter the third decade of the new millennium it is not impossible that political shifts and changes will (again) prompt significant shifts and large changes in the manner in which global corporations manage and govern their global partnerships and productive relations. However, the analyses set out above will also inform corporate decision-making and trajectories of governance.

In the next chapter I also pick up the question of the wider impact on policy making of the supply chain's distortion of global trade data; although seldom made explicit, the manner in which trade is recorded has a clear impact on how (some) macroeconomic, or economic developmental policy decisions are made and/or justified. Given the data is influenced and (re)shaped by the political economy of the global supply chain, understanding the impact on trade flow data of how global production networks operate is of some importance. It is worth also noting that while trade in intermediate goods (and services) may account for around a half of all international trade, as a proportion of all global economic activity (to include those products and services not traded internationally) supply chains accounts for under a fifth (Baldwin and Lopez-Gonzalez 2015: 1718). This is not to under-play the importance of the global supply chains and production networks discussed above but rather to remind ourselves that even for (global) corporations much activity remains focused on their home states (or the states where their subsidiaries are located). In this sense, the 'death of distance' has yet to arrive.

Key questions for research(ers)

How does introducing issues of governance and a democratic deficit to the analysis of global supply chains transform our understanding of their political economy?

How might we better measure/assess the overall impact in developing countries of engaging with corporate supply chains?

How might we better understand the potential for labour agency in global production networks?

Is the control of access to supply chain contracting a significant site of non-price-based corporate political power?

Can states shape their legal infrastructure to enhance their abilities to capture value-added from the supply chain?

If we are entering a period of less 'frictionless' trade, how will the global supply chain be transformed?

Notes

1. Elsewhere I have discussed the manner in which the World Bank Connecting to Compete Reports have framed and encouraged economic policy development to focus on the establishment and maintenance of efficient/effective logistic capacity as an essential element in building an effective national supply chain strategy (May 2019).
2. Adapted from Steffik and Pereira (2011) with some modification for use in the corporate realm (without, I hope, violating the original analytical intent).
3. The long history of the export processing zone and its origins in the legal establishment of freeports is critically analysed in some detail in Orenstein (2019).

5 The corporation's political agency

As Michael Moran once stated, 'all business is political: that is, the state is constantly present in various guises in the life of business' (Moran 2009: 82). While the role of corporations and other business enterprises in modern democracies is the subject of considerable argument, the facilitative role of law and regulation alongside the economic policy interests of governments across the political spectrum mean that there is no aspect of business that does not intersect with politics in one way or another. However, it is only relatively recently that scholars and researchers (as opposed to activists) have begun to pay attention to the *political* aspects of global corporate practices (Geppert and Dörrenbächer 2011: 7). Moreover, little work in political theory has had much to say about the corporation as a *political* actor, or with a couple of exceptions has much to say about how corporations have changed the contemporary political realm. While David Ciepley has explored the interaction between the development of the US constitution and the parallel development of corporate law (Ciepley 2017) and asked whether corporations might be held to account where their activities intersect with the public interest (Ciepley 2018; see also Ciepley 2013), little else has been developed on these topics from a starting place in political theory. For instance, Scott Bowman's survey of *The Modern Corporation and American Political Thought* for the most part focuses on analysis from adjacent fields, such as economics or law, rather than identifying an extensive *political* tradition of thought about the corporation (Bowman 1996). Therefore, while there is much to say about politics and the corporation, it has seldom been political theorists who've been saying it.

As will be clear from the following discussion, the character of such politics is dynamic and changing. However, in the critical study of the contemporary global system or global political economy, it is also difficult not to start by saying something about neoliberalism and its connection with corporate politics. Having mostly avoided it so far, I begin with a short discussion of the link between neoliberalism and the political economy of (global) corporations. Indeed, in one sense the manner in which political analysis has engaged with the corporation is by seeing it as the privileged beneficiary of *neoliberalisation*. There is an excellent volume in this series by Kean Birch, which explores the complexities of the various accounts of neoliberalism itself (Birch 2017), and therefore, for the sake of simplicity, here I will adopt Ray Kiely's recent approach which focuses on three key social dimensions that neoliberalism engages with in a particular way.

The first of Kiely's three dimensions of neoliberalism is between freedom and social constraint; neoliberals in Kiely's view adopt an individualist view of freedom defined as the absence of coercion by others, leaving the state's key role to 'coerce, coercive behaviour' (Kiely 2018: 105); this is secured by the enjoyment of property rights. For the neoliberal, collective action is acceptable but only when it is organised round a collective individualised interest, not when used to seek to expand a common good. Neoliberalism's second element for Kiely is the manner in which the state is constrained by the rule of law. This reflects a specific (and limited) view of the rule of law shorn of any significant normative content – sometimes referred to as a thin view of the rule of law (May 2014). Very clearly drawing on the influence of F. A. Hayek, this aspect of neoliberalism is concerned with the limitation of arbitrary or particular rule and requiring that the state should only govern on the basis of general rules/ laws (Kiely 2018: 109). Thirdly, and to some extent leading on from this prior understanding of the rule of law, neoliberals have sought to ensure that power (social and economic) cannot be concentrated, but with a particular focus on such concentration by the state (Kiely 2018: 114). For Kiely, a key paradox of neoliberalism is that it is both explicitly against state power, but equally seeks to deploy the state to achieve its ends. Recognising that markets, while an effective and efficient technology of social allocation, are not natural, neoliberals require the state to legislate to support and/or facilitate marketisation, but are also quick to blame such regulation for distorting the market and producing crises that if neoliberalism had been 'properly' implemented could have been avoided. This has considerable importance for how we understand the interaction between the politics of neoliberalism and the political economy of the corporation.

For Kiely, corporate power under neoliberalism involves a further important paradox. Neoliberalism is a 'movement' in which the 'price mechanism was championed because of incomplete knowledge existing within each individual, but increasingly it became a supporter of expert knowledge residing in the concentrated power of large corporations' (Kiely 2018: 325). Originally, the market was celebrated as a conduit by which collective information, driven by the requirements of market exchange, would lead to socially beneficial results that were beyond even the most talented planners. However, some neoliberals began to argue that corporations, by virtue of their extensive in-market operations, were able to develop knowledge resources that allowed them to deliver the social benefits that neoliberals celebrated (focused on individual – negative – freedoms) in the absence of extensive competition. Thus, while earlier neoliberals were sceptical of all concentrations of power, more contemporary variants are less concerned with the concentration of power in the corporate sector, while still arguing such concentration within the state (or within the labour market via unionisation) is detrimental to the good society.

Interestingly, John Braithwaite sees these developments somewhat differently. He has argued that rather than something we might identify as *neoliberalism*, the contemporary political economic settlement might be better characterised as *regulatory capitalism*. Rather than seeing the current political economic system as having been hijacked by corporate interests (with the collusion of neoliberals), for Braithwaite regulatory capitalism is more a case of 'reciprocal causation': the growth in size in power of corporations prompts political development of regulatory interventions, called for by political critics, but also importantly by corporate interests themselves. However, the expansion of such regulatory aspects of the states' involvement in markets, then supports and prompts the further expansion of the largest corporations, best placed to both respond to, and thrive, in a regulated market environment (Braithwaite 2008: 21). Furthermore, as he points out:

> Many states simply forfeit domains of regulation to global corporations that have superior technical capability and greater numbers of technically competent people on the ground. For example, in many developing nations the Big Four accounting firms effectively set national accounting standards. (Braithwaite 2008: 25)

In other words, for Braithwaite the contemporary regulated form of capitalism has corporate interests at its heart, not due to any form of capture or reformulation by neoliberals but because corporate interests have been central to its development in the first place. Indeed, corporations are now often regulated by other corporations, such as credit rating agencies and global accounting firms, whose judgements states' governments often defer to, in what has sometimes been referred to as a form of 'private authority' (see Hall and Biersteker 2002; Mayer and Phillips 2017). Here, regulatory capitalism represents an intertwined form of political governance that sees corporations as complicit in regulation, not merely passive recipients of regulatory actions or constraints.

For both characterisations of the contemporary political economy, be it either *neoliberalism* or *regulatory capitalism*, this is where the interaction between corporations, their representatives and public governance (national or regional in the case of the European Union) is a vital issue. In general and following the lead of America, many regulators now seem to accept an argument, often linked to a series of cases in the 1970s won by Robert Bork at the US Supreme

Court on behalf of his corporate clients, that monopolies may actually cause little harm. Bork argued that the goal of anti-trust laws should not be the control and dissolution of monopolies but rather to ensure where monopolies cohered that they served the 'protection of consumer welfare'; provided monopoly offered clear benefits to consumers the fact they were monopolies was immaterial. As Tim Wu rather archly notes, at the end of the 1970s the US Supreme Court 'almost casually abandoned the foundation of [anti-trust] law' (Wu 2018: 103). The acceptance of Bork's argument (supported and publicised by corporate interests) denuded much anti-trust, pro-competition market regulation into the new millennium, not least as 'consumer welfare' was increasingly narrowly conceived to mean only new products and low prices.

However, in the decade since the financial crisis of 2008, this acquiescence has become a little less general. Recent research by the European Central Bank suggests that since the global financial crisis of 2008, there has been a divergence between the extent of market concentration in the USA and in the largest members of the EU. While in America there has been a growth of market concentration, in Germany, Spain, France and Italy while there are a number of markets in which concentration remains evident, this has not got 'worse' in the last decade. The researchers suggest that this demonstrates that the more robust regulatory response to corporate domination taken by the EU (and the states concerned) seems to have had a material impact on maintaining competition (Cavalleri et al. 2019). Whether this difference is sufficient to satisfy critics of global corporate power is quite another matter. Indeed while the EU may have forestalled further concentration, powerful multinational or global corporations have still managed to maintain a dominant position in many European markets. Contemporary neoliberalism or regulatory capitalism remains both comfortable with corporate power and sees it as politically unproblematic.

So, as large and dominant corporations are a commonplace, as such, their role in the international or global *political* system requires analysis. Writing some decades ago, John Stopford and Susan Strange identified what they referred to as a triangular diplomacy to highlight a certain form of large-scale corporate practice. Examining the contours of the global political economy at the end of the last century, and in a world where competition between states had intensified, they argued that multinational corporations had become key to the delivery of governments' economic priorities. Moreover, as large international actors, themselves often now dealing with intermediate goods and/or services, many corporations had extensive interactions with similarly scaled enterprises. This, Stopford and Strange argued, had led to a transformation of the patterns of interaction across the global system: a set of patterns they referred to as 'triangular diplomacy'. This diplomacy included the standard patterns of inter-state relations; the new(er) forms of state–corporate relations; and the hitherto under-appreciated corporation-to-corporation relations (Stopford and Strange 1991; Strange 1992 [2002]). Of course, this analysis was partly framed as a critique of the academic discipline of International Relations as being too narrowly focused, but this need not detain us here.

This identification of corporations having a diplomatic function both in their relations with states but also between themselves has been under-developed in the subsequent decades, even as critical analysis focused on neoliberalism has recognised the privileging of corporate interests (Babic et al. 2017). The relations between enterprises are in this analytical frame subject to similar considerations of power, influence and legitimacy that would shape other forms of diplomacy. Indeed, for Strange, it is the interplay of 'transnational bargaining' across these three dimensions of diplomacy that drives the global political economy (Strange 1992 [2002]: 168–9). It is not that inter-corporate diplomacy is unrecognised, but rather that its analysis is kept within accounts of the corporate sector (and rendered as merely *management*) rather than linked through the notion of triangular diplomacy to the interactions between states and enterprises, and therefore part of the central political characteristics of the contemporary global capitalist system. The notion of *governance* I have focused on in this volume enables analysis to include easily these sorts of hitherto under-analysed relations.

Everyday politics and corporations

This political power of global corporations has been the focus of both critical academic analysis and a more popular campaigning literature. This should be no real surprise because as Guido Palazzo and Andreas Scherer rather succinctly put it over a decade ago: 'the politicization of the corporation is [an] unavoidable result of the changing interplay of economy, government and civil society in a globalizing world' (Palazzo and Scherer 2006: 76). The populist, campaigning literature is best represented by Joel Bakan's book *The Corporation* (Bakan 2004) and the work of Naomi Klein (most recently Klein 2018). These authors are probably the best known and perhaps most coherent in their critique of the current forms of corporate capitalism. For both (albeit differently argued), the corporation has developed considerable power without any linked responsibility or accountability in the modern capitalist system. Likewise, following on from Noreena Hertz's *The Silent Takeover* (Hertz 2002) and other books warning of the corporation's negative impact on democracy, there has been a continuing stream of commentary expressing concern about the extent and strength of corporate interests in national, international and global politics. However, equally, much of this critique since 2008 has been subsumed within a more general negative analysis of *neoliberalism* (see above), even as scholarly analysis of the (global) corporation has grown in both extent and sophistication, most recently focusing on the technology sector (see, for instance, Zuboff 2019).

One recent (academic) survey of the issue concluded that the growing political power of global corporations has had three clear implications. Firstly, John Mikler argues that corporate power is deployed to stifle competition and remove the traditional idea of separate markets in which economic exchange takes place; rather, corporations are now controlling or managing much of the ecology of market exchange (Mikler 2018: 133–6). This includes the areas of the economy where social interactions have become the basis of capital accumulation by 'Big Tech'. Secondly, corporations actually still wield their power from national bases; they remain multinational rather than truly transnational or global. As was pointed out in the introduction, the corporation works closely with (and indeed may often heavily influence) its home state to ensure that its political interests are furthered in the multilateral forums of international economic governance (Mikler 2018: 137–40). However, and thirdly, Mikler also suggests that if the first two implications hold true, then there remains a range of opportunities for the reassertion of political control over corporate practices (Mikler 2018: 140–44). That this is not always obvious demonstrates how corporations and their allies utilise their structural or discursive power (see discussion of Doris Fuchs' work below) to shape and maintain a political economy that serves their best interests (Mikler 2018: 40–49). In other words, corporations and their political allies have worked hard to shape a global system that serves their interests.

To take one high-profile sector, and following Shoshana Zuboff's recent intervention foregrounding the manner in which large technology corporations have gathered and commodified personal data to enhance their profits (Zuboff 2019), the question of the manner in which social media corporations govern the social media space/territory in which they operate is now being discussed in *political* terms. Previously such an analysis only appeared in mainstream accounts when there was an impact on other areas of 'high politics' such as its utilisation by terrorists or where other corporate interests (such as the large entertainment firms) have been impacted via the lack of concern to protect intellectual property rights. However, as the example of Facebook suggests, what drives the focus of this new governance is the dependence for profits on social interactions; as Oli Schwarz observes when 'human interactions becomes sources of profits, they can also be *maximised through their rational governance*' (Schwarz 2019: 121). This can be understood as parallel to large shopping mall owners seeking to control the retail space (not public space, but privately owned space) to maximise the opportunities and minimise the constraints for purchase(s).

Like shopping mall owners, Facebook governs its space through the application of the sanction of exclusion, which has significant consequences due to the social capital now represented by the social ties mediated via (in this case) Facebook. Thus

> Facebook's power relies on its status as an emergent central bank of generalised social capital . . . Since Facebook streamlines the accumulation and maintenance of social capital, those who avoid using it are disadvantaged. Yet those who deposit their social capital in Facebook become increasingly dependent on Facebook Inc. and cannot withdraw their capital against its policy. (Schwarz 2019: 127)

This is to say that Facebook is able to define and control the means by which social capital (as mediated through its services) both appears and is reinforced, thereby both grounding its value and also establishing a credible threat of loss if exclusion is enacted.

While shoppers may have other shopping options, on the one hand Schwarz wants to argue that Facebook is so central to the reproduction of social capital that it has significant social exclusionary power. On the other hand, even if other social media platforms offer plausible sites of social capital production and accumulation for users, it is likely that they will adopt similar forms of governance (Schwarz 2019: 136). This form of governance of consumer activity is not necessarily new; in the realm of intellectual property, and specifically digital copyright, forms of digital rights management (DRM) systems have a relatively long and contested political economy (May 2007). However, while DRMs are a form of technically facilitated governance, Facebook and others have actually returned to much more human-mediated forms, with rules enacted by a prolitarianised 'judicial labour' force (Schwarz 2019: 129) with significant parallels to the labour issues explored in Chapter 4's discussion of the governance of the supply chain. That said, the relationship between the corporation and state remains a key nexus of political concern, not just in the realm of privacy or the regulation of intangible assets.

The 'problem' of investor–state dispute settlement

As has already been noted, states, especially economically under-developed states, have a fraught and often difficult political relationship with powerful global corporations. Nowhere is this clearer than in the highly contentious issue that has received extensive coverage both in the academy *and* from campaigning groups: the processes of Investor–State Dispute Settlement (ISDS). This has been frequently identified by critics as an avenue whereby corporations have been able to 'discipline' states that are hosting inward investments. This is accomplished through a two-step process: firstly, the corporations' 'home' state (and as noted, global corporations remain tied to a home state in some way) concludes a bilateral investment treaty (BIT) with the prospective investment hosting state. Secondly, when the corporation encounters a difficulty (ranging from policy changes that undermine the profitability of the investment, to issues of effective appropriation of corporate property, quite widely defined), the corporation uses the dispute settlement mechanism to try to extract damages (and/or the threat of such action to try to change state policy). One commentator has referred to the tribunals that decide ISDS cases as 'shadow courts' (Edwards 2016) which gives a flavour of their general reception.

This form of dispute settlement finds its origins in the period of decolonialisation after the 1950s. Conventionally, the development of ISDS is ascribed to two different (but complementary) issues; firstly, the desire of developing (post-colonial) states to attract investment for (economic) development required them to make credible commitments that once corporations had undertaken foreign direct investment (FDI), with attendant sunk costs, that governments would not be able to appropriate such assets with impunity. Here, ISDS is part of a package intended to reassure investors and make FDI attractive to developed country multinational corporations, most often consolidated into a BIT. On the other hand, BITs have also been identified as an instrument used by post-imperial developed countries seeking to perpetuate their influence and/or control over the political economy of FDI once the formal governance controls of colonialism had been dismantled (Behn et al. 2018: 339–42). As newly independent states sought control of their natural resources, but equally required foreign corporations' expertise to exploit these resources, so the renewal of previous 'rights' of major corporations secured during the colonial period became a fraught and contentious political issue.

However, there is a third element to the story of the development of ISDS, which presents it as the result of early aspirations for global governance.

As Taylor St John observes, the 'corporations and law firms that dominate investor–state arbitration today were not present at its creation' (St John 2018: 3). However, neither were states particularly intensive lobbyists for the development of investor protection, often seeing already established forms of investment insurance as effective. Rather, international administrators responding to the experiences of the Second World War sought to develop a legal system to govern international investments (St John 2018: 4). This reflected the more general acceptance of the idea of the rule of law as the common sense of global politics (see May 2014) that was in ascendance during the decades following 1945, and the professionalization of global (regulatory) politics in the twentieth century.

Perhaps, most crucially, as St John sets out in his extended history and analysis of ISDS, the more recent acceleration of arbitration cases and the subsequent rise in the profile of the instrument(s), and the critical response, followed on from a significant period in which the system was developed and normalised. St John therefore divides the development of ISDS into two initial phases and then the contemporary period of a more fraught political economy of ISDS. The first stage was essentially constitutional: the development of a legal grounding for and then of the establishment of the International Centre for Settlement of Investment Disputes (ICSID). The Centre was more of a recognition that the World Bank, which hosted many of the initial discussions, would facilitate disputes that were to be litigated under the convention's various articles (St John 2018: 6–8, part I *passim*). Reflecting early concerns about (im)partiality, the ICSID was portrayed by the World Bank (and others) as a neutral body and as a 'trusted' forum for dispute resolution. The Centre still acts as the facilitator of specific dispute settlement tribunals with its procedures and norms widely adopted (while also being adapted to each particular circumstance) across a range of treaties that include ISDS clauses and influencing other forums available and/or nominated in BITs.

This adoption of the ICSID's procedures took place in a second phase: the integration of the convention into the various BITs negotiated as world trade recovered from the upheavals of the first half of the twentieth century. Three dimensions were involved: individual agreements between investing corporations (or other enterprises) alongside the (voluntary) integration of the convention's requirements into state law; the development of BITs between investors' home states and the states hosting (or hoping to host) investment; and regional and multilateral investment agreements (St John 2018: 8–9, part II *passim*). For St John, a clear constituency (albeit aspiring to a neutral technocratic involvement) based in the ICSID Secretariat then sought to set an agenda for the international protection of investors' rights through the mechanism of socializing states' policy makers into the approach and legal instruments of the ICSID convention. While at any one time particular states might seem to dominate the development of ISDS, St John's central contention is that, actually, at the centre of the process sat a stable set of actors, using their position at the ICSID to further the development of ISDS in a particular direction (St John 2018: ch. 4, *passim*). This is perhaps best confirmed by the proliferation of BITs over the subsequent decades. Moreover, given that many of these developments pre-dated the expansion of the *neoliberal* state, this might be better identified as part of the development of *regulatory capitalism* (to use Braithwaite's term). Here we might recognise the 'reciprocal causation' of a regulatory institution that has expanded through a process of interaction between social actors focused on regulation and corporations, with each responding to initiatives and developments by the other.

These new bilateral treaties included clauses regarding the settlement of investment disputes (as is normal for any international treaty). However, as Pablo Leandro Ciocchini and Stéfanie Khoury (reflecting a now common critique) put it: these clauses have 'a neocolonial rationality because it is not only a mechanism to protect foreign investments, but also a means for states to engage politically outside of the diplomatic sphere' by seeking to further and protect the foreign interests of corporations based in that sphere (Ciocchini and Khoury 2018: 980–81). Most significantly, over the period in which BITs have become commonplace, there has been a move away from a focus on the problem/threat of expropriation and towards the recognition of the principle of protection against 'regulatory takings'; the loss of income/return on property, while not the total loss of expropriation, represents a significant loss against expectations. This led to the principle of fair and equitable treatment increasingly becoming a key part of BITs signatories' obligations (Sornarajah 2015: ch. 5). These treaty clauses are intended to allow corporations to gain recompense for unforeseen domestic political changes that so transform the investment environment that the corporation is unable to gain the expected returns on its investment. Prompted by the experience of expropriation, the field/scope of political action included in such clauses became an indication of the corporate expectations of protection from the domestic political processes of regulatory change and democratic responses to their activities in-country. In the new millennium, fair and equitable treatment has become the most frequent basis for ISDS claims (UNCTAD 2012: 10). The key issue, then, which has dominated the recent history of ISDS arbitration is the justification of such claims: what is the baseline for fairness and equity, and what are the legitimate levels of 'damage' that might be successfully claimed?

The widespread adoption of ICSID practices therefore has been the subject of considerable attention as regards the operation of these arbitration activities. This reflects the significant growth of cases entering the ISDS process since the beginning of the new millennium: the cumulative total of cases had grown from less than 100 in 2000 to over 500 by 2012 and reached over a thousand four years later, after years of relative inactivity (UNCTAD 2014: 19; Langford et al. 2017). The ICSID's key original aims were to reduce the risk of national bias (particularly in favour of the host state) in arbitration of disputes; address the ineffectiveness of normal diplomatic protections as regards non-national investor interests; and to reduce the perceptions of the illegitimacy of arbitration decisions due to claims of their arbitrary character (Muchlinski 2007: 745–6). However, as Peter Muchlinski has pointed out, due to the expansion of 'harms' that are regarded as within its scope, it has become a 'mechanism for the control of governmental discretion and not merely a system of international commercial dispute settlement' (Muchlinski 2007: 718). This raises important political issues about the delocalised control over the priorities and practices of national economic development in developing countries (partly) dependent on investments from abroad.

It also highlights, for its critics, the most notable aspect of the ISDS process: its unbalanced and exclusionary character. Cases can only be initiated by foreign investors and not by states' parties to the treaty; the cases are heard by a closed community of international arbitrators, whose neutrality (as discussed below) is regarded widely as severely compromised; and cases are frequently progressed without publicity or transparency. Indeed, Ciocchini and Khoury conclude that: 'what might ordinarily have been state–state negotiations can be carried out through private–state arbitration with the result of conditioning domestic markets in a forum removed from the people directly impacted by the decisions taken' (Ciocchini and Khoury 2018: 982). This has led UNCTAD to conclude that, as regards the principle of legitimate expectations, the utilisation of the standard of fair and equitable treatment (FET) had in fact demonstrated

> a risk that tribunals may evaluate the FET standard only in terms of an investor's expectations, without due consideration given to a State's wider political and social obligations, although on the whole, tribunals have paid attention to distinguishing legitimate regulation from governmental conduct that violates the standard. (UNCTAD 2012: 91)

As this suggests, it is the frequent (but not universal) lack of recognition of the legitimacy of political and regulatory activity by host states that lies behind the significant disquiet around ISDS.

In addition, there are continuing complaints about inconsistency between arbitral decisions, the partiality of supposedly independent arbitrators as well as the costs and lengthy procedure of settling claims/cases (UNCTAD 2014: 23–9). This is compounded by the arbitrators' claim that the ISDS process is an unproblematic form of contract law and is a key element of accepted international law. However, at the very same time the idea that as such there might be therefore competing international legal principles and norms that should enter the process of arbitration is denied or obscured (Sornarajah 2015: 134). For many critics, therefore, the problems of arbitrary and inconsistent awards in the ISDS process are because this appeal to international law remains partial and as such driven less by legality than by the ad hoc justification for the advancement of corporate interests. Seldom are mores derived from other international legal instruments (for instance those dealing with human rights) accorded any effective weight in the panel deliberations. This has led to a focus on the make-up of panels and background of arbitrators themselves; over 20 years ago it was already clear that these arbitrators were building a community of expertise (Dezalay and Garth 1996). This community of arbitrators had both captured the development of the processes and norms of ISDS, but perhaps more significantly has now established a virtual monopoly in providing arbitration panel members. Moreover, through panel members' close connection with corporate plaintiffs (across successive arbitrations) many of the commentators (including those cited above) regard the system as institutionally skewed towards the interests of the global corporation who make use of the system *as* plaintiffs.

For many developing states, the difficulty in extracting themselves from this system (even if it often seems to be unbalanced and favour corporate rights) is that the complexities of BITs make stepping out of the agreements almost impossible. Ranging from the problem that unilateral withdrawal is often 'illegal' due to the length of sunset clauses (making withdrawal a long-term process) likely to have been included at the original ratification, to corporate threats of disinvestment to investment 'strikes', many developing states are caught in a system that seldom clearly serves their interests. While not the only site of the exercise of global corporate power, this is a useful example (which has been subject to some excellent analytical work) to precede a more general discussion of the forms and dimensions of the political and economic power of global corporations in global governance.

The global governance of (global) corporations

The history of global governance, especially in the period after 1989 is patterned by a growing level of openness of international organisations to the involvement of non-state actors of various types. The earlier term 'international organisation' has shifted into a recognition and wide use of the terminology of *global governance*, and this might broadly be said to reflect the expansion of such organisations' expected interlocutors. Early international organisational politics privileged the interests and requirements of states (as members or as subjects of regulation) and while not deaf or closed to other actors, regarded such engagement(s) as secondary. Into the new millennium, however, the organisations now playing a part in what has become 'global governance' are open to, value and expect engagement from non-state actors; this includes, crucially for this volume, the acceptance of extended engagement from the corporate sector (Talberg et al. 2014). This involvement has often been mediated by the legal profession who, as Sol Picciotto put it, have become central due to the techniques they 'have developed as creative ideologists of the texts which define the institutions and terrains through which economic activity is conducted' (Picciotto 2011: 457). Elsewhere I have developed an account of lawyers as a key global epistemic community (May 2014: 68–73), and here merely note that the development of global governance generally, and how it relates to the corporate sector, have not 'emerged' but been driven by specific and identifiable groups of agents, including the legal profession. While corporate involvement in global governance is a growing aspect of international organisations' everyday practices it would be mistaken to regard this as outside the more general development of global governance networks and a more decentralised 'networked governance'.

Nevertheless, researchers for the United Nations Intellectual History Project concluded a decade ago that the UN had 'retreated from setting the intellectual agenda regarding [multinational corporations] and their role in the global economy, ecology and polity' (Jolly et al. 2009: 113). Indeed, the plight of the UN specialised agency that researched the global corporate system and made policy recommendations exemplifies the *political* actions by certain powerful state members of the UN to ensure critical analysis was not conducted *within* the UN system (a location that added weight to such analysis) (May 2017). In the end, the office of the UN Secretary General (UNSG) decided on pragmatic grounds to seek to establish at least some form of corporate oversight, even if this had to be under the auspices of their office and not the United Nations itself (Coleman 2003). That the United Nations Global Compact seems as good as it is likely to get for now in the global governance *of* global corporations tells us much about the global corporate political economy and the market/ economic environment it has been able to develop and maintain.

Following a speech by the UNSG at the World Economic Forum the previous year, the UN Global Compact was launched in 2000. The Global Compact is organised on the basis of reputational incentives and benchmarks, a set of carrots rather than sticks; it encompasses a set of principles that have been developed in the public realm but are to be enacted privately. The Compact is intended to put human rights, labour standards, 'environmental stewardship' and the reduction of corruption at the centre of global corporations' practices and planning. Rather than offering a code of conduct, the Compact offers, in the words of George Kell and John Ruggie (its chief architects), 'a framework of reference and dialogue to stimulate best practice and to bring about convergence in corporate practices around universally shared values' (Kell and Ruggie 2001: 323). Corporations are asked to adopt the Compact, integrate the values it expresses into their mission statements and management practices, and regularly report on their progress towards fulfilling the aims of the compact itself; the only firm commitment they need to make is to supply information about their practice(s).

As Ruggie explained, not long after its establishment, the Global Compact is a 'social learning network [that] operates on the premise that socially legitimated good practices will help drive out bad ones through the power of transparency and competition' (Ruggie 2003: 113). This voluntary approach reflects a presumption that it would prove difficult, if not impossible, to generate a robust multilateral code of conduct for corporations; a recognition that the Compact may be all that it is presently possible to achieve. The Compact is intended to peg corporate practice to internationally recognised 'best practice', and thus may allow some 'ratcheting up' of standards, related to its ten principles.

The Compact's ten principles in the areas of human rights, labour, the environment and anti-corruption are derived from

- The Universal Declaration of Human Rights;
- The International Labour Organization's Declaration on Fundamental Principles and Rights at Work;
- The Rio Declaration on Environment and Development;
- The United Nations Convention Against Corruption.

It requires member corporations and enterprises to embrace, support and enact, within their sphere of influence, a set of core values in the areas of human rights, labour standards, the environment and anti-corruption. The actual principles are:

1. Businesses should support and respect the protection of internationally proclaimed human rights; and
2. make sure that they are not complicit in human rights abuses.
3. Businesses should uphold the freedom of association and the effective recognition of the right to collective bargaining;
4. the elimination of all forms of forced and compulsory labour;
5. the effective abolition of child labour; and
6. the elimination of discrimination in respect of employment and occupation.
7. Businesses should support a precautionary approach to environmental challenges;
8. undertake initiatives to promote greater environmental responsibility; and
9. encourage the development and diffusion of environmentally friendly technologies.
10. Businesses should work against corruption in all its forms, including extortion and bribery.[1]

The Compact itself was originally conceived as a relatively small contribution to the general aim of changing the practices of corporations, but as it has developed, more weight has been laid on its ability to affect significant change by itself. The formal adoption of the Compact allows corporations, in theory at least, to be held to account through the surveillance of civil society groups; a form of moral suasion rather than regulation.

The Compact also contains four mechanisms through which the modification of corporate practices may be achieved: Dialogue, Learning, Projects and Local Networks. Policy Dialogues bring together corporate managers with representatives of various labour and civil society groups, to work with governments on the development of policies to further the aims of the compact. The Learning Forum is intended to allow (through its website and at meetings) the sharing of experiences and the identification of 'knowledge gaps' between the best practice of compact participants and those seeking advice on how to improve their own practices. Partnership projects provide opportunities for groups (specifically among the 'poor') to develop research and advocacy projects related to corporate activities, again publicised through a website. The Global Compact also explicitly supports outreach efforts to establish and maintain local networks, through which its aims can be articulated and supported by civil society (May 2014: 74–5). Overall, therefore, the compact is facilitative of political action, but is predicated on a central role for corporations themselves: it is an inclusive forum, rather than an external regulatory mechanism.

Given its voluntary character, in its first two decades it has been subject to considerable critique (often suggesting corporations are using it to associate themselves with the UN and thereby 'bluewash' their activities). Even initially supportive NGOs have expressed concerns about the weakness of the Compact's influence on its signatories' practices (Gregoratti 2012). Indeed, the Compact's very character suggests that efforts at more formal control have been undermined by the ability of corporations to mobilise significant resources to compromise political control (or extensive regulation) of their activities. As Jackie Smith summed up this critique:

> The Global Compact is ultimately an arrangement that privatizes relations between the UN and transnational corporations [*sic*], thereby insulating corporations from public scrutiny while tying the hands of the UN, thereby limiting its capacities to ensure implementation of international law and norms. (Smith 2010: 113)

Certainly this sort of criticism is not uncommon, prompting some shifts in its organizational practices after its first decade and the use of specific demands including new conditions on the use of the Compact's logo, and stricter rules on how partners communicate their progress towards the Compact's goals (Gregoratti 2012: 102–3). Interestingly, the tightening up of the regulatory aspect of the Compact – not least of all the publication of those Compact members not offering an annual 'Communication on Progress' (CoP) – has led to some financial impact on non-compliant corporations.

Estefania Amer has suggested that investors have started to take the undertakings made by corporate members of the Compact seriously enough to mark-down their shares where a CoP has been missed. She argues the Compact provides investors with

> knowledge that they can use, together with other sources of information about companies, to identify good and bad [corporate social responsibility] CSR performers within the [Compact], to monitor the companies' implementation of the initiative's 10 principles into their operations, and to pressure bad CSR performers to 'walk the talk'. (Amer 2018: 281)

This sort of normative and private regulatory effect is exactly the manner that the Compact's originators hoped and expected that it would develop, and may indicate that greater exposure for some global corporations to threats to their brand reputation (or as we will discuss in Chapter 6, their implied social 'licence' to operate) can encourage shifts in practice(s).

Away from the United Nations, the Organisation for Economic Co-operation and Development (OECD) has since 1976 been slowly developing a set of 'principles' for the responsible conduct of multinational corporations (or enterprises). Now in their sixth revised form (most recently having been expanded in 2011), the principles remain in the form of guidelines which may be voluntarily adhered to but maintain no *regulatory* intent (Reinert et al. 2016). Indeed, as is often pointed out, where corporations have rights there seems to be a considerable appetite for global governance (the introduction of intellectual property into the trade regime on the establishment of the World Trade Organization, for instance). Conversely, where there is a desire to establish formal responsibilities around (global) corporate behaviour, little is achieved beyond guidelines and voluntary principles, not least due to a well-organised political resistance to such (potential) regulations.

As I noted in Chapter 1, John Ruggie has suggested that the 'disjuncture between [the corporation's] economic reality and legal convention is the single most important contextual factor shaping the global institutional status of multinationals' (Ruggie 2018: 329). This is to say, to understand the manner in which corporations can or should be governed in the global realm, attention needs to be paid to the 'dynamic interaction' between the legal and the economic spheres in which corporations operate. In the field of corporate taxation, this 'dynamic interaction' has become particularly evident in recent years.

Taxing (or not) global corporations

Corporations' political agency has had a significant pay-off in the area of their global tax affairs. While their networks are increasingly global, by working closely with political elites (often also directly linked to firms through directorships and other roles), corporations (and their representatives) have been able to contain tax affairs to within national jurisdictions. As Ronen Palan puts it:

> Rather than view the discrepancy between legal personality of the corporation and the economic rationale of the firm as a problem, firms have learned to take advantage by rearranging their legal presence in such a way as to minimise taxation. (Palan 2016: 105)

This is to say, the tension between legal and organisational form is not seen as a problem requiring a solution, but rather as an opportunity to be exploited, prompting significant tax planning efforts to enhance corporate 'tax efficiency'. The mismatch between the formal regulatory environment (still based on national jurisdictions) and corporations' global organisational networks has presented an opportunity for corporations to distinguish in their governance work between legal and practical organisational characteristics. Exploiting this opportunity mainly takes place across two dimensions that allow profits to be moved around networks and to appear in low tax or no tax jurisdictions. Firstly, intra-group loans that shift earnings/profits via the payment of interest and other debt servicing; secondly (as discussed in Chapter 4) the manipulation of transfer pricing in their supply chain networks enables profits to appear in the network where they will be taxed the least, or not at all (Zucman 2015: 103). In both cases, the manner in which formalised/legal reporting and actual practical organisation of the network diverge is to the advantage of the corporation.

Capitalising on the fluidity in formalised financial reporting, global corporations have also utilised the incidence of tax competition to reduce and retain low levels of exposure to taxation. This reflects their purported interest in seeing free market competition (sovereign states have the right to compete to offer competitive tax rates) alongside the corporation's ability to make reasonable claims that they are abiding by the legal requirements in any specific jurisdiction. A common strategy is for corporations to request the status of foreign corporation in a jurisdiction in which they operate, to obtain low or nil rate taxation; this location then becomes the recipient of transferred profits via intra-network transactions (Yang and Metallo 2018). Moreover, as intangibles (various forms of intellectual property) have become key assets transferred/ exchanged around the network, so corporations have established interpretive expertise in valuing and defining such assets. They have also 'encouraged' states to offer tax incentives to lodge intangibles in their jurisdiction, thereby allowing the state to tax activity, albeit it at a lower rate, that has no direct link with their jurisdiction. It is difficult for regulators to establish grounds on which they may be able to make a compelling challenge to the value allocated (and thus tax exposure engineered) for such intangibles; indeed states enjoying the tax benefits of harbouring intangibles are unlikely to cooperate with wider attempts to formalise such standards of valuation.

Nevertheless, one key question, as global tax affairs emerge from the shadows is: what is the reputational status in corporate boards' calculations around the conduct of their tax affairs, especially in a governance environment that would indicate it is in shareholders' interest to minimise any global corporation's tax exposure? Ainsley Elbra and John Mikler conclude that: 'If corporations do not primarily judge their standing and brand value on the basis of social responsibility, being less concerned with an obligation to society than shareholders, then they are unlikely voluntary payers of tax' (Elbra and Mikler 2017: 188). This is to say, while a range of political campaigns (such as Tax Justice Network) have sought to shame corporations into reforming their tax affairs, the attendant publicity has done little to shift behaviour unless the corporation has significant consumer brand value exposed to such publicity (see, for instance, recent tax 'concessions' by Amazon and Starbucks, both consumer facing brands). However, the publicity around 'strategic tax planning' *has* led to growing clamour for global tax (re)regulation to constrain what for many are abuses of the system, even if they do not necessarily amount to illegal practice(s) (Eccleston 2018; Morgan 2016). While corporations will no doubt mobilise to defend their position using their discursive power to try to shape political agendas around global taxation, equally it is clear this will be less easy or straightforward than it has been in the past (discursive power is discussed below).

Nevertheless, for now the basic assumptions of international corporate taxation remain in place. Firstly, each enterprise, firm or contracting corporation in a global production or service network is treated as a separate legal entity, not least as each is incorporated (or legally regulated) within specific national jurisdictions. Secondly, transactions between various network-members are regarded (for calculation purposes) as on average being priced as if the exchange was being conducted at 'arms-length'. While these assumptions make little sense in a world in which global corporations actively govern their networks and the ownership of subsidiaries (even if obscured though legal means) is widespread, reform efforts seem to have been unable to dislodge them from the international tax regime (such as it is) (Avi-Yonah 2019: 77–8). This is evident in the recent Group of 20 states (G20) and OECD project to address tax 'base erosion and profit shifting' (BEPS). This initiative has identified a wide range of political moves that need to be made to address the problem of corporate taxation, but as yet has had little practical effect, nor has it fundamentally shifted these two basic norms (Avi-Yonah 2019: 124; Eccleston 2018: 58–9).

At the centre of most demands for reform of global taxation is the notion of 'unitary taxation'. Here the global corporation would be treated as a single enterprise for tax purposes, its tax assessed on overall activity and then payment divided between the states in which the corporation operates by a formula intended to be equitable as regards the share of profit contributed by each segment of the network. This might be based on sales in that jurisdiction, or perhaps workforce numbers. This solution has widespread support in the activist and legal communities (Morgan 2016), but would require significant international coordination and, of course, an agreed formula for the division of the assessed taxation. Although current global tax arrangements were a response to a reasonable concern by internationally active corporations that they would be subject to double taxation if there was no clear limitation on states' abilities to tax their profits, the current situation remains something more like double non-taxation for large corporations with complex global production or service networks. Unitary taxation is one (seemingly) simple solution to this problem.

It is also worth noting here an associated problem caused by 'tax planning'; manipulations of (or arbitrage between) tax jurisdictions has an adverse impact on the way corporate operations are recorded in international financial data, and thereby on the ability of states' governments to make reasonable assessments of fiscal requirements or their likely economic impact. Regulation becomes difficult when the information on which it is to be based is manipulated and distorted by the likely subjects of at least part of the regulatory focus (Zucman 2015: 109). This is compounded by the manner in which this data is also rendered unreliable by the share of value-added for those countries hosting plants/enterprises dealing with intermediary products passing along the supply chain, alongside the problem of valuing intangibles 'correctly'.

As Dominik Boddin of the International Monetary Fund warns, basing national development policy or strategy on unmodified gross output trade measures would likely be mistaken. Rather, utilising figures from the *World Input-Output Database* (that focuses on sectors rather than aggregated state-level data) he detects a variance of over 20 per cent when measuring overall economic share between the two methods (Boddin 2016; see also Linsi and Műgge 2019: 373).[2] The key issue here is that using the basic output figure may flatter and indeed distort (to the advantage of corporations) their contribution to the economic developmental expansion associated with participation in supply chains, and by doing so support more favourable policy allowances than some might regard as warranted when the (lower) share of global value added is identified. Indeed, this is a major (but not only) aspect of the increasing unreliability of globalised macroeconomic data utilised for national and global economic policy deliberation, analysis and decision-making (Linsi and Műgge 2019), and as such may be a further under-recognised impact of the development of complex global production networks.

Lastly, it is also worth noting that more fine-grained analysis of flows around global production networks demonstrates, especially for stages that involve considerable value-added, networks can be quite regionally concentrated (Baldwin and Lopez-Gonzalez 2015). Therefore, while developing countries may be able to establish links with the far end of supply chains, and engage in political relations with corporations to do so, their ability to 'upgrade' (as discussed in Chapter 4) may not be significant. Thus, the tax advantages wrested by corporations from states seeking to establish an export/supply-chain processing route to economic development may actually again reflect asymmetries in power and knowledge, and undermine the ability of developing states to establish a robust tax base support for their public sector(s).

This highlights the overall problem that critics of corporate taxation identify: rather than merely tax existing behaviour, corporate taxation can have a major impact on how corporations organise their activities. Additionally, those corporate taxes that are successfully levied, are in effect often passed on to workers and consumers through the manner in which corporations manage their financial affairs (Desai and Dharmapala 2018). This leads some critics to conclude that corporation tax, despite its current political appeal, may actually be regressive and as such establishing a global unitary tax would not solve the problem of how to 'fairly' tax corporations. Unsurprisingly, in the current political climate this remains a minority position, but given the past inability to reform current taxation models, dissolution (with tax exposure transferred to a consumption tax perhaps) may seem no less plausible than other reforms being proposed.

Corporate politics: a preliminary note of caution

Many commentators claim that corporations' ability to (illegitimately) influence policy at national and multinational levels to reflect their interests is hardly limited to taxation. For instance, Kevin Farnsworth has argued that since the 1970s the shifting (global) political economy has underpinned an expansion of the structural power of business to shape welfare and social policies towards forms that support corporate interests, from increased flexibility in workforce regulation, to the privatisation of social provision, thereby offering new business opportunities for the private sector. This can be observed, he argues, both at the multilateral level where organisations like the European Round Table of Industrialists have had significant input into European policy making and the national level, where (in the UK for instance) business groups have been able to influence the shape of national social and welfare policies (Farnsworth 2004; 2012). However, equally, it is not always easy to conclusively prove that influence has been wielded as often policy shifts (or consolidations) may be over-determined, being caused by a complex of different factors.

Indeed, in their study of the influence of business on the workings and policies of the European Union, Andreas Dür and his co-authors concluded that, despite frequent claims (in the UK at least) that the EU is an organ of corporate neoliberalism, the business lobby in Europe has been unable to make significant shifts in European public policy, when it has lacked support from other groups. This is partly because the corporate sector lacks substantial allies in both the European Commission and Parliament, while the Council, if more attuned to business interests, seldom prioritises them above the normal tripartite negotiations between the EU's main organs. Dűr and his colleagues suggest the assumption of influence is partly caused by a perception that access to policy makers and legislators *means* influence (Dűr et al. 2019: 161, *passim*); this is a useful corrective to much critical literature which *does* equate access and influence. Rather, corporations may only be influential when they can build alliances with non-governmental groups and political parties or other groupings. To some extent this is what one would expect in a democracy, and while in particular instances one might suggest that corporations have successfully built an alliance on the basis of a specific and partial framing of an issue, this needs to be demonstrated via research and analysis, not asserted at a more general level.

What this *does* suggest, however, is that the ecology of the global corporate political economy is now quite complex. Not only would we want to open out our frame to include what Strange refers to as 'triangular diplomacy', but we need to recognise that there is a wide range of other non-state actors that inform, influence and shape the governance of the global corporate political economy. This pluralisation of politics means that there are many more routes and avenues along which power relations and structures flow and manifest, and therefore there is a wide range of power relations that any account of the global corporation has to recognise (Backer 2017). As this suggests, analyses like Luigi Zingales' exploration of the possibility of a *political theory of the firm*, which focuses almost exclusively on how corporations utilise their resources to influence and frame regulation and governance while certainly identifying a key and important element of corporate political power, remain partial at best (Zingales 2017). Corporate politics is now (and perhaps always was) much more complex than a focus on lobbying and direct influence would indicate.

Even if we assume (not unreasonably, when many corporations have extended supply chains and global production networks) that business prefers free trade in general (even if some firms may seek trade protection in some sectors), the rise in populist nationalism in the second decade of the new millennium has undermined the common sense of free trade in political elites. Indeed, the decade since the global financial crisis of 2008 seems to have led to trade being (re)'weaponised' by some governments and older ideas of 'strategic trade' (where trade agreements and arrangements are used for explicitly political ends) becoming mainstream once again (Harding and Harding 2017). While some corporations may well be able to benefit from these moves, for those who require (relatively) frictionless trade to facilitate their cross-border production networks, this move exemplifies a loss of influence on leading political parties. In a range of countries, politicians have moved to a more 'populist' set of policies that have little regard for corporate claims for the advantages and benefits of free trade.

Corporate politics and the transnational corporate class

It is pretty clear that the corporation has had a varied reception politically across the last century. Writing in the late 1970s, Irving Kristol (at the time embarking on his trajectory as one of America's best-known neoconservatives) suggested that the politics of that time had swung decisively against business, with voters and politicians being suspicious of corporations' motivations and practices. For Kristol, while capitalism has undoubtedly delivered prosperity and freedom(s), it had also led to a 'spiritual malaise'. This was because capitalism was no longer dominated by the free play of competition, but rather was increasingly dominated by big business (corporations) that did not behave in a way that preserved the values and benefits of a liberal society. Indeed, most strikingly (and perhaps reflecting his earlier leftist views), this led him to argue for a form of social responsibility; corporations (as legally constituted individuals) should 'behave like a citizen when circumstances seem to require it, and regardless of whether or not the law demands it' (Kristol 1978: 93). Given this repeated and often revived criticism of corporate behaviour (of which the contemporary call for CSR is merely the latest reiteration), what is striking is how well the corporate sector in many countries has been able to resist the calls for regulation, or has in Braithwaite's analysis turned regulatory interventions to their own advantage.

In some areas regulations may have expanded significantly over the last century, but here the corporate interest has either been able to limit sanctions, forestall full enforcement or through the establishment of 'private authority' has brought the regulatory function inside the corporate sector itself. In this sense, the move to keep CSR mostly outside the formal legal system is a clear corporate victory over who governs their activities. The maintenance of CSR's essentially elective or voluntary character (as I have already noted) demonstrates the ability of the (global) corporate sector to establish relatively strong rights (over intellectual property rights) while managing to keep their (social) responsibilities to the form of guidelines, principles and voluntary undertakings. Clearly, this would seem to be the result of the influence corporations have been able to hold over the shape of regulatory capitalism or (if you prefer) the neoliberal state.

Certainly, individual business owners and rich investors have always had the ear of government, but in the 1970s and 1980s there was a major expansion of corporate political activities. This led, in Michael Useem's term, to an inner circle of corporate influencers who inhabit the 'leading edge' of corporate political activity, partly driven by their class position, partly by the needs of the corporations which they manage (or own), but also by the wider interests of corporations seen as a distinct social grouping (Useem 1984). This early and prescient analysis of the shape of (global) corporate political activity has been largely confirmed by subsequent analyses which have identified the development of a global, interconnected business community, meeting regularly at events such as the World Economic Forum (WEF) in Davos every January (see, for instance, George 2015: 132–44). At the WEF and elsewhere the corporate and political elites intermingle, developing communal links and shared understandings.

More particularly, the regional corporate sector has managed to secure significant advantage in the developing regulatory structure of the European Union, even if, as noted above, this is often uneven. Since the Single European Act, the European Commission has itself shifted from a role of mediation (at the regional level) between organised labour and industrial capital, to a position that seeks to support the continuing development of an environment that supports the needs and requirements of internationally active corporations (Horn 2012: 156). The facilitation of the single market has subsequently been focused on ensuring coordination and alignment around corporate governance and market facilitation to ensure not only that there is a single European market, but that this market is an economic environment which large corporations find amenable, if competitive. Working at the regional level has enabled the Commission (and others) to effect a de-politicisation of corporate governance so as to depict coordination to specific standards not as an acquiescence to corporate interest but rather as necessary convergence for a single market (a set of technical regulatory solutions) (Horn 2012: 163). For many this adoption of a market-enhancing business agenda by European Union legislators suggests that business and political groupings share a class identity of some sort, and indeed, much critical analysis of the global corporate sector takes as a given that global business is a self-aware class.

So, for instance, in Leslie Sklair's well-known exploration of this 'transnational capitalist class' the interests of the corporation take central place within a complex group of actors (from professionals in various jurisdictions to global bureaucrats) and a range of formal and less formal institutions. This *transnational* class works together to further the interests of capitalists, consolidate and institutionalise corporate influence over global politics and also to ameliorate and neutralise resistance to such an agenda (Sklair 2001). As Stephen Gill has argued (see discussion below) its political programme is to construct and maintain a global system that is safe for capital investment and reproduces the interest/advantages of the capitalist class (Gill 2003). This is hardly a new argument; for instance, John Scott has been arguing since the late 1970s in similar terms that there was a well-connected global business class shaping and reproducing the global business environment (Scott 1997). In the new millennium, however, analytical focus has shifted to the manner in which this 'community' maintains its coherence and connectivity, and the mechanisms by which its interests are then translated into practice and policy.

As briefly discussed in Chapter 3, the pattern of interlocking directorships reveals much about the patterns of corporate power. James Angresano (2016) has termed this set of relations a 'powerful ruling nexus' that in his analysis stretches far beyond the boardroom and shareholders, to include policy makers and other influential groups (including but not limited to commentators and journalists). Moreover, as Doris Fuchs has pointed out, a key function of this nexus is the articulation of the 'discursive power' of the corporate sector. She argues that business groups and individual corporations for at least three decades have recognised the need for the development and deployment of the ability to frame discussion of corporations and that this power can be often deployed in the realm of regulation (Fuchs 2007). Fuchs defines this form of power as the ability to (re)define norms and values that serve a particular interest as being emerging or ascendant *general* norms and values, alongside a developed capacity to (re)produce these norms beyond the immediate confines of corporate interrelations.

However, while this discursive power may be articulated through the media and other communicative channels (with corporations mobilising large communications and advertising budgets), global corporations have also sought to establish, or perhaps more accurately maintain, a specific set of narratives around the roots of innovation and economic development through more direct means. Corporations and their allied analysts, scholars and researchers (often located in university business schools) have worked to promote a perception of the 'rules of the game' that limits the discussion of corporate practice (and the criticism thereof) to a relatively narrow field of acceptable issues. This might lead us to say that corporations' representatives have been active in seeking to define the new millennium's global political economy in ways that follow the interests of a specific (corporate) form of practice. This is far from uncontested and the success of such a venture varies from sector to sector of the global economy.

Fuchs develops this argument by arguing that the power of corporations (in her work, directly related to global governance) is composed of three elements. Firstly, instrumental power offers direct and material means and modes of influence. Secondly, she identifies structural power as revolving around rule-making which can be rather more indirect, as (both at national and global levels) the rules concerned require legislation and thus corporate influence is often linked primarily to national jurisdictions (or national diplomatic and negotiating teams in the international arena). Thirdly, as previously noted, she posits a form of discursive power, linked to the manner in which certain settlements are politically legitimated outside the formal processes of policy adoption (Fuchs 2007: 66). It is worth noting that Fuchs' treatment of *structural* power (while related to Susan Strange's argument(s) laid out in Chapter 1) is a little different in its articulation. While we might relatively easily identify the extent of direct/instrumental power of corporations (their economic 'weight' as it were), it is the discursive, legitimating element that underpins their indirect influence. This latter element can be much harder to identify in the global realm, not least as it may be developed in casual and hidden interactions at least partly facilitated by the contacts required for interlocking directorships.

However, Fuchs also notes that one of the reasons that corporations have managed to expand their influence over debates concerned with the forms of political economic relations and global governance is that the policy discourse now encompasses a clear narrative of competitiveness, economic growth and efficiency, which can be observed in the European Union's adoption of such an agenda. These are all aspects of social practice that corporations have claimed as reflecting their own particular competences and skills (Fuchs 2007: 153). It is unlikely that these developments have been accidental or organic; rather, they are more likely directly related to a relatively explicit campaign by corporations and analysts to normalise their positive and constructive role in the growth and development of the global economy.

Indeed, the ability to keep the corporate interest, for the most part, as a set of issues of low political salience and thus of little concern to vocal political groupings is a key successful outcome of this form of discursive power. Where political salience grows, for instance, as in the area of executive pay, or taxation, then the corporate sector may find themselves exposed to unwelcome political attention (Culpepper 2011: ch. 6). However, for the most part, the business sector manages to limit the political attention (in the mainstream, at least) paid to their activities, although at times of crisis (around the global financial crisis of 2008 for instance) the political salience of business activity and its social impact can shift relatively swiftly.

Again, Useem's prescient analysis identified the role of interlocking directorships in the development of a wide *business* view (albeit favouring the perspective of large enterprises) rather than a more particularised corporate view (i.e. the interest of individual corporations) (Useem 1984: 55–8). In a study of global interlocking directorships, Eelke Heemskerk and Frank Takes come to a similar conclusion seeing 'board interlocks as an opportunity structure for the reproduction of existing beliefs and ideas, as well as for the dissemination of new ones' (Heemskerk and Takes 2016: 94). This community of corporate directors interacts and engages regularly and is a key source for the ideas and knowledge that are articulated and deployed though corporations' *discursive* power. However, Heemskerk and Takes are also careful to distinguish the contours of this global community, identifying eight regional groupings where interlocks are more closely clustered: Asian, Nordic and Baltic, Latin American, Middle Eastern, Eastern European, North Atlantic and Commonwealth, French, and European Mediterranean (Heemskerk and Takes 2016: 106–11). As this suggests, the corporate networks that are visible at this level of generality are both global (with clear interactions between corporate communities) and also specific to cultural/geopolitical groupings. As with all communities, especially those with this sort of variable and complex geometry, it is difficult to be sure how power, information and influences may flow across such linkages, although equally it seems sensible to assume there is some significant level of community inculcation, socialisation and collective self-identity.

While these networks are often quite difficult to map in detail, interestingly in the UK, the establishment of an open register of beneficial ownership has made one aspect of these networks more visible. In 2018, Global Witness examined this data and concluded that while it is currently incomplete and there are still significant areas where corporations and their owners have been able to manipulate the system to maintain secrecy, the records did reveal some notable trends in information opacity. Interestingly, their report indicates that the establishment of an open data regime (however compromised) prompted a massive decline in incorporation using the Scottish Limited Partnership model, which is notorious for its association with corruption, organised crime and tax evasion (Global Witness 2018: 10). However, for the discussion of corporations herein, two key findings emerge from this report. Firstly, over 10,000 of the corporations in the register have beneficial owners that are foreign corporations, of which nearly three quarters are domiciled in countries that Global Witness regards as 'secrecy jurisdictions' which offer little or no information on company owners. Secondly, even with the incomplete data it was possible to identify over 300 companies on the register whose ownership structures are 'circular', which is to say, a network of companies hold their shares in a circle with no final owner identified (which is actually illegal in the UK) (Global Witness 2018: 14–15). As this suggests, the simple model of shareholding and ownership frequently presented in analysis of the corporate sector has little real relevance to the real corporate political economy.

The concern for how (political) power over (and within) corporations can be solidified through 'interlocking directorships' has a significant historical pedigree. Over a century ago Louis Brandeis responded to the US House of Representatives' Pujo Committee's report into the predatory practices of the 'bankers trust' (led by J. P. Morgan) raising similar concerns. He set out in detail how the interlocking directorships centred on a small number of investment banks had led to an unhealthy concentration of power, to the cost of society generally and consumers more specifically (Brandeis 1914 [2009]). Thus, the question of corporations controlling other corporations to reduce (or at least control) competition and market access is not a function of globalisation but rather seems more tied up with the character of (certain types of) capitalism, which have now been globalised. Indeed, by the mid-1980s Brandeis' concern had become more clearly expressed in the discussion of the importance of networks of directorships between various corporations, and how this contributed to the development of a generalised business interest (Useem 1984). In the intervening years, focus had moved from the concentration of market power to the assembling and deployment of extensive *political* power.

This political power can be wielded in a wide range of policy areas; sometimes this will be directly through bribery, and/or improper influence over particular policy makers. However, perhaps more difficult to judge is when the activities of large global corporations have political impacts which do not involve illegality. Where developing countries are dependent on investment programmes from one, or a small number of corporations, policy makers may not need to be directly asked to follow policies that favour (or privilege) these investors' interests. It is also often the case, where corporations control public-facing services, that key political decisions about the management of these services are no longer made locally or even in the host state. Likewise, where heavily involved in domestic activities, corporations may also be a window through which sensitive information leaks out of host economies and into the wider corporate sphere, potentially disadvantaging the host state's governance capacity (Gabel and Bruner 2003: 140). It is these and other forms of influence that any *research agenda* for corporations needs to put centre stage.

Why corporate politics matters

To have a fully rounded view of the extent of corporate politics, as outlined in this chapter, any analysis has to recognise three dimensions of this power. Two common perspectives are usually used to conceptualise the relationship between corporations and political actors/organisations (including states); as input (shaping the agendas of such governance institutions) or as output (the impact on corporations of institutional decisions) (Brühl and Hofferberth 2013: 354). However, as I have been stressing, the global corporation itself should be considered an institution of (global) governance with a clear realm of interest in which it operates. The corporations' supply networks have been built to enhance or extend a range of explicit economic and non-economic benefits, and given the network itself is a significant (organisational) asset we should not be surprised that corporations' governance of such networks is likely to be more sophisticated than merely an exclusive focus on market relations (Dunning and Narula 2004: ch. 9). Moreover, as with any asset the 'owner' seeks to maintain its value and manage its deployment to gain further advantage, as well as seeking *political* protection from external pressures.

It is this desire for protection that has contributed to the development of what a growing number of critics have referred to as a Corporate Welfare Economy (see Angresano 2016; Farnsworth 2012). When he coined the term, Ralph Nader described it as encompassing the 'enormous and myriad subsidies, bailouts, giveaways, tax loopholes, debt revocations, loan guarantees and other benefits conferred by government on business' (Nader quoted in Angresano 2016: 11). This perspective suggests that corporations (acting individually and collectively) have levered their political influence to (re)shape contemporary markets in two dimensions; firstly, they have ensured that the regulatory structures that might constrain their activities are relatively under-developed or weakly enforced, while those structures that they depend on are significantly strengthened. This is sometimes summarised as a set of strong rights and weak responsibilities. It is here that whatever their particular actions (for instance adopting CSR standards), the results of (collectivised) political influence to which they contribute are likely more consequential. Secondly, the corporate sector has managed (as perhaps best typified by the bank bailouts during the global financial crisis) to capture significant support to ameliorate financial problems; sometimes referred to as privatising rewards while socialising risks, or perhaps more snappily: socialism for the rich and capitalism for the rest of us.

The idea of the corporate welfare economy, therefore, has focused analysis on the manner in which corporations have managed to capture or influence policy to protect their position, and in Angresano's terms 'trade favours within the nexus' (Angresano 2016: ch. 5). It is also clear that both corporations and states' governments have been reticent in acknowledging the manner in which such activity continues to support the success of the corporations involved and more widely the local capitalist systems where it is most developed. This creates a critical political problem: business interests and their political supporters claim that state involvement is detrimental to economic activities and corporate success, while at the same time benefitting from support that is obscured (Farnsworth 2012: 198–9). As Mariana Mazzucato has stressed, there is actually significant evidence that the involvement of the state in a range of sectors has had widespread benefits, both for corporations in terms of innovation and profitability and for voters/consumers in terms of support for ongoing economic development (Mazzucato 2013). Therefore, the problem lies not so much with the provision of corporate welfare by states' governments, but the diversion of resources from social welfare activities with little or no democratic accountability or deliberation.

This reflects many critics' concern that states' governments often seem to privilege the interests of the private/corporate sector at the expense of less-organised social groupings (who lack the immediate access to policy makers and legislators often available to a country's business leaders and their representatives). Quiet political privilege may be the result of the relatively low political salience of many policy decisions that are of direct interest to business and the corporate sector. When issues are regarded as technical or difficult to appreciate, both national electorates and the media on whom they largely rely for information may for the most part take little notice of many aspects of corporate welfare (Culpepper 2011). Of course, political salience is far from natural, or fixed; businesses and their representatives may spend much time seeking to maintain aspects of the interaction between the corporate sector and the state hidden in plain sight (not least by arguments that these are technical, *not* political, issues, related to the warranted support of economic development). For Stephen Gill this reflects a wider (global) political programme to establish specific rights and protections for global capital and its local representatives.

Therefore, in Gill's analysis of the 'new constitutionalism', globalisation has involved the establishment of a globalised 'market civilisation'; the latest phase of an expanding capitalist system rooted in the nascent liberal state that emerged in Britain in the seventeenth century and the subsequent internationalisation of liberalism in the nineteenth century (Gill, 1998: 27–9; 2003: 118).

Drawing on Foucault, Gill sees the increasing marketisation of social relations as driven by a set of 'disciplinary practices' (Gill 2003: 130) centred on the use of legal institutions to structure and shape political forms of regulation and governance. This form of contemporary governance 'mandates a particular set of state policies geared to maintaining business confidence through the delivery of a consistent and credible climate for investment and thus for the accumulation of capital' (Gill 1998: 38). This 'involves *pre-commitment mechanisms* to lock in not only present governments and citizens into the reforms, but more fundamentally to prevent *future* governments from undoing the reforms' (Bakker and Gill 2003: 30, original emphasis). Emphasising 'market efficiency; discipline and confidence; economic policy credibility and consistency; and limitation[s] on democratic decision-making processes' this new discipline establishes 'binding constraints' on fiscal and economic policy (Gill 2003: 132). Crucially, this 'new constitutionalism' seeks to confer privileged rights of citizenship on global corporate capital, and establish mechanisms by which the commitment to these values is embedded in current and future political practice. Thus, at a local level, the new constitutionalism that Gill identifies is manifest through forms of corporate welfare that normalise positive support practices and mechanisms for the corporate sector, while (largely) removing them from political scrutiny.

However, while interest in political activities has ebbed and flowed over the last century, and certainly varies across the political spectrum, equally as should be clear from the above discussion, in the new millennium the political salience of a range of issues around corporate practice and behaviour has risen. While the manner in which the contemporary global system is characterised may vary, from *neoliberalism* to *regulatory capitalism* for instance, what I have tried to establish in this chapter is that any account of the contemporary global political economy must include a coherent analysis of the power and activities of (global) corporations. This centrality then leads us in the final chapter to examine the question of reform of the (global) corporate sector and the manner in which this might be achieved.

Key questions for research(ers)

Can analyses that characterise the global system as *neoliberal* or a form of *regulatory capitalism* or define political practices as a form of *new constitutionalism* be brought into a fruitful engagement with each other?

How have specific policy areas and the related specific governance institutions been subject to corporate influence?

How might the disparity between strong global corporate rights and weak corporate responsibilities be more equitably resolved?

How do interlocking corporate directorships inform the transnational business community's mores and norms of behaviour?

Are there better ways to arbitrate and manage disputes between global corporate investors and national host states' governments?

What would be a fair form of tax on global corporations that avoids the danger of double taxation, but equally no longer facilitates double *non*-taxation?

Notes

1.   See https://www.unglobalcompact.org/what-is-gc/mission/principles.
2.   See http://www.wiod.org/home.

6 Can the corporation be reformed? Should it be?

In this last chapter, the normative element of the earlier discussions becomes more explicit; here I look at possible directions of reform of the (global) corporate sector. As Laura Horn has pointed out, interestingly, the way science fiction depicts corporations reproduces our anxieties and fears about contemporary corporate power. However, even when escaping realism, resistance to the corporate form (and its practical impact on society) is still often presented as only possible through individualised resistance, and not through the development of different forms of economic organisation. While identifying a small number of science fictions that present a more 'utopian' view of the possibilities for different economic organisation(s), Horn warns that if (following Frederic Jameson) science fiction is an 'archaeology of the future', then the options for reform look constrained by the dominant model of incorporation (Horn 2018). This chapter draws together and develops further much that has been discussed above to address exactly this issue: can the corporation be reformed to deal with its often observed social inadequacies? Conversely, is it so dominant that it has become difficult to identify a route to a future economic settlement not dominated by something like the contemporary corporate form? These important questions can only be answered plausibly by carefully and fully analysing corporations' contemporary political economy.

That said, like Kendy Hess I start from the position that corporations (and other business enterprises) are not outside our normal moral universe; they do not get a free pass due to the special circumstances of their organisational logic. Thus, it is worth emphasising Hendy's clear position: she has summarised this in three statements that I concur with, and which therefore underpin much of what follows:

1. The members of firms have standard moral obligations that are not somehow invalidated by the fact that they have joined a firm or engaged in business activity.
2. Firm actions (the collective action of firm members) should likewise meet moral standards.
3. Our accounts of firm moral action (the morally significant collective actions of firm members) need to incorporate both individualist and holistic aspects [related to the firm as an actor itself]. (Hess 2017: 185)

Hess argues that these three statements would be acceptable to anyone considering the morality of corporate activities and their outcomes. If we do not care about morality at all then this would be different, but if we are concerned with the manner by which we understand, justify and legitimate specific corporate practice, then Hess' point is that there is no reason why we should dispense with or ignore our normal moral considerations. As Colin Mayer puts it: 'Profits are the product of the purpose of the corporation, they are not its purpose per se' (Mayer 2016: 64); a justification for immoral behaviour on the basis that it is profit maximising is not sustainable.

At the heart of any call for reform of the (global) corporation is the recognition that its current political economy is not the teleological refinement of economic relations, but rather that the current forms of corporate capitalism have their own distinct histories. These histories are patterned not only by the careful development of economic analyses that privilege corporate interests (from property law to market regulation), but also work to ensure the continued accumulation of capital by a small wealthy segment of financial capital. So, for instance, Alexander Styhre has detailed the history of the 'Shareholder Welfare Society' at length (Styhre 2018), while parallel analyses of global *financialisation*, the development of the politics of *neoliberalism* or the rise of *regulatory capitalism* can also all be (re)read as stories of how corporations and their owners have managed to establish an economy that rewards (rentier) 'investment' and hides its contingent (politicised) character to assert that 'there is no alternative'. This chapter is, of course, predicated on the assertion that actually there is an alternative!

First, it is as well to be clear that the question of reforming or modifying global corporations' practices does not confront a legal vacuum or regulatory blank page. Rather, throughout the world, national jurisdictions contain laws that (however incompletely and ineffectively) purport to protect aspects of human rights and socially valuable practices that corporations might wilfully or accidentally violate (Kinley 2009: 187–8). Indeed, the history of the idea of 'corporate governance' (both as a subject for academic analysis, and attracting activists' attention) is rooted in the establishment of a reform agenda for the management of corporate activity in the United States during the early 1960s (Mees 2015). The governance of the corporation only came into focus fully when it became clearly (partly) dysfunctional. Therefore, regulatory mechanisms and institutions to attend to such concerns do not have to be built from scratch, but may rather need (sometimes, of course, quite extensive) reform.

The key issue is to close what Nadia Bernaz calls the 'accountability gap'. At the global level this would involve establishing corporations as legal subjects of international law, and by extension, holding them accountable in the same (albeit imperfect) way that states are held accountable for human rights violations. On a more incremental basis, but complementing the move to subject-hood, provisions against corporate violation of human rights could (and indeed have in some instances) be added to investment and other bilateral and/or multilateral treaties (Bernaz 2017: 8–10, chs 5 and 6). Problems of allocating responsibility in complex global supply networks would remain, alongside finding ways around claims for limited liability based on cross-shareholding, but the political dynamic, if slowly, is moving in this direction.

For some commentators, such top-down regulatory reform can only be achieved in time of crisis, such as that which followed the global financial crisis of 2008 (see, for instance, Cioffi 2010; Mayer 2013) or perhaps (at the time of writing) in the aftermath of a global pandemic. However, recent experience has suggested that generally the window for action may never be that wide, and indeed in the second decade of the new millennium specifically, seemed to snap shut rather quickly as the financial sector largely managed to avoid blame for the crisis (at least within policy elites, if not in the more popular commentary). This leaves the question, where might efforts at reform be best targeted?

The continuing 'problem' of incorporation

For some authors and activists, while reform may be helpful in alleviating particular key problems with corporate practices, in the end what is required is a dismantling of the (extra) protections that incorporation (and allied legal structures) extend to the economic actors behind the 'corporate veil' (Tombs and White 2015). While shareholders are protected, not least of all by the institutionalisation of limited liability, others who are impacted by corporate problems, be they the enterprise's workers, or those whom the enterprise's activities touch in some way, do not enjoy anything like the same levels of protection from the negative effects of business activity (Mayer 2016: 62). This disparity is driven by the identification of what Bryn Jones has called 'corporate over-reach', by which he means the manner in which corporations (by virtue of technological developments and the changes in consumption patterns engineered by the corporate sector) have reached further and further into our lives (Jones 2015). This over-reach means that the tightly constrained forms of corporate governance need to be democratised; Jones argues that it is unjust to limit control (and protections) to shareholders, investors and their proxies in light of the widespread effects of corporate decisions.

Behind many calls for reform are similar if differently articulated claims that corporations 'over-reach' through commodification, financialisation or (neo-liberal) privatisation leading to an ever more problematic democratic deficit at the heart of the corporate political economy. If we accept, as argued earlier, that corporations are themselves governance institutions, then the political question of how the governors themselves should be restrained is of significant political importance (Driver and Thompson 2018: 9). If we are making a claim that as a society we are to accept the rule of law (May 2014) then the notion that those that govern are themselves constrained by the norms of the rule of law would seem to be both apposite and uncontroversial. Thus, reform of the corporation is directly related to the manner in which corporations work with and act within (or outside) the broader mores and values of the societies within which they operate.

As mentioned in Chapter 2, Joel Bakan (2004) has argued that therefore incor-poration should return to its origins as a *privilege* accorded as recognition of the delivery of a public good, and should not be a right to incorporate shorn of any associated responsibilities. Indeed, as Koji Yamamoto notes, 'early cap-italists promoted their new schemes by highlighting their public service' and as such the early history of business is patterned by 'negotiations among stake-holders, repeated under the burden of mistrust' that could only be dispelled by promises of wider benefit (Yamamoto 2017: 234–5). This is to say, the interest in attaching a public-regarding purpose to incorporation is not some unprec-edented innovation in capitalist organisation but rather represents a long term and significant historical continuity.

One way of attaching some public-regarding purpose to incorporated enter-prises is through the idea of the social licence and associated regulatory steps. These, it is claimed (see discussion below), can shape corporate actions and practice, but conversely may be seen by some as merely another way of seeking to establish the legitimacy of corporations' business activities. However, once we focus on the social licence to operate, then a key and prior question becomes, what are the more general concerns that undermine such legitimacy in the first place? Here, perhaps, the very character of the corporation is the difficulty.

The impetus for reform often seems to accept that there is a single legal form of the corporation (which may vary by jurisdiction) but can be subject to renewed or reformed legislative focus. However, Jeroen Veldman and Martin Parker (2012) have argued that rather, in America (and implicitly in those jurisdictions that have adopted or been influenced by American forms of incorporation), the corporation is actually a 'shape-shifter'. While the idea of the corporation has led to a reified depiction of a single legal entity (as set out in the introduction to this volume, and as would be inferred from the process of incorporation), Veldman and Parker argue that corporate managers toggle between different models of the corporation depending on what they are seeking to achieve.

In the first model (referred to as 'identification') the corporation is understood as being like a human with a head and limbs which are controlled by the brain. This model is often used to both justify the large salaries of executives (as they are directing the whole business) and lies behind the idea in corporate criminal investigations of needing to find (or more often failing to find) the 'directing mind'. This latter search often reveals (as executives may argue) that *really* decisions are taken at all levels of the organisation, and as such the directing mind may well not be in the boardroom or executive suite. The (second) 'aggregated model' therefore sees the corporation as a nexus of contracts, as a collection of individuals, certainly cooperating, but legally distinguishable and organised in complex structures. However, depending on the sort of responsibility being assigned, corporate management may move between these two models. When it comes to assigning rights (such as ownership of intellectual property) or being a counter-party in contractual relations, then a third model is deployed: personification, where the corporation is treated as a single legally constituted 'person' for legal purposes independent of its personnel (Veldman and Parker 2012). From a different perspective, Tony Lawson also identifies this lacuna when it comes to assigning responsibility for corporate actions. In his view,

> from a shareholder point of view, all doings – including harmful ones – are the responsibility of the directors, and in any case shareholders are not liable. From the directors' point of view, moral concerns cannot come into it, because their only (or primary) responsibilities are to seek profits to the advantage of the shareholders. (Lawson 2019: 145)

Contemporary accounts of incorporation often miss this indeterminacy, and so also miss some of the (ethical) strategies corporations and their managers may use to avoid the impact of reforming (legal) measures, and avoid demands for their moral responsibility for particular outcomes to be recognised. Equally, dissatisfaction with this indeterminacy drives many calls for formal legal reform to deal with the 'problem' of effectively holding corporations to account.

Reform of the law of (and affecting) corporations

Reflecting on the development and enacting of a global constitutionalism Larry Catá Backer suggests that because corporations have perverted the international legal system to their own ends 'by strategically using [their] private status to avoid public obligation, then the constitutionalization of the enterprise sector, now a lawless zone, is the necessary next step' (Backer 2016: 179). This essentially turns Gill's concern about the establishment of a global constitution for capital (discussed earlier) on its head. Constitutionalisation becomes an opportunity rather than a threat to welfare and justice. At the centre of this constitutional approach is the need to replace the fiduciary principles at the heart of the regulatory system focused on shareholder value with the recognition that corporations and commercial enterprises actually articulate a form of public power and therefore should have a responsibility to act in the public interest. This in one sense harks back to the original 'bargain' of incorporation – protection from prosecution for monopoly in return for the delivery of a public good of socially beneficial economic organisation. For this form of constitionalisation to work there would need to be a significant shift in the normative underpinnings of approaches to (global) corporate regulation. Here, the various codes of conduct and the UN Global Compact that have gained some traction in the new millennium would likely play a vital role (Backer 2016: 186). However, as political discussions and disputes around various contending normative programmes reveal, there is a range of views on how a global constitution for corporations might be established, what its character might be and even whether this would be an approach that for the critics of global corporate practices can deliver the sorts of reforms deemed urgently necessary.

In the next section, we will look at reforms at the global level, but the corporation remains a creature of national law through its incorporation and the range of laws that regulate the form and substance of corporate practice in each jurisdiction. Therefore, it is as well to look, albeit briefly, at the routes towards reform in the developed states where most (but not all) globally active corporations are domiciled. For example, recently in France the *Pacte Statute* has introduced a requirement for corporate management to consider social and environmental impact(s) of enterprises' activities alongside the possibility of a legally recognised statement of the corporation's *raison d'etre* (Robé et al. 2019). This move reflects the 2014 European Union directive to require various forms of non-financial reporting as part of corporations' annual reports, and may be an opportunity to establish a wider range of operational assessments, which could focus on aspects of a putative social licence. This

French legal initiative seeks to require corporations (domiciled in France) to maintain and report on a 'Vigilance Plan', which details their actions to ensure that their supply chain fulfils a range of social commitments. Responding in part to the Rana Plaza fatal building collapse, such Vigilance Plans are required to detail how the corporation would enact its duty of care across its global supply chain (Lyon-Caen and Sachs 2016). The approach seeks to lever the governance function discussed earlier but subject it to the forms of political regulation other forms of public power come under; it is a form of partial (micro-) constitutionalisation. While this falls short of Bakan's aspiration of incorporation to be contingent on 'good behaviour' it does move such a subset of these considerations, in France at least, into statutory law.[1]

Focusing less on the supply chain and more on general issues of market power, in America (but more widely relevant) there is an increasing recognition that the country's early twentieth-century history of anti-trust and pro-competitive regulatory instruments has been compromised and in some sense dismantled. If modern capitalism can only deliver its claimed benefits through competition, as is often claimed or asserted, then the significant levels of monopolistic or oligarchic control of industrial or commercial sectors (including online) has led critics to argue that what is required is a revival of America's anti-trust regulatory politics (Eichar 2017; Tepper and Hearn 2019; Wu 2018). The ability of large corporations to control (and plan) the sectors that they operate in either largely untroubled by competitors or working implicitly or explicitly with oligopolistic groups has, these critics argue, been behind rising levels of income and wealth inequality in the USA, and has also been responsible for a slow-down in innovations and productivity growth. These reformers argue for a return to the form of market intervention, to break up large-scale and dominant enterprises, that US Supreme Court Justice Louis Brandeis championed in his early twentieth-century classic *The Curse of Bigness* (Tepper and Hearn 2019: 237). Interestingly, the work of EU competition commissioner Margrethe Vestager over recent years has adopted a similar agenda and has had some impact on the power of large (often American) corporations, even if she has had to pick her battles carefully. One might argue that this call for a renewed move to anti-trust, competition regulation is about the corralling of outsized economic power(s) and as such is about the forms of countervailing power at the centre of J. K. Galbraith's work for years.

Originally set out in his book *American Capitalism* (Galbraith 1952; see also Galbraith 1985), the key point that Galbraith makes is that if (as he believed) modern capitalism almost invariably led to a concentration of economic power in large corporations then there was a clear requirement in a liberal democracy to establish and support 'countervailing powers'. These balancing social 'powers' ranged from unions and organised labour, through community pressure organised via social grouping to legal powers enacted by the state. The balances between these various countervailing powers might change across time and between socio-economic sectors but they were necessary to check the unaccountable power of private business and to address market failures (primarily but not exclusively a lack of competition) that led to monopolies and allied market concentration (oligopoly). From this perspective the new millennial period of (so-called) *neoliberalisation* has involved a successful programme of erosion and removal of such countervailing power, and therefore implies a return to focusing on anti-trust, competition regulation as the most important reform of the corporate sector (see, more recently, Tepper and Hearn 2019; Wu 2018). However, there has not merely been a diminution of countervailing power in America and across the global system; there has also been an often identified expansion in the 'rights' enjoyed by and accorded to corporations.

In America, reformers have especially focused on the Supreme Court's decision in *Citizens United*. An extensive assessment of this case is beyond the scope of this book, but its key impact was to render the difference between natural persons and legally constituted persons (corporations) null and void as regards political donations (see Chapter 1 for a discussion of this distinction). This facilitated a major expansion of political donations protected under the US constitution as (political) free speech – a right previously limited to natural persons. While it is unlikely that the Supreme Court will reverse itself any time soon (Eichar 2017: 329), nevertheless it has become an instructive case of both the effects of constitutional change in the USA and an example of a form of *political* 'over-reach' to complement the technical/market over-reach noted above. More generally, there has been considerable concern voiced about how corporate donations to political parties have moved politics in a more 'business friendly' policy direction (Moran 2009: ch. 7). Corporate donations range from direct support for particular legislators through to more general payments to parties and campaigns to further the corporate agenda, and (for critics) to expand the reach of corporate welfare.

Unsurprisingly, then, one key area for attention by reformers has been the influence that corporations apparently wield over national legislative development, both narrowly in the form of regulating corporate governance and more widely through corporations' ability to help shape wider market and economic regulation. This might of course also be constrained by a form of self-denying ordinance. For instance, a number of states across America have passed laws to allow for the formation of 'benefit corporations': the key innovation of the 'B Corp' is the extension of managers' fiduciary duties beyond the purely financial (i.e. related to profit and/or shareholder value), to include specified non-financial public or social benefits. The intent is to offer the choice of a form of incorporation that allows companies both to manage according to specified non-financially linked goals in addition to any financial ends, and to establish a clear standing for auditing and reporting on such goals or ends. In one sense, this makes more explicit the sorts of understanding of incorporation that Joel Bakan and others have argued would allow corporations to be judged according to the public benefit they deliver (or fail to deliver).

Certainly, this might well dovetail with other forms of private regulation centred on voluntary codes or principles, and civil society auditing of corporate behaviour (including certification programmes) and could also work in tandem with the idea of the social licence to operate, both discussed below. However, in its short history there has also been a move to 'encourage' non-profit organisations, which might gain from adopting the B Corp form, to seek incorporation. While the benefits of widening corporate managers' fiduciary duties to explicitly include formal social responsibility framed goals and outcomes seem relatively clear to reform-minded commentators, the introduction to the non-profit sector of fiduciary duties focused on financial goals seems less progressive (see Baudot et al. 2019). As yet, this development has not spread much beyond America, other than as an inspiration for legislative consideration, but it would clearly be one way to reform corporations beyond the current more socio-normative regulatory initiatives.

If the influence of corporations is sometimes difficult to discern clearly in developed countries due to their complex and multifaceted politics, in developing countries the influence of corporations is relatively easier to see (if not to counter) through the support and cooperation they require to expand enrolment of domestic enterprises in global production networks. Here an account of instrumental corporate power covers most of what would seem to be happening; the direct application of resource-based power to bring about political change (here related to inward investment). In the developed countries, however, corporations' discursive power is much more important and suggests that reform will require a programme of engagement and critique of corporate agendas. To some extent this can be seen to be happening (albeit quite slowly) in the decade since the 2008 financial crisis; as noted earlier new populist governments across the world seem a little less willing to accord the business interest unalloyed privilege in policy and legislative deliberation. However, whether this will bring about effective regulatory change and/ or legislative change remains at the time of writing unclear. Certainly some governments have been looking at aspects of corporate practice (from supply chain issues, to the question of the gender pay gap), but while corporations remain able to play state off against state, there would seem to be a limitation to how much national reforms might achieve. As a result, reformists' attention often remains focused on global governance.

Reforming the global governance of the corporate sector

Reflecting on previous attempts to establish codes of conduct for global corporations in the international legal arena, Karl Sauvant concludes that one of the key difficulties that confronts such attempts is both the number of states that would need to be party to any negotiation alongside the expansion of the non-governmental, civil society sector expressing interest in corporate behaviour. While self-interest may encourage various groups, states and representatives of the corporate sector to initiate discussions, for Sauvant it has proved impossible to establish anything stronger than relatively weak 'soft law' of advisory guidelines due to the difficulty (or even impossibility) of resolving the complex of conflicting and often contradictory interests among these parties (Sauvant 2015). Behind this situation is the fact that corporations, acting in the realm governed by international law, remain neither objects nor subjects of international law, despite clear evidence that their practices and behaviour have significant effects in this realm.

Although recent developments in international criminal law have expanded the subjects of international law to include (some) individuals, in the main international law (which underpins global governance) still only recognises states as the subjects of the law; corporations only have international legal personality as nationals of states. At the time of writing there is a significant ongoing effort hosted by the UN Human Rights Council (UNHRC) to develop a new regulatory instrument covering the international activities of corporations. Indeed, as Jens Martens and Karolin Seitz declare:

> It was a truly historic decision, when, in 2014, the Human Rights Council granted a new intergovernmental working group the mandate to develop a legally binding instrument on TNCs [sic] and other business enterprises with respect to human rights. For the first time since the closure of the United Nations Commission on TNCs in 1992, a UN intergovernmental body was to dedicate itself to the international regulation of corporations. (Martens and Seitz 2016: 43)

Led by Ecuador, a clear statement of intent by developing countries to develop formal international regulation of their relations with multinational corporations was adopted by the UNHRC in 2015. It is too early to say whether the complex and contentious politics of attempting to formalise corporate obligations (towards human rights) will be successful, but it is clear that for many states the current legal system is unbalanced by virtue of the (engineered) lacuna around the corporation's *international* legal subjectivity.[2] Corporations remain important yet anomalous actors in the international system, meaning that forms of regulation (at least currently) are either ad hoc or *sui generis* (Lowe 2004), a combination of bilateral and plurilateral contracting, alongside more comprehensive guidelines that lack any prospect of robust enforcement. However, this *does* leave significant scope for the operation of the forms of political pressure surveyed in Chapter 5.

Nevertheless, although states are international law's immediate subjects, corporations' everyday activities are subject to a myriad of regulations established through a wide range of global governance institutions and as such there is considerable debate about the extent of corporations' exposure to international legal instruments (Pentikäinen 2012). These regulations have not necessarily been forced onto corporations; rather, as global corporations' operations have become more complex and *global* their senior management teams have often sought action in the international arena from their home states to establish a more ordered and standardised environment for economic activity (Haufler 2006: 91). The impact of global governance on the corporation can be both facilitative of its economic activity and/or represent a constraint on corporations' preferred activity, for instance in the realm of environmental rules. The key issue is that such regulations are dynamic, responding to corporations' perceived needs, and thereby represent an ongoing regulatory developmental process where reform would require (merely) a widening of issues to which regulatory development responded.

Investment and trade regulations that impact on corporations have already been discussed, but here I want to emphasise that corporations can also have their actions regulated (directly or, more often, indirectly) in other areas of activity. One important example is the impact on corporate practices of the various climate change governance regimes of which the Kyoto Protocol is likely the most important but not only mechanism requiring amendments to practice in light of their impact on the environment (usually mediated through state-level laws). Here, the role of corporations has generally followed experience from other sectors: while offering support for the aims, corporations and their supporters (including those in governments) have limited actions to those that do the least to disrupt 'normal' corporate practices. Another example is the regulation of the international banking industry through the Basel Committee on Banking Supervision, which is an organ of the Group of 10 (G10) developed countries. Here, even after the disruption of the financial crisis in 2008, banks and the financial sector-based corporations have forestalled serious reform and shifts in regulatory focus, leaving rules on capital adequacy and the control of risk largely untouched (if modified at the edges). Overall, then, one might conclude (again) that Fuchs' notion of discursive power, alongside Strange's idea of agenda-setting as structural power, can be deployed to understand the difficulty of achieving meaningful change in the face of corporate resistance.

Of course, reform may also be about the regulation of aspects of the global system that then offer considerable benefit to the corporate sector. Thus, very clearly, the negotiations in the Uruguay Round of international trade talks, that led to the establishment of the World Trade Organization (WTO) can be presented as a major shift (reform) of the regulation of global corporations' everyday, supply chain-related activity. This is because the WTO is an important regulator of a number of aspects of the global political economy of direct relevance to global corporations, not least because much global trade flows through global corporations (Lanz and Miroudot 2011). The WTO's primary concern is to open up markets to freer competition, and thus one key focus of its activity which impacts on corporations operating in any members' jurisdiction is the progressive reduction in barriers to international competition in domestic markets by reducing import tariffs and other impediments.

Additionally, there are four specific areas of concern to corporations' management, and for each we can identify aspects of the WTO regulatory regime that have some impact on decisions about corporate practices and activities.

1. *Location of production*: national treatment as a norm – non-national corporations must be treated no worse than local firms (and of course can be treated better) – via the WTO's principle of non-discrimination; the General Agreement on Trade in Services (GATS) (related particularly to national procurement practices); and provisions of the Trade-Related Investment Measures (TRIMs) agreement;
2. *Access to markets*: the general provisions of the WTO; more specifically, GATS as related to non-product markets for services; the reduction of tariffs; the reduction of barriers to imports (the removal of localised regulations, regarded as discriminatory by the WTO);
3. *Structure of industries*: the reduction of subsidies; procurement practices again;
4. *Management of corporate functions*: the protection of intellectual property under the Trade-Related Aspects of Intellectual Property Rights (TRIPs) agreement, as regards corporate resources (and their 'location'); the regulation and facilitation of technology transfer (TRIPs); GATS relating to

visas for personnel moving around international corporate structures (list adapted and amended from Brewer and Young 2009: 291, and *passim*).

As this indicates there are a wide range of areas where the WTO has some impact on how corporations manage and develop their international activities (from investment, to internal management of the organisation).

However, that impact can be widely different across different elements of the WTO's 'single undertaking' (by which state members accede to *all* aspects of the WTO's regulatory complex). What this shows is that one key area of reform of the global governance of the corporate sector may be achieved via the operation of the WTO's continuing development of its own legal regime. Here the role of dispute resolution and precedent at the Appellate Body would be key, not least as non-state actors and organisations have the ability to file *amicus curiae* briefs representing civil society views on disputes, and thereby having a potential ability to (re)shape effective regulation of trade-related corporate activity.[3] However, the rights that are accorded corporations through the mechanisms and rules of the WTO are not matched, as critics never tire of pointing out, by similarly robust (social) responsibilities. Rather, the responsibilities of global corporations remain in the softer form of guidelines, principles and voluntary codes of conduct.

Although as we would expect, the architects of the UN Global Compact saw it as a major advance (Ruggie 2013), and equally many critics seem to have misunderstood the focused/limited character of its (political) project, the Compact remains more of a potential instrument of transformation than a major mechanism for reforming the global corporate sector. Certainly, as I have already noted, it may have shifted some corporations' practices by presenting them with some investment risk where they have signed up to the commitments entailed in the Compact. However, while there is little enforcement mechanism involved in the Compact, other than external reputational threats mobilised through external actors/communities, the Organisation for Economic Co-operation and Development (OECD) guidelines do have an (albeit 'consensual') enforcement mechanism. The OECD guidelines' National Contact Points (NCPs) are intended to allow complainants to seek a finding of facts and when corporations are willing to work within the process, where such findings detect violations of the OECD principles the NCPs can 'require' ameliorative actions. However, for this process to work, corporations need to engage with this *voluntary* process, and in reviewing over 400 cases over a decade Stéfanie Khoury and David Whyte conclude that this is not happening to any meaningful extent (Khoury and Whyte 2019). This is to say, once again, by limiting regulatory oversight to voluntary mechanisms, either a lack of political will, or effective political pressure brought to bear on state signatories by corporations (or their representatives), corporations retain strong (economic) rights but are subject only to weak responsibilities. This then leads to the question: are there any effective mechanisms for effecting reform of the corporate sector? One response has been the development of the idea of the social licence to operate.

A social licence for corporations?

This notion of the (social) responsibilities that might be attached to corporate activity has figured quite extensively in the previous chapters, and these concerns have (recently) prompted calls for the development of a 'social licence' to operate for the corporation. This would potentially include the ability to withdraw the privileges of incorporation in light of unacceptable behaviour or its effects. The question of the legitimacy of business activity lies behind these calls both implicitly and, in some cases, quite explicitly; indeed, while there are a number of models for the social licence, each of them invokes legitimacy in one way or another (Gehman et al. 2017). This is to say, a social licence to operate may only be as useful as the corporation's need to construct a level of legitimacy around its practices (generally and specifically) in the jurisdiction(s) in which it is operating. If this is so, an important question becomes, who is included in the constituency of stakeholders who will accord such legitimacy?

From the discussions of private authority, we might take this most plausibly to be well-informed civil society organisations who have built up trust in their authoritative evaluations. Conversely, if we regard the potential scope for deliberations in liberal democracy as crucial, then we might prefer a state legislation-based licence to operate. However, for John Morrison the social licence is a form of social contract, which shapes how corporations operate and how/whether various stakeholders grant a form of consent to their operations based on both trust and legitimacy. For Morrison, this is a way of rethinking how corporations should be managed, and not necessarily a call for forms of regulatory intervention (Morrison 2014). Therefore, it may be that we accept different forms of licence depending on the character of the economic sector.

The Foundational Economy Collective (FEC) have argued that a social licence to operate is most clearly required in those areas of the economy that are foundational, which is to say those areas where spending (by consumers) can hardly be regarded as elective or discretionary but is rather linked to their welfare and well-being (FEC 2018: 105–6). They argue that this should be *constitutional* and therefore embedded within the basic regulatory mechanisms of national law. However, as an interim solution, they also model a more contractual approach based on the mining/extractive industry social licences that have been developed in some countries (FEC 2018: 111–12). Key to this approach is the recognition that for many foundational services (delivered on behalf of the welfare state, through outsourced provision), the corporation (or enterprise) delivering the service does not have to contend with a competitive environment once the contract has been awarded. Therefore, the social licence would recognise this bargain: the protection of profitability gained from a non-competitive environment linked to the requirement to deliver a clear foundational output and benefit (FEC 2018: 112–13); again a parallel to Bakan's more general point about incorporation as social bargain.

To some extent Colin Mayer's recent argument that the regulation of corporate governance should foreground the purpose of the corporation, not only shareholder or investor rewards and control, also can be seen as a form of social licence argument. Meyer highlights a number of examples, but most extensively that of Handelsbanken; the Swedish multinational bank only pays bonuses, to all staff, on retirement and devolves almost all decision-making to branch level. By being embedded in their local community, both Mayer and the bank itself contend that these branches are able to respond to the mores of that community (Mayer 2018: 192ff.). He goes on to argue that while there are a number of alternatives to the Anglo-Saxon model of regulation, what these have in common is a recognition of a diversity of stakeholders within the corporations' ambit and a range of acceptable/normal forms of ownership. This stakeholder model is not novel, but while often discussed by reformers (see, for instance, Hutton 1996: 298–319; Cooper 2004) it has failed to gain traction in the UK and USA.

Much of the stakeholder literature implies that those within the corporation and those identified as stakeholders share a cultural background, allowing them to communicate easily (even if they disagree and clear power disparities are evident). For global corporations operating across a wide range of societies/ situations, however, this may not always be the case. There may be significant areas of operation where the stakeholders are indigenous groups that share few if any of the social mores of the corporate staff/managers, and express their interests in ways that are not seen (or understood) by even the most willing corporate interlocutors. In such socio-political environments the demand to see a corporation acting in a socially responsible manner may be either hindered by local populations and corporate staff talking past one another, or by the imposition of well-meaning (or in some cases cynically) misconceived 'solutions' to stakeholder involvement (Whiteman 2009). This is not necessarily a response to a particular form of capitalism; equally, when seeking to establish a reform agenda for corporate activities in developing countries, many also call for much better integration of local stakeholders into decision-making. This includes a need to recognise that ideas of justice and well-being *within* the corporations' own governance culture may need to be more responsive to local *difference* if the idea of global corporate responsibility is to be a realistic prospect and not merely a top-down modification of dominant practices.

This leads Martin Brueckner and Marian Eabrasu (2018) to conclude that the idea of a social licence to operate is relatively indeterminate, subject (still) to considerable variance in definition in conception, and normatively complex. However, one way around this issue is to make market failure the centre of the licence requirements. Therefore, Pierre-Yves Néron suggests that a social licence to operate would be conditional on corporations not undertaking activities or strategies that were explicitly intended either to enable profit from market failure or even to engineer such failure of markets in the first place. This would therefore preclude actions intended to maintain or establish monopolies, or to seek to politically control (via legislative means) market entry to competitors (Néron 2016), or in the term deployed by Anastasia Nesvetailova and Ronen Palan (2020) actions intended to 'sabotage' competitive markets. The advantage of aspects of 'market failure' being a significant element of the condition for licence renewal is that there has been a substantial literature and significant legislative deliberation about what would count as market failure and also the character of actions/practices intended to bring such failure about for corporate advantage. Moreover, this would make a very useful and fruitful link between the development of the social licence to operate and the existing and extensive political context of anti-monopoly competition regulation on both sides of the Atlantic (albeit differently organised).

Nevertheless, it seems likely that its future as an element of corporate governance can really only go in two directions (as already evident from this brief discussion): firstly, while there might be general legal requirements for such a social licence to be in place, its development would need to be focused on individual enterprises. This would involve some form of consultation with all stakeholders and a referendum (of some sort) to attach democratic legitimacy to the social licence so developed. Here issues of constituency would be apposite, as would the issue of vocal minorities and silent majorities as regards the recognition of a legitimate political settlement on the content and scope of the social licence (Gehman et al. 2017: 310). As with the discussion of the democratic deficit *within* corporate supply chains networks (in Chapter 4), again corporations may need to consider models and forms of deliberative processes as part of the establishment of a legitimated social licence. As Guido Palazzo and Andreas Scherer point out, 'the more active citizens in their different stakeholder roles become, the greater the need to deal with their demands in a discursive way' (Palazzo and Scherer 2006: 81). However, unlike the supply chain, it may be less clear who the appropriate constituency is; even a national population may be too narrow for some (environmental) impact(s) of corporate activity.

Given the clear potential difficulties here, conversely, and secondly, a standardised form of social licence to operate could be developed, and enshrined in national laws; adoption of the licence then would become a condition of incorporation (or even activity) within that jurisdiction (and one would expect some form of Bakan-like sanction) (Brueckner and Eabrasu 2018: 223–4). The key element would be the (relative) ability of states to make this a requirement of operation in their national markets, and given power imbalances around such decision-making there would be many opportunities for the complexity Brueckner and Eabrasu identify to be retained and exploited by (larger, more powerful) corporations. This may imply that to work as a reforming instrument, given the contemporary global organisation of global capitalism, logically a *global* social licence to operate is required. Whether the UN Global Compact would be a foundation for such a global licence depends to a large extent on an assessment of whether more robust legal regulation is possible at the international level, and the outcome of the discussions at the UN Human Rights Council.

Another way of achieving the ends sought by supporters of a social licence model is the separation of primary and secondary aspects of the share-capital approach to investment. As has been clear from the previous chapters, much of the pressure on business incentives around 'shareholder value' derives from the manner in which the (secondary) market for shares operates. This is to say, *financialisation* and the contemporary dominance of largely uninterested aggregated investment firms owning shares has led to (sometimes) perverse incentives around the management of corporations' economic activity. However, if the secondary market were more firmly regulated with the emphasis on shareholder influence/control directly linked only to the primary investors (those that originally bought the shares) then it is possible that at least some of the problems a social licence is intended to solve would be ameliorated (Macaulay 2015). To some extent, this would see the extension of the approach to continued family control often presented as the dominant practice in Germany. Here, the problem is presented not so much as the manner in which corporations are operated, but rather the corrosive impact of uninterested absentee owners (Veblen 1923 [1997]). Again, however, given that stock markets compete (to some extent) to gain listings of global corporations, and indeed transfers of stock market listings are not uncommon, coordinated efforts would be required to instigate such a shift in regulatory focus, which leads us back to the current shortcomings of inter/transnational attempts to regulate corporations.

Private regulation and corporate social responsibility

In some ways, the discussion of a licence to operate is a subset of the more general debates around supporting and developing corporate social responsibility. Indeed, the Fair Tax Mark, an accreditation issued by the Tax Justice Network to corporations that fulfil a number of criteria around their tax payments, including but not limited to the non-use of tax havens to shelter income and profits, reflects this social licence approach. The Mark also recognises transparency of the process of corporate tax planning, including a good match between the jurisdictions in which activity is undertaken and the payment of tax on the returns from such activity (Christians 2018). There are some clear potential interactions and links between the award of a Fair Tax Mark and the adherence to the sorts of priorities around base erosion and profit shifting that are being developed at the OECD. Nevertheless, the Fair Tax Mark represents an example of how the social licence to operate can drive developments in the private regulation of corporations.

Indeed, alongside the general sets of guidelines proposed by the OECD and included within the UN Global Compact, there are various standards organisations with industrial sector-related or an issue area focus, which also seek to regulate corporate behaviour in various ways. Organisations working with guidelines often involve a range of stakeholders seeking to govern or control the behaviour of corporations around specific politically sensitive issues, for instance involving the environment or labour and employment practices or corporations' impact on host countries' economic development or the (global) environment, or around the conduct of extractive industries' frontline operations. Here, governance can be relatively weak with a lack of formal enforceable constraints only partly balanced by the power of normative engagement, and the sanction of publicity, with questions of verification and 'real' corporate commitment to codes offering critical weaknesses that are difficult to resolve (Haufler 2006; Utting 2012). As this indicates, there is an extensive and mixed ecology of private regulatory institutions of governance that potentially have some impact on global corporations' day-to-day activities.

On the other hand, we might question how legitimate such attention can be. Quite famously, as noted in Chapter 3, Milton Friedman argued in 1970 that the only social responsibility of the corporation was to make a profit for its shareholders; while there might be other social benefits to corporate activity this was incidental to this primary concern (Kitzmueller and Shimshack 2012: 52). Indeed, Friedman argued on a broadly utilitarian basis that by maximising the profit/return on investment, the corporation's incidental social benefit would be maximised, and is partly how the expansion of shareholder value as a key metric of evaluation of corporate success has been justified. This also prompts two different (but perhaps complementary) responses as regards the social impact of corporate activity. Firstly, it may be that shareholder value or the financial success of the enterprise is best served by being attuned to a corporation's social responsibilities, not least as brand reputation stemming from these activities may have a direct effect on the bottom line. Secondly and alternatively, Friedman's view is too thin a view of the corporation's social role, disregarding the social benefits accruing from state-instituted incorporation and the subsequent social responsibility to balance the receipt of such benefits. Nevertheless, at its most basic, we might say that reform of the way corporations understand their relations with 'stakeholders' has led to the general acceptance that corporations should be held to account for the social impact of their activity, most often articulated under the rubric corporate social responsibility and a rejection of Friedman's argument.

Corporate social responsibility (CSR), due to the range of activity and practice it might encompass, is necessarily a complex concept; as it is also evaluative and freighted with considerable political meaning (both positively and negatively), establishing an accepted definition remains difficult. Certainly, most if not all definitions of CSR focus on corporate behaviour and/or practices – on what corporations *actually* do beyond any claim(s) they may make. However, for some this primarily concerns their impact on the environment, while for others it encompasses labour and workforce relations, or cultural impact, or a social role beyond their core commercial sphere. For Stephen Wilks this misses the point: questions about CSR are in the end not about the practices themselves but rather prompt the question: 'who governs'? Is it the corporation's internal governance mechanisms that establish the acceptability of its practice or is it an external authority, be it state or other actor, that makes these judgements, and importantly is able to enforce them (Wilks 2013: 205–10)? As this suggests, the regulation and 'encouragement' of CSR is merely a subset of the problem of the location of legitimate authority in contemporary capitalism.

Other critics have come to see CSR as essentially a signalling function, to consumers (around brand differentiation), to workers (to attract and retain certain sorts of prospective employees) and to governments (to forestall more legalistic and formal regulation). Corporations adopting CSR are trying to say something about themselves even if some critics regard such invocations of social responsibility as being articulated in bad faith, and a mask for the operation of a rapacious global capitalism (Sklair and Miller 2010). Indeed, we might say that the assessment of risk has moved from a primary concern with impact of actions on others, to a concern for the risk that the *publicity* around adverse impacts may have economic costs to the corporation itself. Where this corporate-risk aspect becomes central, critics understandably see CSR as merely marketing or a cynical interest in brand values. However, equally, Naomi Klein (2001) and others have identified this brand vulnerability as one way to move corporations towards more responsible behaviour.

From the perspective of private regulation (or governance), standards-setting organisations such as Fair Trade accreditation organisations and sustainably sourcing certification regimes (such as the Forest Stewardship Council) play a key role, with the corporation's managers taking a more proactive and fine-grained interest in how their network(s) is/are governed. However, it is also clear that in this form of regulation, the issue of moral legitimacy can be double-edged, as both the legitimacy of the corporation, *and* that of those who seek to evaluate and accredit corporate behaviour are in play. Whether the focus is on environmental degradation and sustainability, on workers' rights, human rights, global corporations' political role in host states or on wider concerns around their socio-cultural influence, the legitimacy of those seeking to hold corporations to account is as important as the activity being judged. This was Friedman's point; this variability and even inconsistency in ethical positions indicates that it is the liberal democratic state's responsibility to set the 'rules of the game', not well-meaning but minority groups of citizens.

Nevertheless, the continuing expansion of CSR, both as rhetoric and practice, still exposes corporations to more extensive interest in their activities. As corporations engage more openly with political processes (through lobbying/influence, but also by delivering social services via the privatisation of state functions) questions about their social standing, including CSR, play an increased part in the discourse around domestic and global politics (Hanlon 2011: 82; Wilks 2013: 216). As I have already observed, however, this has not been matched by any major expansion in formal (as opposed to voluntary) modes of compliance monitoring over and above those required by domestic company law (including those related to corporate governance) or, perhaps more importantly, by any framework for sanctioning non-compliance. In this sense, reform remains in the areas of activity and practice often included within CSR as an issue of moral suasion, voluntary compliance and reputation management.

Perhaps a little surprisingly, Robert Reich in his analysis of what he called *supercapitalism* before the 2008 financial crisis, adopts a relatively similar position to Friedman. Reich argued that focusing on a particular corporation's practice(s) and behaviour(s) missed the larger structural issue about economic incentives. As such, while having perhaps a more rounded, socially progressive view of what the 'rules of the game' might comprise, like Friedman he saw this as a job for democratic institutions, not for private regulation (not least of all to allow proper deliberation of the norms to be supported) (Reich 2007). Thus, while agreeing with other critiques of corporate practice(s), for Reich state regulation remains the key to reform, not the deployment of private regulation or civil society initiatives; this top-down approach, of course, may reflect his experience of being Labour Secretary in the administration of President Bill Clinton.

This may also reflect a relatively common critique of CSR: that corporations have co-opted the language of their erstwhile civil society critics to construct a narrative of responsibility, which, while having some salience in developed countries, is often merely empty rhetoric when it comes to corporate practices in the Global South (Orock 2013). Certainly, considerable effort is expended within global civil society to identify activities and conduct that violate the self-professed codes of CSR adopted by various corporations. However, this raises the issue of whether non-governmental organisations (NGOs) and other civil society actors have sufficient resources and/or knowledge to monitor corporate activity.

Implicitly reflecting Braithwaite's analysis of the development trajectory of *regulatory capitalism*, interestingly, Gillian Hadfield has suggested that the independent regulation of global corporate practices, currently often under-taken by NGOs, might be more effectively facilitated through market provision (and thus competitive) of standards regimes (Hadfield 2017: 330–35, *passim*). In this approach, if innovation is required in regulatory approaches to the global corporate networks of production and supply, then the private sector rather than 'politicised' NGOs might offer a better solution. Corporations could choose between market providers although as Hadfield recognises these private regulators would be subject to some legal oversight as part of the more general global 'legal infrastructure'. For the corporate sector, this would mean that regulation then becomes another entrepreneurial opportunity and as such expands further the market reach of the corporate sphere. Thus, even if Hadfield is correct that innovative regulatory approaches might be developed through a competitive market provision, this in many ways assumes away the *political* problem that the NGOs have built their reputations on – the very fact they are *not* part of the corporate sector. In this sense, the deeper issue is the questions of legitimacy and trust that remain at the heart of the politics of CSR and its private regulation. This leads us back to the question of the social licence as an indicator of exactly the social legitimacy and trust that would be required for a corporation to approach a form of regulation uncontaminated by the social perception of the provider.

It is clear that such an approach depends to a significant extent on the utilisation of non-political *professional* assessment and auditing. However, the audit sector has been often criticised since the global financial crisis of 2008, with much of such criticism focused on the dysfunctional relations between providers of various auditing and reporting services and their corporate clients. For John Coffee these problems reflect a 'Catch 22' form of dilemma that precedes the financial crisis:

> absent of a litigation threat, professionals acquiesce in dubious and risky practices that their 'client' wants; but once subjected to an adequate litigation threat, professionals insist upon narrow duties, hopelessly specific safe harbours and a rule-based system that often seems devoid of meaningful principles. (Coffee 2006: 371)

This suggests that approaches to corporate reform that rely on an extension of current auditing and assessment practices are unlikely to deliver the significant reforms deemed necessary by those most critical of global corporate practices and their social impact. Indeed, David Vogel concluded his wide-ranging assessment of CSR practice by arguing that not only is 'CSR not a substitute for effective government, but the effectiveness of much civil regulation depends on a strong and well-functioning public sphere' (Vogel 2006: 170). As this confirms (reflecting much of the discussion in this and previous chapters), private regulation may well have a significant role to play in the governance of the practice(s) of the corporate sector, but only when it complements not replaces state-level legal instruments and regulations.

As has also been clear from the discussion in this volume, corporations have significant potential for exercising political influence, and this can sometimes be most obvious in the manner in which preferred assemblages of private and public/state regulation are normalised. This is to say, and as I have made clear, the corporate sector is dependent on the state for a range of facilitative regulations but is also adept at influencing the scope and range of regulatory interventions to minimise their impact on corporate profitability. Corporations also frequently use such regulations as are deemed 'acceptable' to raise barriers to entry to market segments in which they operate when threatened by (potential) new entrants or technological changes (Picciotto 2011: 4). In the end, private regulation may be a route to reform, but reform-minded critics need to accept that such methods have inherent limits and will fail to reach the worst offenders without extensive state involvement.

Alternative organisational logics

In the final two substantive sections, I will briefly examine the reform, not of corporate behaviour but of the organisational logics of enterprise. Firstly, I will look at how corporations and enterprises might be reformed as regards their internal organisation, before then looking at one contemporary (and much commented on) shift in external relations: the development of platform capitalism (or the gig economy).

In Chapter 3 we looked at alternative modes of organising economic activity, and therefore one way of reforming the corporate sector is through the pluralisation of its organisational logic(s). In one sense, this works within the competitive ethos of contemporary capitalism inasmuch if these forms were more successful an optimistic analysis might suggest they would start to 'crowd out' corporations. For James Angresano this involves the (re)establishment of a 'community-friendly economy' starting with the recognition of, and dismantling of the corporate welfare economy. This would start with comprehensive reform of financial services (and thereby a transformation in the logics of investment), followed by significant expansion (especially in America) of the welfare safety net for individuals, job creation schemes and investment in public infrastructure, the reform of the tax system and the reinvigoration of local food and product markets (Angresano 2016: 164–72). This is an all-encompassing scheme of social renewal intended to unpick the various aspects of the corporate welfare economy (his primary concern is the USA), but here I want to focus on how we might more incrementally reform the (direct) organisation of activities currently dominated by the contemporary corporate form.

For David Ciepley, one reform would be the establishment of Industrial Foundations; these foundations are common in Denmark, hold a controlling interest in large firms and work to a set of goals not limited by the maximisation of 'shareholder value'. In Denmark these foundations have usually been established when a founder's family no longer has descendants willing to take up the control of the enterprise. Ciepley argues that the relatively simple legal change to allow such foundations to hold controlling stakes and not be held to financially defined fiduciary responsibilities would likely be of some appeal to successful entrepreneurs seeking to maintain their vision for their enterprise after their departure or demise (Ciepley 2018: 13–14). This reform, he argues, would reduce short-termism, reduce incentives and temptations for corporate misconduct, and reduce the fluctuation of corporate strategy driven by stock market pressures. This would, of course, leave the basic organisation of the corporation unreformed, and as such, for some critics and activists, may not go far enough.

Pushing reform further, Isabelle Ferreras has developed a strategy based around the argument that while it is true that capital invests, the labour force also invests time, initiative and other forms of personal 'capital' in the enterprise. At some length Ferreras develops an argument that focuses on the democratic deficit in the corporation and concludes that without formalised representation for the workforce, corporations (and other firms) will remain political dictatorships, which elsewhere in society would be regarded as unacceptable. This leads her to propose an 'economic bicameralism' where both capital and labour are represented democratically in two representative assemblies and the management (playing the metaphorical role of political executive) is answerable to both (Ferreras 2017: 141, *passim*). While for many this may be only a step on the road to economic transformation, equally where large investments are needed, it is a clear complement to more direct forms of worker self-management.

In the UK, while not formally adopting Ferreras' model, Julian Richer's management of his hi-fi retail chain has encompassed a clear role for his workforce, alongside an obligation to conduct a more ethical capitalism (see Richer 2018). Ranging from a commitment to the development and valuing of his workforce, to his argument for the social necessity of a mixed economy with extensive government involvement (funded via fair taxation), Richer offers a model of business-led reform. Depending on your view this offers some interesting precedents for how contemporary corporate capitalism could reform itself, or conversely is merely the 'exception that proves the rule' of a sociopathic mainstream corporate culture. Like previous 'enlightened' employers, Richer plans to transfer ownership of his business (at least partly) to his workforce on his retirement (whether this will be achieved via an Industrial Foundation or a reorganisation as trust or partnership model remains to be seen). This route to employee ownership is one way that the work-owned enterprise has become established (an earlier British example being the now celebrated John Lewis & Partners retail chain).

However, workers do not need necessarily to wait for employer largesse to establish alternative forms of economic enterprise. One well-known alternative to corporate organisation is the large federation of Basque social enterprises, collectively known as Mondragon. A complex network of semi-autonomous enterprises, Mondragon was originally both a response to economic adversity, and in a period when the Basques were marginalised in Spanish society, also part of a strategy to retain a level of regional/cultural distinction in a socio-political environment perceived as hostile (Jones 2015: 136). Mondragon is a complex organisation that in one sense mirrors conglomerate corporate arrangements even while its organisational ecology is dominated by cooperatives (although not all its constituent enterprises are run as co-ops). If Mondragon is perhaps a differently scaled example, nevertheless there are in most developed countries significant numbers of cooperative enterprises even if these remain much smaller. Certainly the idea of enhanced workplace democracy has gained significant traction in the academic community (Dejours et al. 2018) and with unions. Of course, for workers in the supply chains run by global corporations, even independent union representation would be a step forward in the representation of their interests (Selwyn 2013). Nevertheless, reorganising the workplace to include wider involvement by workers is hardly revolutionary, with worker representation on corporate boards already mandated legally in Germany.

Certainly, in the USA and to some extent elsewhere (where similar shareholder forms are dominant), there is nothing formally to stop workers seeking to own shares in their employers. This has led to some reformers suggesting that one way to enhance democracy in corporations is for workers to become more directly involved in the ownership of the corporations that employ them. For critics this can be both a positive move towards reform but also (and not inconsistently) an example of co-option and the inculcation of workers into the mores and behaviours of capital; 'learning to own' in Daniel Souleles' terms (Souleles 2019). This may move corporations towards a more shared prosperity, but also might be seen as a distraction from inequalities of power – can minority shareholders' voices really be heard in corporate decision-making? More importantly, where workers have shares but are unable to affect corporate decision-making this may both expose them to financial risk (with no agency to ameliorate it) as well as act as a mode of required acquiescence as workplace disruption may have short-term effects on their share-holding(s).

In the interests of democratic control, at its most extreme there have been calls for all, or at least socially crucial corporations, to be nationalised, removing them from the incentive structures that have led them to act in ways that are regarded by their critics as detrimental to social well-being across the global system. This idea of democratic capitalism would see corporations owned by (democratic) states and working to a set of ends that are defined not by shareholders but by a much wider group of stakeholders (Barak 2017). This has remained an option in times of crisis even for governments that have broadly adopted a privatisation agenda, for instance the re-nationalisation (albeit temporary) of regional rail services in the UK in the second decade of the new millennium or, at the time of writing, in response to a society-wide health crisis. In certain sectors, especially where this would see previously nation-alised and the subsequently privatised utility services re-nationalised, this is clearly popular among a segment of the electorate. However, a major and widespread programme of bringing (national *and* globally active) corporations into state ownership seems to be such a major political move that it remains outside (what might be termed) mainstream politics. As the above discussion suggests, corporate reform can encompass a set of incremental and partial moves that modify, and in some cases change considerably, the organisational logic of enterprises, sometimes to be achieved by changing existing enterprises and sometimes by establishing new enterprises on a new organisational model.

The future: platform capitalism, the gig economy and the end of the hope for a responsible capitalism?

Perhaps the most obvious reform/reorganisation of the corporate sector in the second decade of the new millennium has been the development of a 'new' way of organising commercial activity that reduced the corporations' obliga-tions to, and responsibility for, their workforce. For some, the gig economy is a new form of capitalism focused on the manner in which new technologies can establish an intermediary platform that brings together independent con-tractors and service users in a more efficient manner than hitherto possible. Conversely, for critics, the gig economy returns capitalism to the labour struc-tures of the nineteenth century with workers only able to bid for work on a spot market and shouldering most (if not all) of the risk(s) of economic volatility.

Reflecting the issues raised in regard of a social licence to operate, revela-tions about how workers in the gig economy are managed may in the end undermine platform corporations' implied licence (Stanford 2017: 397). This is to say, as users of various platform services become increasingly aware of the manner in which the corporation has been able to distance itself from any social responsibility for their workforce(s), these users may be less than impressed by what is revealed. However, it is less clear what the implications of such loss of licence would be unless it was formal – for instance, taxi-hailing firm Uber losing its taxi-operating licence, as it has done in some cities. Would there be a mass consumer boycott or does the political will exist (which may now be developing) to regulate the working conditions of contractors more positively (rather than more passively via contract law)? If not, then the loss of an informal 'licence' may have little impact on a gig economy that seems to have grown at least partly outside formal regulatory regimes.

In one sense, this is a reform of the global corporate sector as it significantly shifts the character of corporations' engagement with its stakeholders. By doing so, it may fragment further the ground on which forms of social responsibility might rest. A key and often asked question is whether this is a new development, or whether it merely re-invents the early capitalist system of *putting out* – the utilisation of self-employed contractors to deliver aspects of the overall business function (Crouch 2019: 21–4)? For corporations there is much to be gained from side-stepping the post-1945 standard employment contract, primarily around both enhanced flexibility and cost(s) reduction. Thus, Jim Stanford concludes his historical contextualisation of the gig economy by arguing that these 'new' arrangements are 'simply facilitating the application of long-standing management labour extraction strategies that are as old as capitalism' (Stanford 2017: 396). While the standard employment contract (or post-war capitalism) coped with the challenge of extracting value from the workforce through a combination of oversight and trust (given complex work is often difficult to manage tightly), the gig economy has allowed a return to a more disciplinary environment with a swing back to monitoring and financial sanction. For workers, this has increased the power imbalance in the workplace and as such has led to call for renewed (different, more appropriate) regulation as well as calls for gig economy workers to be re-included within the regulatory structures of the standard employment contract.

Some potential reforms seek to offer a middle way between a formalised worker–employer relationship and the 'new' contract, gig, relationship. For instance, Colin Crouch has suggested extending notions of flexicurity developed in Europe where the state (public sector) undertakes to offer both unemployment support but also significant (re)training opportunities to allow displaced workers to find new work aside from their previous experience, an approach often referred to as Active Labour Market Policy (ALMP) (Crouch 2019: 103–10). Here, the state takes up some of the risk and costs of labour market changes, which the gig economy and a more general move to precarious working have allowed corporations to shrug off. Crouch also suggests that in return for this avoidance of risk, there needs to be a renewed form of corporate social insurance contribution(s). This should be based not on the worker's contractual relations but on the actual labour hours contracted for – a tax that would contribute to the maintenance of the ALMP he regards as crucial to rebalance the share of economic rewards in contemporary capitalism (Crouch 2019: 113–16). However, as noted before, the corporate sector has been adept at avoiding hard responsibilities while arguing for its rights to be protected; there is little reason to think gig economy corporations (especially given their size and the extent of their assets) would be any different.

In 2020, it remains unclear whether platform capitalism (the gig economy) will be able to continue to function at least partly beyond the regulatory reach of developed states. However, given in the end such enterprises, whatever their claims for technical innovation, are to a large extent merely reviving a business model from the nineteenth century, the question is: will the same political forces which eventually required and obtained significant reform from early corporations do so again, and (re)instigate a form of more responsible capitalism for the new millennium?

Final remarks

Although I have been talking about corporations in general, behind this general discussion lies the suggestion that a research agenda for corporations needs to take the range of issues raised and discussed in this volume and apply them to the actual practices of specific corporations. Just for the avoidance of doubt, my own position is not that corporations necessarily rule the world, as David Korten (1995) once claimed, nor that it is impossible to reform their practices or effectively regulate their behaviour. Rather, perhaps against many critics (especially those with neoliberalism in their crosshairs) I believe that capitalism can be reformed. It seems to me corporations can be remade and that business can (even if it currently does not always) play a positive role in the global political economy. However, equally, reform is not easy, the corporate interest in retaining a set of privileges and advantages is strong, and much of the time what is really going on in the business environment is obscured or misunderstood by both the corporation's supporters and fellow travellers, as well as by its most trenchant critics. The premise of this book, therefore, is if we all knew more about how actual, really existing corporations work, and the ways specific corporations further their specific aims, then not only can we work to reform the global corporate political economy, but we can make it work better, by which I mean in a fairer way. This is not a call for the case-study approach beloved of management schools, so much as a warning that without a clear appreciation of actual corporate practices, calls for reform will likely fall on stony ground.

So, of course, the first step is to find out what is actually going on. This book-length research agenda has been intended to help those working to develop a critical perspective on the global corporation make hitherto unseen or obscured connections between a range of issues too often kept apart through the operation of disciplinary boundaries and attempts to limit discussion of corporate politics to a set of seemingly *technical* issues. There is unlikely to be one consensual view of the global corporate political economy. However, by examining the issues raised in these chapters, and by applying the questions raised to a range of case studies of corporations, we are likely to understand the corporate sector better, be clearer about where reforms may be necessary and be able offer a more compelling analysis of some of the most powerful actors in the global political economy.

Notes

1. Space precludes a detailed discussion of this important recent political development; however, Alice Evans (2019) provides an excellent and detailed account of the context and campaign that lies behind this legislative innovation.
2. A comprehensive survey of the prospects, difficulties and potential elements that might be developed through this process can be found in the contributions to Deva and Bilchitz (2017).
3. That said, at the time of writing the Trump administration has obstructed the appointment of new appointees to the WTO Appellate Body, leaving dispute settlement among members moribund.

References

Ahlquist, John H. (2017), 'Labor unions, political representation, and economic inequality', *Annual Review of Political Science* 20: 409–32.

Amer, Estefania (2018), 'The penalization of non-communicating UN Global Compact's companies by investors and its implications for this initiative's effectiveness', *Business and Society* 57, 2: 255–91.

Anderson, Elizabeth (2017), *Private Government: How Employers Rule Our Lives (and Why We Don't Talk About It)*, Princeton, NJ: Princeton University Press.

Angresano, James (2016), *A Corporate Welfare Economy*, Abingdon: Routledge.

Archer, Rory and Musić, Goran (2017), 'Approaching the socialist factory and its workforce: considerations from fieldwork in (former) Yugoslavia', *Labor History* 58, 1: 44–66.

Arrighi, Giovanni, Barr, Kenneth and Hisaeda, Shuji (1999), 'The transformation of business enterprise', in G. Arrighi and B. J. Silver (eds), *Chaos and Governance in the Modern World System*, Minneapolis: University of Minnesota Press.

Avi-Yonah, Reuvan S. (2019), *International Tax Law* (Elgar Advanced Introduction), Cheltenham: Edward Elgar Publishing.

Baars, Grietje (2015), 'From the Dutch East India Company to the Corporate Bill of Rights: corporations and international law', in U. Mattei and J. D. Haskell (eds), *Research Handbook on Political Economy and the Law*, Cheltenham: Edward Elgar Publishing.

Baars, Grietje (2016), '"It's not me, it's the corporation": the value of accountability in the global political economy', *London Review of International Law* 4, 1 (March): 127–63.

Baars, Grietje and Bair, Jennifer et al. (2016), 'The role of law in global value chains: a research manifesto (The IGLP Law and Global Production Working Group)', *London Review of International Law* 4, 1: 57–79.

Baars, Grietje and Spicer, André (2017), 'Introduction: why the corporation?', in G. Baars and A. Spicer (eds), *The Corporation: A Critical, Multi-Disciplinary Handbook*, Cambridge: Cambridge University Press.

Babic, Milan, Fichtner, Jan and Heemskerk, Eelke M. (2017), 'States versus corporations: rethinking the power of business in international politics', *The International Spectator* 52, 4: 20–43.

Baccaro, Lucio and Howell, Chris (2017), *Trajectories of Neoliberal Transformation: European Industrial Relations since the 1970s*, Cambridge: Cambridge University Press.

Backer, Larry Catá (2008), 'Multinational corporations as objects and sources of transnational regulation', *ILSA Journal of International and Comparative Law* 14, 2: 499–523.

Backer, Larry Catá (2016), 'The concept of constitutionalization and the multi-corporate enterprise: from body corporate to sovereign enterprise', in J.-P. Robé, A. Lyon-Caen and S. Vernac (eds), *Multinationals and the Constitutionalization of the World Power System*, London: Routledge.

Backer, Larry Catá (2017), 'The evolving relationship between TNCs and political actors and governments', in A. de Jonge and R. Tomasic (eds), *Research Handbook on Transnational Corporations*, Cheltenham: Edward Elgar Publishing.

Baglioni, Elena, Campling, Liam and Hanlon, Gerard (2019), 'Global value chains as entrepreneurial capture: insights from management theory', *Review of International Political Economy*, available at https://doi.org/10.1080/09692290.2019.1657479.

Bairoch, Paul (1993), *Economics and World History: Myths and Paradoxes*, Hemel Hempstead: Harvester Wheatsheaf.

Bakan, Joel (2004), *The Corporation: The Pathological Pursuit of Profit and Power*, New York: Free Press [and associated DVD].

Bakan, Joel (2015), 'The invisible hand of law: private regulation and the rule of law', *Cornell International Law Journal* 48: 279–300.

Bakker, Isabella and Gill, Stephen (2003), 'Ontology, method, and hypotheses', in I. Bakker and S. Gill (eds), *Power, Production and Social Reproduction*, Basingstoke: Palgrave Macmillan.

Baldwin, Richard and Lopez-Gonzalez, Javier (2015), 'Supply-chain trade: a portrait of global patterns and several testable hypotheses', *The World Economy* 38, 11: 1682–721.

Barak, Gregg (2017), *Unchecked Corporate Power: Why the Crimes of Multinational Corporations Are Routinized Away and What We Can Do About It*, Abingdon: Routledge.

Barff, Richard (1995), 'Multinational corporations and the new international division of labour', in R. J. Johnson, Peter J. Taylor and Michael J. Watts (eds), *Geographies of Global Change: Remapping the World in the Late Twentieth Century*, Oxford: Blackwells.

Baudot, Lisa, Dillard, Jesse and Pencle, Nadra (2019), 'The emergence of benefit corporations: a cautionary tale', *Critical Perspectives on Accounting*, available at https://doi.org/10.1016/j.cpa.2019.01.005.

Beder, Sharon (2006), *Suiting Themselves: How Corporations Drive the Global Agenda*, London: Earthscan.

Behn, Daniel, Laudal Berge, Tarald and Langford, Malcolm (2018), 'Poor states or poor governance? Explaining outcomes in investment treaty arbitration', *Northwestern Journal of International Law and Business*, 38, 3: 333–89.

Bernaz, Nadia (2017), *Business and Human Rights: History, Law and Policy – Bridging the Accountability Gap*, London: Routledge.

Bierce, Ambrose (1911 [1958]), *The Devil's Dictionary*, Neal Publishing [reprinted, New York: Dover Publications].

Birch, Kean (2017), *A Research Agenda for Neoliberalism*, Cheltenham: Edward Elgar Publishing.

Blanchflower, David G. (2019), *Not Working: Where Have All the Good Jobs Gone?* Princeton, NJ: Princeton University Press.

Boddin, Dominik (2016), 'The role of newly industrialised economies in global value chains', IMF Working Papers 16/207, Washington, DC: International Monetary Fund.

Bowman, Scott R. (1996), *The Modern Corporation and American Political Thought*, University Park: Pennsylvania University Press.

Braithwaite, John (2008), *Regulatory Capitalism: How it Works, Ideas for Making it Work Better*, Cheltenham: Edward Elgar Publishing.

Brandeis, Louis D. (1914 [2009]), *Other People's Money and How the Bankers Use It*, New York: Frederick A. Stokes Co. [reprinted: Mansfield Centre: Martino Publishing].

Braverman, Harry (1974), *Labour and Monopoly Capital: The Degradation of Work in the Twentieth Century*, New York: Monthly Review Press.

Brewer, Thomas and Young, Stephen (2009), 'Multilateral institutions and policies: implications for multinational business strategy', in A. Rugman (ed.), *The Oxford Handbook of International Business*, Oxford: Oxford University Press.

Brown, Bruce (2003), *The History of the Corporation (Vol. 1)*, Sumas, WA: BF Communications.

Brueckner, Martin and Eabrasu, Marian (2018), 'Pinning down the social license to operate (SLO): The problem of normative complexity', *Resources Policy* 59 (December): 217–26.

Brühl, Tanja and Hofferberth, Matthias (2013), 'Global companies as social actors: constructing private business in global governance', in J. Mikler (ed.), *The Handbook of Global Companies*, Chichester: Wiley-Blackwell.

Buckley, Peter J. and Chapman, Malcolm (1997), 'The perception and measurement of transaction costs', *Cambridge Journal of Economics* 21, 2: 127–45.

Burawoy, Michael (1979), *Manufacturing Consent: Changes in the Labour Process under Monopoly Capitalism*, Chicago, IL: University of Chicago Press.

Burczak, Theodore (2006), *Socialism after Hayek*, Ann Arbor: University of Michigan Press.

Casson, Mark (2018), *The Multinational Enterprise: Theory and History*, Cheltenham: Edward Elgar Publishing.

Cavalleri, Maria Chiara, Eliet, Alice, McAdam, Peter, Petroulakis, Filippos, Soares, Ana and Isabel Vansteenkiste (2019), 'Concentration, market power and dynamism in the euro area', European Central Bank Working Paper series No. 2253 (March).

Christians, Allison (2018), 'Tax justice as social license: the Fair Tax Mark', in R. Eccleston and Ainsley Elbra (eds), *Business, Civil Society and the 'New' Politics of Corporate Tax Justice: Paying a Fair Share?* Cheltenham: Edward Elgar Publishing.

Ciepley, David (2013), 'Beyond public and private: toward a political theory of the corporation', *American Political Science Review* 107, 1: 139–58.

Ciepley, David (2017), 'Is the US government a corporation? The corporate origins of modern constitutionalism', *American Political Science Review* 111, 2: 418–35.

Ciepley, David (2018), 'Can corporations be held to the public interest, or even to the law?' *Journal of Business Ethics*, available at http://dx.doi.org/10.2139/ssrn.3173810.

Ciocchini, Pablo Leandro and Khoury, Stéfanie (2018), 'Investor–state dispute settlement: institutionalising "corporate exceptionality"', *Oñati Socio-legal Series* 8, 6: 976–1000, available at http://ssrn.com/abstract=3194643.

Cioffi, John W. (2010), *Public Law and Private Power: Corporate Governance Reform in the Age of Finance Capitalism*, Ithaca, NY: Cornell University Press.

Coase, Ronald H. (1937 [1993]), 'The nature of the firm', *Economica* N.S. 4 (reprinted in O. Williamson and S. G. Winter (eds), *The Nature of the Firm: Origins, Evolution and Development*, New York: Oxford University Press).

Coe, Neil M. and Yeung, Henry Wai-Chung (2015), *Global Production Networks: Theorizing Economic Development in an Interconnected World*, Oxford: Oxford University Press.

Coffee, John C. (2006), *Gatekeepers: The Professions and Corporate Governance*, Oxford: Oxford University Press.

Cohen, George M. (2017), 'Law and economics of agency and partnership', in F. Parisi (ed.), *Oxford Handbook of Law and Economics (Volume 2: Private and Commercial Law)*, Oxford: Oxford University Press.

Coleman, David (2003), 'The United Nations and transnational corporations: from an inter-nation to a "beyond-state" model of engagement', *Global Society* 17, 4: 339–57.

Connelly, Brian L., Haynes, Katalin T., Tihanyi, Laszlo, Gamache, Daniel L. and Devers, Cynthia E. (2016), 'Minding the gap: antecedents and consequences of top management-to-worker pay dispersion', *Journal of Management* 42, 4 (May): 862–85.

Cooke, C. A. (1950), *Corporation, Trust and Company: An Essay in Legal History*, Manchester: Manchester University Press.

Cooper, Stuart (2004), *Corporate Social Performance: A Stakeholder Approach*, London: Routledge.

Crouch, Colin (2019), *Will the Gig Economy Prevail?* (Future of Capitalism series), Cambridge: Polity Press.

Culpepper, Pepper D. (2011), *Quiet Politics and Business Power: Corporate Control in Europe and Japan*, Cambridge: Cambridge University Press.

Dallas, Mark P. (2015), '"Governed" trade: global value chains, firms, and the heterogeneity of trade in an era of fragmented production', *Review of International Political Economy* 22, 5: 875–909.

Dallas, Mark P., Ponte, Stefano and Sturgeon, Timothy (2019), 'Power in global value chains', *Review of International Political Economy* 26, 4: 666–94.

Davies, William (2017), 'Elite power under advanced neoliberalism', *Theory, Culture and Society* 34, 5–6: 227–50.

Davis, John P. (1905), *Corporations: A Study of the Origin and Development of Great Business Combinations and of their Relation to the Authority of the State*, New York: G. P. Putnam's Sons.

Deakin, Simon (2017), 'Tony Lawson's theory of corporation: towards a social ontology of law', *Cambridge Journal of Economics* 41: 1505–23.

Deakin, Simon, Gindis, David, Hodgson, Geoffrey M., Huang, Kainan and Pistor, Katharina (2017), 'Legal institutionalism: capitalism and the constitutive role of the law', *Journal of Comparative Economics* 45: 188–200.

Dejours, Christophe, Deranty, Jean-Phillippe, Renault, Emmanuel and Smith, Nicholas H. (2018), *The Return of Work in Critical Theory: Self, Society, Politics*, New York: Columbia University Press.

Dekker, H. C., Sakaguchi, J. and Kawai, T. (2013), 'Beyond the contract: managing risk in supply chain relations', *Management Accounting Research* 24 (March): 122–39.

Desai, Mihir A. and Dharmapala, Dhammika (2018), 'Revisiting the uneasy case for corporate taxation in an uneasy world', *Journal of the British Academy* 6 (sl): 274–84.

Deva, Surya and Bilchitz, David (2017), *Building a Treaty on Business and Human Rights: Context and Contours*, Cambridge: Cambridge University Press.

Dezalay, Yves and Garth, Bryant G. (1996), *Dealing in Virtue: International Commercial Arbitration and the Construction of a Transnational Legal Order*, Chicago, IL: University of Chicago Press.

Dollar, David (2017), 'Global value chains provide new opportunities to developing countries', Brookings: Order from Chaos, available at https://www.brookings.edu/blog/order-from-chaos/2017/07/19/global-value-chains-provide-new-opportunities-to-developing-countries/.

Donaghey, Jimmy, Reinecke, Juliane, Niforou, Christina and Lawson, Ben (2014), 'From employment relations to consumption relations: balancing labour governance in global supply chains', *Human Resource Management* 53, 2 (March–April): 229–52.

Dong, Lingxiu and Kouvelis, Panos (2019), 'Impact of tariffs on global supply chain network configuration: models, predictions and future research', *Manufacturing and Service Operations Management*, available at https://doi.org/10.1287/msom .2019.0802.

Driver, Ciaran and Thompson, Grahame (2018), 'Corporate governance and why it matters', in C. Driver and G. Thompson (eds), *Corporate Governance in Contention*, New York: Oxford University Press.

Dubey, Vinod (1975), *Yugoslavia: Development with Decentralisation: Report of a mission sent to Yugoslavia by the World Bank*, Baltimore, MD: Johns Hopkins University Press.

Dugger, William M. (1985), 'The continued evolution of corporate power', *Review of Social Economy* 43, 1 (April): 1–13.

Dugger, William M. (1988), 'An institutional analysis of corporate power', *Journal of Economic Issues* 22, 1 (March): 79–111.

Duménil, Gérard and Lévy, Dominique (2018), *Managerial Capitalism: Ownership, Management and the Coming New Mode of Production*, London: Pluto Press.

Dunning, John H. (1988), *Explaining International Production*, London: Unwin Hyman.

Dunning, John H. and Narula, Rajneesh (2004), *Multinationals and Industrial Competitiveness: A New Agenda*, Cheltenham: Edward Elgar Publishing.

Dür, Andreas, Marshall, David and Bernhagen, Patrick (2019), *The Political Influence of Business in the European Union*, Ann Arbor: University of Michigan Press.

Durand, Cédric and Milberg, William (2020), 'Intellectual monopoly in global value chains', *Review of International Political Economy* 27, 2: 404–29.

Eccleston, Richard (2018), 'BEPS and the new politics of corporate tax justice', in R. Eccleston and Ainsley Elbra (eds), *Business, Civil Society and the 'New' Politics of Corporate Tax Justice: Paying a Fair Share?* Cheltenham: Edward Elgar Publishing.

Edwards, Haley Sweetland (2016), *Shadow Courts: The Tribunals that Rule Global Trade* (Columbia Global Reports), New York: Columbia University Press.

Eichar, Douglas M. (2017), *The Rise and Fall of Corporate Social Responsibility*, New York: Routledge.

Elbra, Ainsley and Mikler, John (2017), 'Paying a "fair share": multinational corporations' perspectives on taxation', *Global Policy* 8, 2 (May): 181–90.

Evans, Alice (2019), 'Overcoming the global despondency trap: strengthening corporate accountability in supply chains', *Review of International Political Economy*, available at https://doi.org/10.1080/09692290.2019.1679220.

Farnsworth, Kevin (2004), *Corporate Power and Social Policy in a Global Economy: British Welfare Under the Influence*, Bristol: The Policy Press.

Farnsworth, Kevin (2012), *Social Versus Corporate Welfare: Competing Needs and Interests within the Welfare State*, Basingstoke: Palgrave Macmillan.

FEC [Foundational Economy Collective] (2018), *Foundational Economy: The Infrastructure of Everyday Life*, Manchester: Manchester University Press.

Ferreras, Isabelle (2017), *Firms as Political Entities: Saving Democracy through Economic Bicameralism*, Cambridge: Cambridge University Press.

Fischer, Andrew Martin (2018), *Poverty as Ideology: Rescuing Social Justice from Global Development Agendas*, London: Zed Books.

Forsgren, Mats (2013), *Theories of the Multinational Firm: A Multidimensional Creature in the Global Economy*, Cheltenham: Edward Elgar Publishing.

Forsgren, Mats, Holm, Ulf and Johanson, Jan (2005), *Managing the Embedded Multinational: A Business Network View*, Cheltenham: Edward Elgar Publishing.

Fridell, Gavin and Walker, Chris (2019), 'Social upgrading as market fantasy: the limits of global value chain integration', *Human Geography* 12, 2: 1–17.

Friedman, Milton (1970), 'The social responsibility of business is to increase its profits', *New York Times Magazine*, 13 September: 32–3, 122–4.

Fuchs, Doris (2007), *Business Power in Global Governance*, Boulder, CO: Lynne Rienner.

Gabel, Medard and Bruner, Henry (2003), *Global Inc. An Atlas of the Multinational Corporation*, New York; The New Press.

Galbraith, John Kenneth (1952), *American Capitalism: The Concept of Countervailing Power*, Boston, MA: Houghton Mifflin Co.

Galbraith, John Kenneth (1985), *The New Industrial State* (4th edn with a new Introduction), Boston, MA: Houghton Mifflin Co.

Gehman, Joel, Lefsrud, Lianne M. and Fast, Stewart (2017), 'Social license to operate: legitimacy by another name?' *Canadian Public Administration* 60, 2 (June/July): 293–317.

George, Susan (2015), *Shadow Sovereigns: How Global Corporations are Seizing Power*, Cambridge: Polity Press.

Geppert, Mike and Dörrenbächer, Christoph (2011), 'Politics and power in the multinational corporation: an introduction', in C. Dörrenbächer and M. Geppert (eds), *Politics and Power in the Multinational Corporation: The Role of Institutions, Interests and Identities*, Cambridge: Cambridge University Press.

Gereffi, Gary (2019), 'Economic upgrading in global value chains', in S. Ponte, G. Gereffi and R. Raj-Reichert (eds), *Handbook on Global Value Chains*, Cheltenham: Edward Elgar Publishing.

Gill, Stephen (1998), 'New constitutionalism, democratisation and global political economy', *Pacifica Review* 10, 1: 23–38.

Gill, Stephen (2003), *Power and Resistance in the New World Order*, Basingstoke: Palgrave Macmillan.

Giuliani, Elisa and Macchi, Chiara (2014), 'Multinational corporations' economic and human rights impacts on developing countries: a review and research agenda', *Cambridge Journal of Economics* 38: 479–517.

Global Witness (2018), 'The companies we keep: what the UK's open data register actually tells us about company ownership', London: Global Witness, available at https://www.globalwitness.org/en/campaigns/corruption-and-money-laundering/anonymous-company-owners/companies-we-keep/#chapter-0/section-1.

Goodin, Robert E. (1995), *Utilitarianism as a Public Philosophy*, Cambridge: Cambridge University Press.

Goyer, Michel (2010), 'Corporate governance', in G. Morgan, J. L. Campbell, C. Crouch, O. K. Pederssen and R. Whitley (eds), *The Oxford Handbook of Comparative Institutional Analysis*, Oxford: Oxford University Press.

Gray, Mary. L and Suri, Siddharth (2019), *Ghost Work: How to Stop Silicon Valley from Building a New Global Underclass*, Boston, MA: Houghton Mifflin Harcourt.

Gregoratti, Catia (2012), 'The United Nations Global Compact and Development', in D. Reed, P. Utting and A. Mukherjee-Reed (eds), *Business Regulation and Non-State Actors: Whose standards? Whose development?* London: Routledge.

Hadfield, Gillian K. (2017), *Rules for a Flat World: Why Humans Invented Law and How to Reinvent it for a Complex Global Economy*, New York: Oxford University Press.

Hall, Peter and Soskice, David (eds) (2001), *Varieties of Capitalism: The Institutional Variations of Comparative Advantage*, Oxford: Oxford University Press.

Hall, Rodney Bruce and Biersteker, Thomas J. (eds) (2002), *The Emergence of Private Authority in Global Governance*, Cambridge: Cambridge University Press.

Hameiri, Shahar and Jones, Lee (2016), 'Global governance as state transformation', *Political Studies* 64, 4: 793–810.

Hanké, Bob (ed.) (2009), *Debating Varieties of Capitalism: A Reader*, Oxford: Oxford University Press.

Hanlon, Robert James (2011), 'Engineering corporate social responsibility: elite stakeholders, states and the resilience of neoliberalism', *Contemporary Politics* 17, 1 (March): 71–87.

Hansmann, Henry (1996), *The Ownership of Enterprise*, Cambridge, MA: Belknap Press/Harvard University Press.

Hansmann, Henry and Kraakman, Reinier (2000), 'The end of history for corporate law', Yale Law School: Law and Economics Working Paper No. 235, New Haven, CT: Yale Law School.

Harding, Rebecca and Harding, Jack (2017), *The Weaponization of Trade: The Great Unbalancing of Politics and Economics*, London: London Publishing Partnership.

Harrod, Jeff (2006), 'The century of the corporation', in C. May (ed.), *Global Corporate Power (IPE Yearbook 15)*, Boulder, CO: Lynne Rienner.

Haufler, Virginia (2006), 'Global governance and the private sector', in C. May (ed.), *Global Corporate Power (IPE Yearbook 15)*, Boulder, CO: Lynne Rienner.

Haufler, Virginia (2018), 'Producing global governance in the global factory: markets, politics and regulation', *Global Policy* 9, 1 (February): 114–20.

Heemskerk, Eelke M. and Takes, Frank W. (2016), 'The corporate elite community structure of global capitalism', *New Political Economy* 21, 1: 90–118.

Heidenreich, Martin (2012), 'The social embeddedness of multinational companies: a literature review (State of the Art)', *Socio-Economic Review* 10: 549–79.

Herrigel, Gary and Zeitlin, Jonathan (2010), 'Inter-firm relations in global manufacturing: disintegrated production and its globalisation', in G. Morgan, J. L. Campbell, C. Crouch, O. K. Pederssen and R. Whitley (eds), *The Oxford Handbook of Comparative Institutional Analysis*, Oxford: Oxford University Press.

Hertz, Noreena (2002), *The Silent Takeover: Global Capitalism and the Death of Democracy*, London: Arrow Books.

Hess, Kendy (2013), '"If you tickle us . . .": how corporations can be moral agents without being persons', *Journal of Value Inquiry* 47, 3: 319–35.

Hess, Kendy (2017), 'The unrecognized consensus about firm moral responsibility', in E. W. Orts and N. C. Smith (eds), *The Moral Responsibility of Firms*, Oxford: Oxford University Press.

Hodgson, Geoffrey M. (2013), *From Pleasure Machines to Moral Communities: An Evolutionary Economics without* Homo Economicus, Chicago, IL: University of Chicago Press.

Hoffman, Richard C. and Shipper, Frank M. (2018), 'Shared core values of high performing employee-owned enterprises', *Journal of Management, Spirituality & Religion* 15, 4: 285–304.

Horn, Laura (2012), *Regulating Corporate Governance in the EU: Towards a Marketization of Corporate Control*, Basingstoke: Palgrave Macmillan.

Horn, Laura (2018), 'Future incorporated?' in W. Davies (ed.), *Economic Science Fictions*, London: Goldsmiths Press.

Husa, Jaakko (2018), *Law and Globalisation* (Elgar Advanced Introduction), Cheltenham: Edward Elgar Publishing.

Hutton, Will (1996), *The State We're In* (revised edn), London: Vintage.

Ireland, Paddy (2016), 'The corporation and the new aristocracy of finance', in J.-P. Robé, A. Lyon-Caen and S. Vernac (eds), *Multinationals and the Constitutionalization of the World Power System*, London: Routledge.

Jensen, Michael and Meckling, William (1976), 'Theory of the firm: managerial behaviour, agency costs and ownership structure', *Journal of Financial Economics* 3: 305–60.

Jolly, Richard, Emmerij, Louis and Weiss, Thomas G. (2009), *UN Ideas that Changed the World*, Bloomington: Indiana University Press.

Jones, Bryn (2015), *Corporate Power and Responsible Capitalism: Towards Social Accountability*, Cheltenham: Edward Elgar Publishing.

Jones, Geoffrey (2000), *Merchants to Multinationals: British Trading Companies in the Nineteenth and Twentieth Centuries*, Oxford: Oxford University Press.

Jussen, Bernhard (2009), 'The king's two bodies today', *Representations* 106, 1 (Spring): 102–17.

Kantorowicz, Ernst (1957 [2016]), *The King's Two Bodies: A Study in Medieval Political Theology* (with a new Introduction by Conrad Leyser), Princeton, NJ: Princeton University Press.

Karp, David Jason (2014), *Responsibility for Human Rights: Transnational Corporations and Imperfect States*, Cambridge: Cambridge University Press.

Katouzian, Homa (1980), *Ideology and Method in Economics*, London: Macmillan Press.

Kay, John (2019), 'The concept of the corporation', *Business History* 61, 7: 1129–43.

Kell, Georg and Ruggie, John (2001), 'Global markets and social legitimacy: the case of the "global compact"', in D. Drache (ed.), *The Market or the Public Domain: Global Governance and the Asymmetry of Power*, London: Routledge.

Kellogg, Paul (2015), 'Geographies of capital accumulation: tracing the emergence of multi-polarity, 1980–2014', *Research in Political Economy* 30A (Theoretical Engagements in Geopolitical Economy): 259–94.

Ketokivi, Mikko and Mahoney, Joseph T. (2017), 'Transaction cost economics as a theory of the firm, management and governance', *Oxford Research Encyclopedia of Business and Management*, Oxford: Oxford University Press, available at https://oxfordre.com/business/view/10.1093/acrefore/9780190224851.001.0001/acrefore-9780190224851-e-6?rskey=8PD8v2&result=1.

Khoury, Stéfanie and Whyte, David (2019), 'Sidelining corporate human rights violations: the failure of the OECD's regulatory consensus', *Journal of Human Rights* 16, 4: 363–81.

Kiely, Ray (2018), *The Neoliberal Paradox*, Cheltenham: Edward Elgar Publishing.

Kinley, David (2009), *Civilising Globalisation: Human Rights and the Global Economy*, Cambridge: Cambridge University Press.

Kitzmueller, Markus and Shimshack, Jay (2012), 'Economic perspectives on corporate social responsibility', *Journal of Economic Literature* 50, 1 (March): 51–84.

Klein, Naomi (2001), *No Logo*, London: Flamingo.

Klein, Naomi (2018), *No Is Not Enough: Defeating the New Shock Politics*, London: Penguin Books.

Kobrin, Stephen J. (2009), 'Sovereignty@Bay: globalisation, multinational enterprise and the international political system', in A. M. Rugman (ed.), *The Oxford Handbook of International Business* (2nd edn), Oxford: Oxford University Press.

Korten, David C. (1995), *When Corporations Rule the World*, London: Earthscan.

Kozul-Wright, Richard (1995), 'The myth of Anglo-Saxon capitalism: reconstructing the history of the American state', in H. J. Chang and R. Rowthorn (eds), *The Role of the State in Economic Change*, Oxford: Clarendon Press.

Kristol, Irving (1978), *Two Cheers for Capitalism*, New York: Basic Books.

Kutz, Christopher (2000), *Complicity: Ethics and Law for a Collective Age*, Cambridge: Cambridge University Press.

Landermore, Hélène and Ferreras, Isabelle (2016), 'In defense of workplace democracy: towards a justification of the firm-state analogy', *Political Theory* 44, 1: 53–81.

Lane, Christel and Probert, Jocelyn (2009), *National Capitalisms, Global Production Networks: Fashioning the Value Chain in the UK, USA and Germany*, Oxford: Oxford University Press.

Langford, Malcolm, Behn, Daniel and Lie, Runar Hilleren (2017), 'The revolving door in international investment arbitration', *Journal of International Economic Law* 20: 301–31.

Langlois, Richard N. (2016), 'The corporation is not a nexus of contracts: it's an iPhone', available at https://ssrn.com/abstract=2856631 (15 November 2019).

Lanz, Rainer and Miroudot, Sébastien (2011), *Intra-Firm Trade: Patterns, Determinants and Policy Implications*, OECD Trade Policy Papers No. 114, Paris: OECD Publishing.

Latham, Earl (1959), 'The body politic of the corporation', in E. S. Mason (ed.), *The Corporation in Modern Society*, Cambridge, MA: Harvard University Press.

Lawson, Tony (2019), *The Nature of Social Reality: Issues in Social Ontology*, Abingdon: Routledge.

Lazonick, William (2018), 'The functions of the stock market and the fallacies of shareholder value', in C. Driver and G. Thompson (eds), *Corporate Governance in Contention*, New York: Oxford University Press.

Lazonick, William and O'Sullivan, Mary (2000), 'Maximizing shareholder value: a new ideology for corporate governance', *Economy and Society* 29 (1): 13–35.

LeBaron, Genevieve and Lister, Jane (2016), 'Ethical audits and the supply chain of global corporations', SPERI Global Political Economy Brief No. 1, Sheffield: Sheffield Political Economy Research Institute/University of Sheffield.

Levinson, Marc (2008), *The Box: How the Shipping Container Made the World Smaller and the World Economy Bigger*, Princeton, NJ: Princeton University Press.

Linsi, Lukas and Mügge, Daniel K. (2019), 'Globalisation and the growing defects of international economic statistics', *Review of International Political Economy* 26, 3: 361–83.

Locke, Richard M. (2013), *The Promise and Limits of Private Power*, Cambridge: Cambridge University Press.

Lowe, Vaughan (2004), 'Corporations as international actors and international law makers', *Italian Yearbook of International Law* 14: 23–38.

Lyon-Caen, Antoine and Sachs, Tatiana (2016), 'The responsibility of multinational enterprises: a constitutionalization process in action', in J.-P. Robé, A. Lyon-Caen and S. Vernac (eds), *Multinationals and the Constitutionalization of the World Power System*, London: Routledge.

Macaulay, Catherine R. (2015), 'Capitalism's renaissance? The potential for repositioning the financial 'meta-economy''', *Futures* 68: 5–18.

McCarthy, Dennis M. P. (1994), *International Business History: A Contextual and Case Approach*, Westport, CT: Praeger.

Macdonald, Kate (2014), *The Politics of Global Supply Chains*, Cambridge: Polity Press.

March, James G. (1962), 'The business firm as a political coalition', *Journal of Politics* 24, 4 (November): 662–78.

Marris, Robin (1998), *Managerial Capitalism in Retrospect*, Basingstoke: Macmillan Press.

Martens, Jens and Seitz, Karolin (2016), *The Struggle for a UN Treaty: Towards Global Regulation on Human Rights and Business*, Bonn: Global Policy Forum.

Masten, Scott E. (1993), 'A legal basis for the firm', in O. Williamson and S. G. Winter (eds), *The Nature of the Firm: Origins, Evolution and Development*, New York: Oxford University Press.

May, Christopher (2002), 'The political economy of proximity: intellectual property and the global division of labour', *New Political Economy* 7, 3 (November): 317–42.

May, Christopher (2007), *Digital Rights Management: The Problem of Expanding Ownership Rights*, Oxford: Chandos Publishing.

May, Christopher (2014), *The Rule of Law: The Common Sense of Global Politics*, Cheltenham: Edward Elgar Publishing.

May, Christopher (2015), 'Who's in charge? Corporations as institutions of global governance', Palgrave Communications, available at http://dx.doi.org/10.1057/palcomms.2015.42.

May, Christopher (2017), 'Multinational corporations in world development: 40 years on', *Third World Quarterly* 38, 10: 2223–41.

May, Christopher (2019), 'The corporate supply chain as global governance', in M. Hofferberth (ed.), *Corporate Actors in Global Governance: Business as Usual or New Deal?* Boulder, CO: Lynne Rienner.

Mayer, Colin (2013), *Firm Commitment: Why the Corporation is Failing us and how to Restore Trust in it*, Oxford: Oxford University Press.

Mayer, Colin (2016), 'Reinventing the corporation', *Journal of the British Academy* 4 (March): 53–72.

Mayer, Colin (2018), *Prosperity: Better Business Makes the Greater Good*, Oxford: Oxford University Press.

Mayer, Frederick W. and Phillips, Nicola (2017), 'Outsourcing governance: states and the politics of a "global value chain world"', *New Political Economy* 22, 2: 134–52.

Mazzucato, Marianna (2013), *The Entrepreneurial State: Debunking Public vs. Private Sector Myths* (Anthem Other Canon Economics), London: Anthem Press.

Meckling, Jonas and Hughes, Llewelyn (2017), 'Protecting solar: global supply chains and business power', *New Political Economy* 23, 1: 88–104.

Mees, Bernard (2015), 'Corporate governance as a reform movement', *Journal of Management History* 21, 2: 194–209.

Micklethwait, John and Wooldridge, Adrian (2003), *The Company: A Short History of a Revolutionary Idea*, London: Weidenfeld and Nicolson.

Mikler, John (2018), *The Political Power of Global Corporations*, Cambridge: Polity Press.

Moberg, Lotta (2017), *The Political Economy of Special Economic Zones: Concentrating Economic Development*, Abingdon: Routledge.

Moore, Karl and Lewis, David (1999), *Birth of the Multinational: 2000 Years of Ancient Business History – from Ashur to Augustus*, Copenhagen: Copenhagen Business School Press.

Moran, Michael (2009), *Business, Politics and Society: An Anglo-American Comparison*, Oxford: Oxford University Press.

Morgan, Jamie (2016), 'Corporation tax as a problem of MNC organisational circuits: the case for unitary taxation', *British Journal of Politics and International Relations* 18, 2: 463–81.

Morrison, John (2014), *The Social License: How to Keep your Organisation Legitimate*, Basingstoke: Palgrave Macmillan.

Muchlinski, Peter T. (2007), *Multilateral Enterprises and the Law* (2nd edn), Oxford: Oxford University Press.

Mukherji, Pradeep and Rawat, Chirag (2017), 'Leveraging business process outsourcing for growth', in D. K. Elms, A. Hassani and P. Low (eds), *The Intangible Economy: How Services Shape Global Production and Consumption*, Delhi: Cambridge University Press.

Narula, Rajneesh and Zhan, James (2019), 'Using special economic zones to facilitate development: policy implications', *Transnational Corporations* 26, 2: 1–25.

Nelson, Julie A. (2016), 'Poisoning the well, or how economic theory damages moral imagination', in G. E. De Martino and D. N. McCloskey (eds), *The Oxford Handbook of Professional Economic Ethics*, Oxford: Oxford University Press.

Néron, Pierre-Yves (2016), 'Rethinking the ethics of corporate political activities in a post-citizens united era: political equality, corporate citizenship and market failures', *Journal of Business Ethics* 136, 4 (July): 715–28.

Nesvetailova, Anastasia and Palan, Ronen (2020), *Sabotage: The Business of Finance*, London: Allen Lane.

Neveling, Patrick (2017), 'The global spread of export processing zones, and the 1970s as a decade of consolidation', in K. Anderson and S. Müller (eds), *Changes in Social Regulation – State, Economy, and Social Protagonists since the 1970s*, Oxford: Berghahn Books.

Noble, David F. (1977), *America by Design: Science, Technology and the Rise of Corporate Capitalism*, Oxford: Oxford University Press.

Nowrot, Karsten (2006), 'Reconceptualising international legal personality of influential non-state actors: towards a rebuttable presumption of normative responsibilities', *Philippine Law Journal* 80: 563–86.

Öncü, Ahmet (2009), 'Wither business ideology: revisiting Veblen's Theory of Engineers as revolutionary actors', *Review of Radical Political Economics* 41, 2 (Spring): 196–215.

Orenstein, Dara (2019), *Out of Stock: The Warehouse in the History of Capitalism*, Chicago, IL: University of Chicago Press.

Orhangazi, Özgü (2015), 'Financialisation and the nonfinancial corporate sector', in U. Mattei and J. D. Haskall (eds), *Research Handbook on Political Economy and the Law*, Cheltenham: Edward Elgar Publishing.

Orock, Rogers Tabe Egbe (2013), 'Less-told stories about corporate globalisation: transnational corporations and CSR as the politics of (ir)responsibility in Africa', *Dialectical Anthropology* 37, 1 (March): 27–50.

Palan, Ronen (2016), 'Corporate power in the global economy: an evolutionary perspective', in J.-P. Robé, A. Lyon-Caen and S. Vernac (eds), *Multinationals and the Constitutionalization of the World Power System*, London: Routledge.

Palazzo, Guido and Scherer, Andreas Georg (2006), 'Corporate legitimacy as deliberation: a communicative framework', *Journal of Business Ethics* 66: 71–88.

Park, Stephen Kim (2016), 'Special economic zones and the perpetual pluralism of global trade and labour migration', *Georgetown Journal of International Law* 47, 4: 1379–1430.

Pentikäinen, Merja (2012), 'Changing international "subjectivity" and rights and obligations under international law – status of corporations', *Utrecht Law Review* 8, 1 (January): 145–54.

Phillips, Leigh and Rozworski, Michal (2019), *The People's Republic of Walmart: How the World's Biggest Corporations are Laying the Foundation for Socialism*, London: Verso.

Phillips, Nicola (2017), 'Power and inequality in the global political economy', *International Affairs* 93, 2: 429–44.

Picciotto, Sol (2011), *Regulating Global Corporate Capitalism: International Corporate Law and Financial Market Regulation*, Cambridge: Cambridge University Press.

Picciotto, Sol (2017), 'Regulation: managing the antimonies of economic vice and virtue', *Social and Legal Studies* 26, 6: 676–99.

Pistor, Katharina (2014), 'Multinational corporations as regulators and central planners: implications for citizens' voice', in G. Urban (ed.), *Corporations and Citizenship*, Philadelphia: University of Pennsylvania Press.

Ramović, Jasmin (2018), 'Looking into the past to see the future: lessons learned from self-management for economies in post-conflict societies of former Yugoslavia', *Civil Wars* 20, 2: 171–92.

Råthzel, Nora, Mulinari, Diana and Tollesfsen, Aina (2014), *Transnational Corporations from the Standpoint of Workers*, Basingstoke: Palgrave Macmillan.

Reich, Robert B. (2007), *Supercapitalism: The Transformation of Business, Democracy, and Everyday Life*, New York: Alfred Knopf.

Reinert, Kenneth A., Reinert, Oda A. and Debebe, Gelaye (2016), 'The new OECD Guidelines for Multinational Enterprises: better but not enough', *Development in Practice* 26, 6: 816–23.

Resnick, Stephen and Wolff, Richard (1989), *Knowledge and Class: A Marxian Critique of Political Economy*, Chicago, IL: University of Chicago Press.

Resnick, Stephen and Wolff, Richard (2003), 'Exploitation, consumption and the uniqueness of US capitalism', *Historical Materialism* 11, 4: 209–26.

Richer, Julian (2018), *The Ethical Capitalist: How to Make Business Work Better for Society*, London: Random House Business Books.

Robé, Jean-Phillipe, Delaunay, Betrand and Fleury, Benoit (2019), 'French legislation on corporate purpose', Harvard Law School Forum on Corporate Governance and Financial Regulation, 8 June, available at https://corpgov.law.harvard.edu/2019/06/08/french-legislation-on-corporate-purpose/.

Robins, Nick (2012), *The Corporation that Changed the World: How the East India Company Shaped the Modern Multinational* (2nd edn), London: Pluto Press.

Rochon, Louis-Philippe and Rossi, Sergio (2017), *A Modern Guide to Rethinking Economics*, Cheltenham: Edward Elgar Publishing.

Rodney, Walter (1972 [2018]), *How Europe Underdeveloped Africa* (new edn with Foreword by Angela Davis), London: Verso.

Rubery, Jill (2010), 'Institutionalising the employment relationship', in G. Morgan, J. L. Campbell, C. Crouch, O. K. Pederssen and R. Whitley (eds), *The Oxford Handbook of Comparative Institutional Analysis*, Oxford: Oxford University Press.

Ruggie, John Gerard (2003), 'Taking embedded liberalism global: the corporate connection', in D. Held and M. Koenig-Archibugi (eds), *Taming Globalization: Frontiers of Governance*, Cambridge: Polity Press.

Ruggie, John Gerard (2013), *Just Business: Multinational Corporations and Human Rights*, New York: W.W. Norton and Co.

Ruggie, John Gerard (2018), 'Multinationals as global institution: power, authority and relative autonomy', *Regulation and Governance* 12: 317–33.

Russell, Steve and Gilbert, Michael J. (2002), 'Social control of transnational corporations in the age of marketocracy', *International Journal of the Sociology of the Law* 30, 1 (March): 33–50.

Sacks, Stephen R. (1983), *Self-Management and Efficiency: Large Corporations in Yugoslavia*, London: George Allen and Unwin.

Sahni, Binda (2005), 'The interpretation of the corporate personality of transnational corporations', *Widener Law Journal* 15 (1): 1–45.

St John, Taylor (2018), *The Rise of Investor-State Arbitration: Politics, Law, and Unintended Consequences*, Oxford: Oxford University Press.

Sapinski, J. P. and Carroll, William K. (2018), 'Interlocking directorships and corporate networks', in A. Nölke and C. May (eds), *Handbook of the International Political Economy of the Corporation*, Cheltenham: Edward Elgar Publishing.

Sauvant, Karl P. (2015), 'The negotiation of the United Nations Code of Conduct on transnational corporations: experience and lessons learned', *Journal of World Investment and Trade* 16: 11–87.

Schrenk, Martin, Ardalan, Cyrus and El Tatawy, Nawal A. (1979), *Yugoslavia: Self-Management Socialism and the Challenges of Development: Report of a Mission Sent to Yugoslavia by the World Bank*, Baltimore, MD: Johns Hopkins University Press.

Schwarz, Ori (2019), 'Facebook rules: structures of governance in digital capitalism and the control of generalised social capital', *Theory Culture & Society* 36 (4): 117–41.

Scott, John (1997), *Corporate Business and Capitalist Classes*, Oxford: Oxford University Press.

Selwyn, Ben (2013), 'Social upgrading and labour in global production networks: a critique and an alternative conception', *Competition and Change* 17, 1 (February): 75–90.

Shaxson, Nicholas (2018), *The Finance Curse: How Global Finance is Making Us All Poorer*, London: Bodley Head.

Sklair, Leslie (2001), *The Transnational Capitalist Class*, Oxford: Blackwells.

Sklair, Leslie and Miller, David (2010), 'Capitalist globalisation, corporate social responsibility and social policy', *Critical Social Policy* 30, 4: 1–24.

Smith, Jackie (2010), 'Power, interests, and the United Nations Global Compact', in T. Porter and K. Ronit (eds), *The Challenges of Global Business Authority: Democratic Renewal, Stalemate, or Decay?* Albany: State University of New York Press.

Sornarajah, M. (2015), *Resistance and Change in the International Law on Foreign Investment*, Cambridge: Cambridge University Press.

Souleles, Daniel (2019), 'Another workplace is possible: learning to own and changing subjectivities in American employee owned companies', *Critique of Anthropology*, available at https://doi.org/10.1177/0308275X19840416.

Spencer, David A. (2020), 'Economics and "bad" management: the limits to performativity', *Cambridge Journal of Economics* 44: 17–32.

Stanford, Jim (2017), 'The resurgence of gig work: historical and theoretical perspectives', *Economic and Labour Relations Review* 28, 3: 382–401.

Steffik, Jens and Pereira, Mariana Gomes (2011), 'Transnational governance networks and democracy: what are the standards?', in O. Dilling, M. Herberg and G. Winter (eds), *Transnational Administrative Rule Making: Performance, Legal Effects and Legitimacy*, Oxford: Hart Publishing.

Stephenson, Sherry and Pfister, Anne-Katrin (2017), 'Who governs global value chains', in D. K. Elms, A. Hassani and P. Low (eds), *The Intangible Economy: How Services Shape Global Production and Consumption*, Delhi: Cambridge University Press.

Stonkuté, Eglé and Vveinhardt, Jolita (2016), 'Key success factors for small and medium sized enterprises in a context of global supply chains', in M. H. Bilgin and H. Danis (eds), *Entrepreneurship, Business and Economics (Vol. 1)*, Basel: Springer.

Stopford, John and Strange, Susan (1991), *Rival States, Rival Firms: Competition for World Market Shares*, Cambridge: Cambridge University Press.

Stout, Lynn (2017), 'The economic nature of the corporation', in F. Parisi (ed.), *Oxford Handbook of Law and Economics (Vol. 2: Private and Commercial Law)*, Oxford: Oxford University Press.

Strange, Susan (1988), *States and Markets: An Introduction to International Political Economy*, London: Pinter Publishers.

Strange, Susan (1991), 'Big business and the state', *Millennium: Journal of International Studies* 20, 2 (Summer): 245–50.

Strange, Susan (1992 [2002]), 'States, firms and diplomacy', *International Affairs* 68, 1 (January): 1–15 [reprinted in R. Tooze and C. May (eds), *Authority and Markets: Susan Strange's Writings on International Political Economy*, Basingstoke: Palgrave Macmillan].

Styhre, Alexander (2018), *The Making of Shareholder Welfare Society: A Study in Corporate Governance*, New York: Routledge.

Suvin, Darko (2017), *Splendour, Misery and Possibilities: An X-Ray of Socialist Yugoslavia*, Chicago, IL: Haymarket Books.

Suwandi, Intan (2019), *Value Chains: The New Economic Imperialism*, New York: Monthly Review Press.

Talberg, Jonas, Sommerer, Thomas, Squatrito, Theresa and Jönsson, Christer (2014), 'Explaining the transnational design of international organisations', *International Organisation* 68, 4 (September): 741–74.

Taylor, Matthew (2017), *Good Work: The Taylor Review of Modern Working Practices*, London: Department for Business, Energy & Industrial Strategy.

Teivainen, Teivo (2002), 'Overcoming economism', *Review (Fernand Braudel Center)* 25, 3: 317–42.

Tepper, Jonathan and Hearn, Denise (2019), *The Myth of Capitalism: Monopolies and the Death of Competition*, Hoboken, NJ: John Wiley & Sons.

Thakur, Vikas and Anbanandam, Ramesh (2016), 'Shift from product supply chain management to services supply chain management: a review', *International Journal of Services and Operation Management* 23, 3: 316–46.

Tombs, Steve and Whyte, David (2015), *The Corporate Criminal: Why Corporations must be Abolished*, London: Routledge.

Udofia, O. E. (1984), 'Imperialism in Africa: a case of multinational corporations', *Journal of Black Studies* 14, 3 (March): 353–68.

UNCTAD [United Nations Conference on Trade and Development] (2012), *Fair and Equitable Treatment*, UNCTAD Series on Issues in International Investment Agreements II, Geneva: UNCTAD.

UNCTAD [United Nations Conference on Trade and Development] (2013), *World Investment Report 2013. Global Value Chains: Investment and Trade for Development*, New York: United Nations.

UNCTAD [United Nations Conference on Trade and Development] (2014), *Investor–State Dispute Settlement*, UNCTAD Series on Issues in International Investment Agreements II, Geneva: UNCTAD.

Useem, Michael (1984), *The Inner Circle: Large Corporations and the Rise of Business Political Activity in the U.S. and U.K.*, New York: Oxford University Press.

Utting, Peter (2012), 'Introduction: multistakeholder regulation from a development perspective', in D. Reed, P. Utting and A.Mukherjee-Reed (eds), *Business Regulation and Non-State Actors: Whose Standards? Whose Development?* London: Routledge.

van der Ven, Hamish (2018), 'Gatekeeper power: understanding the influence of lead firms over transnational sustainability standards', *Review of International Political Economy* 25, 5: 624–46.

van Horn, Rob (2015), 'Reinventing monopoly and the role of corporations: the roots of Chicago law and economics', in P. Mirowski and D. Plehwe (eds), *The Road from Mont Pèlerin: The Making of the Neoliberal Thought Collective*, Cambridge, MA: Harvard University Press.

Veblen, Thorstein (1904 [2002]), *The Theory of Business Enterprise*, New Brunswick, NJ: Transaction Publishers.

Veblen, Thorstein (1923 [1997]), *Absentee Ownership. Business Enterprise in Recent Times: The Case of America*, New Brunswick, NJ: Transaction Publishers.

Veldman, Jeroen and Parker, Martin (2012), 'Specters Inc.: The elusive basis of the corporation', *Business and Society Review* 117, 4: 413–41.

Veldman, Jeroen and Willmott, Hugh (2017), 'Social ontology and the modern corporation', *Cambridge Journal of Economics* 41: 1489–1504.

Vogel, David (2006), *The Market for Virtue: The Potential and Limits of Corporate Social Responsibility*, Washington, DC: Brookings Institution Press.

Wang, Bill, Kang, Yuanfei, Childerhouse, Paul and Huo, Baofeng (2018), 'Service supply chain integration: the role of interpersonal relationships', *Industrial Management and Data Systems* 118, 4: 828–49.

Werner, Marion, Bair, Jennifer and Fernández, Victor Ramiro (2014), 'Linking up to development: global value chains and the making of the post-Washington consensus', *Development and Change* 45, 6: 1219–47.

Whiteman, Gail (2009), 'All my relations: understanding perceptions of justice and conflict between companies and indigenous peoples', *Organization Studies* 30, 1: 101–20.

Whitley, Richard (2000), *Divergent Capitalisms: The Social Structuring and Change of Business Systems*, Oxford: Oxford University Press.

Whitley, Richard (2010), 'The institutional construction of firms', in G. Morgan, J. L. Campbell, C. Crouch, O. K. Pederssen and R. Whitley (eds), *The Oxford Handbook of Comparative Institutional Analysis*, Oxford: Oxford University Press.

Wignaraja, Ganeshan (2015), 'Factors affecting entry into supply chain trade: an analysis of firms in Southeast Asia', *Asia and the Pacific Policy Studies* 2, 3: 623–42.

Wilkins, Mira and Schröter, Harm (eds) (1998), *The Free-Standing Company in the World Economy, 1830–1996*, Oxford: Oxford University Press.

Wilks, Stephen (2013), *The Political Power of the Business Corporation*, Cheltenham: Edward Elgar Publishing.

Williamson, Oliver E. (1985), *The Economic Institutions of Capitalism*, New York: The Free Press.

Williamson, Oliver E. (2013), *The Transaction Costs Economics Project: The Theory and Practice of the Governance of Contractual Relations*, Cheltenham: Edward Elgar Publishing.

Williston, Samuel (1909), 'The history of the law of business corporations before 1800', *Select Essays in Anglo-American Legal History (Vol. III)*, Cambridge: Cambridge University Press.

Wu, Tim (2018), *The Curse of Bigness: Antitrust in the New Gilded Age*, New York: Columbia Global Reports.

Yamamoto, Koji (2017), 'Early modern business projects and a forgotten history of corporate social responsibility', in G. Baars and A. Spicer (eds), *The Corporation: A Critical, Multi-Disciplinary Handbook*, Cambridge: Cambridge University Press.

Yang, James G. S. and Metallo, Victor N. A. (2018), 'The emerging international taxation problems', *International Journal of Financial Studies* 6, 6: 1–10.

Ylönen, Matti and Teivainen, Teivo (2018), 'Politics of intra-firm trade: corporate price planning and the double role of the arm's length principle', *New Political Economy* 23, 4: 441–57.

Zingales, Luigi (2002), 'Corporate governance', in P. Newman (ed.), *The New Palgrave Dictionary of Economics and the Law*, Basingstoke: Palgrave Macmillan.

Zingales, Luigi (2017), 'Towards a political theory of the firm', *Journal of Economic Perspectives* 31, 3 (Summer): 113–30.

Zuboff, Shoshana (2019), *The Age of Surveillance Capitalism: The Fight for a Human Future at the New Frontier of Power*, New York: Profile Books.

Zucman, Gabriel (2015), *The Hidden Wealth of Nations: The Scourge of Tax Havens*, Chicago, IL: University of Chicago Press.

Index

absentee ownership 29–30, 42, 141
accountancy firms (Big Four) 95
Active Labour Market Policy 151–2
Africa, sub-Saharan 80
Amazon 111
Amer, Estefania 108
Anderson, Elizabeth 46–7
Angresano, James 117, 122, 147

Backer, Larry Catá 71, 130
Bakan, Joel 6, 17, 63, 97, 128, 131, 133, 139, 141
Basel Committee on Banking Supervision 135–6
Beder, Sharon 54
Benedictine order(s) 19–20
Bernaz, Nadia 126–7
Bierce, Ambrose 3
bilateral investment treaties (BITs) 10, 100–102, 127
Birch, Kean 93
Blackstone, William 21–2
bluewashing 108
BMW 90
Boddin, Dominik 112
Bork, Robert 95–6
Bowman, Scott 93
Braithwaite, John 95, 101, 115, 145
Brandeis, Louis 120, 131
brands, branding 58, 60, 71, 86–7, 108, 111, 143–4
Braverman, Harry 32
British Petroleum (BP) 60
Brueckner, Martin 140, 141
Buckley, Peter 35
Burawoy, Michael 32
Burczak, Theodore 47

bureaucratic politics 74
business history, the academic (sub) discipline of 37
business to business services (B2B) 71–2

Casson, Mark 29
Chapman, Malcolm 35
Ciepley, David 93, 147–8
Ciocchnni, Pable Leandro 102, 103
Citizen's United, legal case 132
civil society see non-governmental organisations
class analysis 51, 53, 116–20
Coase, Ronald 33–4
Coe, Neil 77–8
Coffee, John 146
Coke, Sir Edward 21–2
competition law/regulation(s) 25, 95, 131–2, 140
containers 3, 28, 67
contract law see law
Cooke, C.A. 20–21
corporate (legal) form 2, 6–12, 14, 19, 24–5, 36, 52, 60, 125, 128–9
'B corp' 132–3
corporate governance 26, 40, 43, 57, 127
corporate shareholding (cross shareholding) 7, 24, 127
corporate social responsibility (CSR) 50, 58–64, 70, 73, 76–7, 85, 86, 108, 115, 121, 130, 139, 142–7, 150–51
Corporate Welfare Economy 121–2, 147
corruption 30, 60, 106–7, 119, 120
countervailing power 131–2
credit-rating agencies 95
cross-subsidy 43–4
Crouch, Colin 151

Dallas, Mark 84, 87–9
Davis, John P. 21
Davos 54, 116
democracy 8, 39–40, 41, 47, 48, 75, 97–8,
    102, 114, 122, 123, 131–2, 138,
    140, 145, 149–50
democratic deficit 47, 72, 75, 127–8, 140,
    148
Denmark 147
depoliticisation 4–5, 39, 116, 126
de-skilling 32–3, 56
developing states 5, 27–8, 31, 77, 78, 80,
    100, 103–4, 112–13, 120, 133, 140
digital rights management (DRM) 99
directors 9, 30, 41, 45, 53–4, 109, 117,
    118, 129
discursive power see power analysis
division of labour 32, 68
Driver, Ciaran 64
Dugger, William 43
Duménil, Gérard 53
Dunning, John 67
Dürr, Andreas 113–14
Dutch East India Company 3, 21, 27, 30

Eabrasu, Marian 140, 141
East India Company [British] 22, 23, 27,
    38
economic development 4, 10, 12, 22, 68,
    77, 78, 80–87, 100, 103, 112, 117,
    122, 142
economics, discipline of 1–2, 15, 25, 35,
    45, 48, 64, 72, 93, 126
    law and economics (sub-discipline
    of economics) 40, 41–2, 44
economies of scale 23, 79
economism 1, 4–5, 11, 39, 40, 45
Ecuador 134
Eichar, Douglas 60
Elbra, Ainsley 110
environmental impact 73, 74, 106–7, 130,
    135, 141–3
European Central Bank 96
European Roundtable of Industrialists
    113
European Union 90, 95, 96, 113–14, 116,
    118, 130, 131
Evans, Alice 153
export processing zones (EPZs) see
    special economic zones (SEZs)

Facebook 45, 98–9
Fair Tax Mark 142
Farnsworth, Kevin 113
feminist approach(es) 11
Fereras, Isabelle 12, 39–40, 47, 148
financialisation 13, 53, 56, 58, 126, 128,
    141
financial reporting/results 30, 52–3, 55,
    56, 110, 112, 130, 133
flexible specialisation 27, 32
Fordism 23, 32, 56
Forsgren, Mats 14
Foundational Economy Collective (FEC)
    138–9
France 73, 96, 130–31
free standing companies see subsidiaries
friction, as an economic concept 35
Friedman, Milton 58, 143, 145
Fuchs, Doris 98, 117–18, 136

Galbraith, John Kenneth 24, 131–2
gender inequality 49, 133
General Agreement on the Trade in
    Services (GATS) 136–7
Germany 24, 62, 96, 141, 149
gig economy 32, 35–6, 72, 150–52
Gilbert, Michael 8
Gill, Stephen 25, 117, 122–3, 130
Giuliani, Elisa 80–81
global governance 73–4, 98, 100–101,
    105–9, 118, 121, 134–5
global production networks see supply
    chains
Global South 84, 145
Global Witness 119–20
Goodin, Robert 61
governance, as corporate practice 5,
    43–8, 64, 69, 71–8, 87–9, 99,
    110–11, 115, 121, 128, 131, 140,
    143
Gray, Mary 35–6
guilds 20–22

Hadfield, Gillian 71, 145
Hall, Peter 26
Handelsbanken 139
Hanseatic League 20
Hansmann, Henry 48–9
Hayek, Friedrich 47, 94

Heemskerk, Eelke 119
Heidenreich, Martin 68
Hertz, Noreena 97
Hess, Kendy 125–6
Hodgson, Geoffrey 55–6
Hoffman, Richard 50
holding companies 7
Horn, Laura 125
van Horn, Rob 42
Hudson's Bay Company 21
human rights 62–3, 73, 104, 106–7, 127,
        134

imperialism 24–5, 27–8, 69, 100
incomplete contracts 42
incorporation 2, 6, 7–8, 9, 20–21, 22, 23,
        32, 37, 40, 74, 125, 127–30, 138,
        141, 143
India 78
Industrial Foundations 147–8
inequality 5, 14, 131
information society 3, 28, 45, 98–9
initial public offering (IPO) 51
intellectual property rights 78, 79, 83, 85,
        98, 99, 109, 110, 115
interlocking (networks of) corporate
        directorships 53–4, 117–20
International Centre for the Settlement
        of Investment Disputes (ICSID)
        101–3
International Labour Organisation 84,
        86, 106
International Monetary Fund (IMF) 112
international trade 3–4, 20–21, 49, 67, 71,
        90–91, 101, 114–15, 136
                data/statistical issues, 4, 91, 112
investor-state dispute settlement (ISDS)
        100–104
Ireland, Paddy 37

Jameson, Frederic 125
Japan 24, 62
John Lewis Partnership 48, 50, 148
Jones, Bryn 127

Katouzian, Homa 11
Kay, John 13–14
Kell, George 106

Khoury, Stéfanie 102, 103, 137
Kiely, Ray 94–5
Klein, Naomi 97, 144
Korten, David 152
Kristol, Irving 115
Kutz, Christopher 61–2
Kyoto Protocol 135

labour standards 74, 76–7, 86, 106–7,
        142, 143
Landermore, Hélène 39–40
Latham, Earl 45
law
        common law 21
        contract law 6–7, 34, 35, 42, 55, 71,
                74, 85, 104, 129, 151
        criminal law 61, 129, 134
        employment law 34, 55, 151
        extraterritoriality 10
        international law 6, 9, 25, 71, 101,
                104, 118, 127, 130, 134–5, 145
        Joint Stock Companies Act (1856)
                22
        legal personality 6–8, 9, 19, 21, 74,
                109, 132, 134
        legal reform 130–34
        lex mercatoria 9, 20–21, 25
        Limited Liability Act (1855) 22
        Roman law 19
        Sherman Anti-Trust Act
                (USA/1890) 23
        soft law 9, 134
law and economics see economics
Lawson, Tony 34, 129
lawyers 9, 12, 105
Lazonick, William 51–2
legal norms 9, 21–2
legitimacy 43–4, 45, 46, 72, 74–7, 80, 138,
        143, 146
Lévy, Dominique 53
limited liability 7, 22, 60, 61–2, 127
lobbying 61, 101, 114, 132, 144
Locke, Richard 76–7
logistics 67
London stock exchange 7, 52

Macchi, Chiara 80–81
Macdonald, Kate 76
management schools 3, 117, 152

managers 4, 15, 29–33, 35, 41, 43–4, 45,
    46, 49, 50, 51–5, 56, 132–3, 139
March, James 45–6
Martens, Jens 134
Masten, Scott 34
Mayer, Colin 59, 126, 139
Mazzucato, Mariana 122
Mechanical Turk 35, 72
Medici family 3, 21
Merchant Adventurers 21
Microsoft 35–6
Mikler, John 98, 110
Modragon 48, 50, 149
monarchy 20
monastic orders 20
monopoly 7, 25, 41, 95–6, 130, 131, 140
monopsony 69–70
Moran, Michael 93
Morgan, J.P. 120
Morrison, John 138
Muchlinski, Peter 103

Nader, Ralph 121
Nelson, Julie 11
neoliberalism 25, 53, 56, 85, 93–6, 98,
    102, 113–14, 116, 123, 126, 128,
    132, 152
Néron, Pierre-Yves 140
Nesvetailova, Anastasia 140
networked governance 9, 105
Neveling, Patrick 28
new constitutionalism 122–3, 130
New York Stock Exchange 7, 52
nexus of contracts, the firm/corporation
    as a 42, 55, 129
non-government organisations 60–61,
    73, 75–6, 107, 108, 114, 133, 134,
    137, 138, 145–6

oligopoly 25, 131, 132
Organisation for Economic Cooperation
    and Development (OECD) 108–9,
    111, 137, 142
Orock, Rogers Tabe Egbe 80
outsourcing 34, 36, 71, 78–9, 139

Palan, Ronen 109, 140
Palazzo, Guido 97, 140–41
Parker, Martin 128–9

Phillips, Leigh 24
Phillips, Nicola 14–15
Picciotto, Sol 10, 105
Pistor, Katharina 44
planning 24, 43, 44, 47, 49, 94, 131
platform capitalism 36, 45, 150–52
political theory, as an academic discipline
    93
Ponte, Stefano 87–9
power, analysis of (corporate) 3, 4,
    12–13, 32, 43, 44, 69, 70, 73, 83,
    87–9, 94–5, 97–8, 104, 113–23,
    130–31, 133, 136, 149
principal-agent analysis 40, 41–2, 54, 57
private governance/authority 59, 60–61,
    72, 76, 86, 95, 108, 115, 133, 138,
    142–7
productivity 4, 23, 131
protectionism 90, 114
public good, public interest 7–8, 22, 93,
    94, 128, 130, 133

Räthzel, Nora 31–2
Rana Plaza 131
regulatory capitalism 95–6, 102, 115–16,
    123, 126, 145
Reich, Robert 145
reification 12, 74, 129
Resnick, Stephen 51
Richer, Julian 148
Robins, Nick 38
Rothschild family 3, 21
Royal African Company 21
Rozworski, Michal 24
Rubery, Jill 56
Ruggie, John 6, 63, 106, 109
rule of law 94, 101, 128
    see also law
Russell, Steve 8

Sacks, Stephen 49
Sauvant, Karl 134
Scherer, Andreas 97, 141
Schwarz, Ori 45, 98–9
scientific management 24, 26–7
Scott, John 117
Seitz, Karolin 134
Selwyn, Ben 86
service sector 71, 77–80

shareholders, shareholding 7, 22–3, 29–30, 39, 40, 41, 42, 46, 48, 52–3, 54, 60, 61–2, 110, 117, 119–20, 126, 127, 129, 139, 141–42, 143, 149
shareholder value 30, 51–3, 54–5, 56, 59, 130, 133, 141, 143, 147
Shipper, Frank 50
shipping 28
short-termism 30, 58, 59, 148
Sklair, Leslie 116–17
small and medium size enterprises (SMEs) 69–72, 76, 81, 85
Smith, Jackie 108
social license to operate 74, 108, 128, 130, 133, 138–42, 146, 150–51
social media see information society
Soskice, David 26
Souleles, Daniel 149
special economic zones (SEZs) 28, 82–4, 85, 90
Spencer, David 15
stakeholders 51, 53, 58, 74, 75, 128, 138, 139–41, 142, 143, 150, 151
Stanford, Ji 151
Starbucks 111
state regulation 4–5, 6–7, 10, 21–2, 26, 29, 31–2, 41, 47, 68, 71, 80–81, 95, 103, 112, 115–17, 123, 131, 139, 145, 146
St John, Taylor 101
Stonkuté, Eglé 70
Stopford, John 96–7
Strange, Susan 2, 12–13, 96–7, 114, 118, 136
structural power see power analysis
Sturgeon, Timothy 87–9
Styhre, Alexander 30, 126
subsidiaries 10, 27, 111
supply chains 4, 5, 14–15, 28–9, 31, 32, 42, 43, 44, 47, 67–92, 110, 112, 114–15, 121, 127, 131, 133, 136, 140–41, 149
Suri, Siddharth 35–6
Suvin, Darko 50
Suwandi, Intan 5, 69

Takes, Frank 119
Tax Justice Network 110–11, 142

taxation 27, 44, 89–90, 110–13, 118, 119, 142, 147, 151–2
unitary taxation, of corporations 111–12
technology 23, 29, 33, 57, 70, 98, 127, 147
technology transfer 5, 81, 82
Teivainen, Teivo 39, 40
Thompson, Grahame 64
Tombs, Steve 8–9, 59–60
Trade-related Aspects of Intellectual Property Rights (TRIPs) agreement 78, 136
transaction cost economics (analysis) 29, 33–6, 37, 43, 45, 49, 55
transfer pricing 4, 49, 89–90, 110
transnational capital class 53, 116–17
triangular diplomacy 96–7, 114

Uber 151
unions 31, 32, 56–7, 86–7, 95, 107, 132, 149
United Nations 105–6
United Nations Conference on Trade and Development (UNCTAD) 80, 103
United Nations Global Compact 63, 105–9, 130, 137, 141, 142
United Nations Human Rights Council 134–5, 141
United States Supreme Court 34, 95–6, 131, 132
upgrading see economic development
Useem, Michael 116, 119

value chains see supply chains
varieties of capitalism, as an approach to analysis 25–9
Veblen, Thorstein 25, 29
Veldman, Jeroen 12, 128–9
vertical integration, of corporate activity 23, 34
Vestager, Margrethe 131
Vogel, David 146
Vveinhardt, Jolita 70

Walmart 24
Washington Consensus 84
Whitely, Richard 26–7, 42
Whyte, David 8–9, 59–60, 137

Wilks, Stephen 143
Williamson, Oliver 29, 33, 34–5
Willmott, Hugh 12
Wolff, Richard 51
workers 23, 31, 39, 43, 46–50, 55–8, 81, 82, 86, 113, 116, 127, 148, 150–51
    workers' cooperatives 2, 47, 149
workplace democracy 47–50
World Bank 49–50, 84, 92, 101
World Economic Forum (WEF) *see* Davos

World Trade Organisation (WTO) 67, 71, 78, 109, 136–7, 153
Wu, Tim 96

Yamamoto, Koji 128
Yeung, Wai-Chung 77–8
Yugoslavia 48–50

Zingales, Luigi 114
Zuboff, Shoshana 98